Advanc₁ ₁-3280

A Peace ₍

A Therapist's Gui
and Other Difficult Emotions

"The Berrys' Anger Management Program has provided a valuable service to our community assisting those with anger problems to make positive changes to improve their lives and relationships. Now the simple wisdom of these important concepts is outlined in a straight-forward understandable manner in *A Peace of My Mind*."

–Don Vogt,
Former Unit Supervisor, Wisconsin Division of Corrections

Praise for
Romancing the Web:
A Therapist's Guide to the Finer Points
of Online Dating,
also by Diane M. Berry, MSW, LCSW, JD

"Diane Berry explains how to write an online profile to attract the type of relationship you are looking for, how to meet partners safely and effectively and how to proceed with your new relationship."

–John Gray, Ph.D,
Author of *Men Are from Mars, Women Are from Venus*

"Diane Berry is the Ann Landers of online dating. Don't hit the SEND button until you've read this book!"
–Jim Barnes, Editor, Independent Publisher Online

"*...Romancing the Web* will help you to point your computer mouse in the right direction and give you invaluable tips along the way."

–Larry James, CelebrateLove.com

Praise for
Child-Friendly Divorce:
A Divorce(d) Therapist's Guide to Helping Your Children Thrive
also by Diane M. Berry, MSW, LCSW, JD

"A roadmap for ending a marriage while inflicting the fewest emotional scars on your children. Don't get divorced without it!"

–Jim Barnes, Editor, Independent Publisher Online

"A quality guide, practical and intuitively written!
"Authoritatively written by Diane M. Berry (a former family law attorney turned psychotherapist who has personally experienced divorce), *Child-Friendly Divorce*...is a straightforward examination of the crisis and trauma that divorce brings to children's lives, and what divorcing parents can do to ease the burden. From helping children adjust to long-term difficulties; to forming a co-parenting partnership with the 'other parent'; to when and how to introduce children to a new partner, *Child-Friendly Divorce* is a quality guide, practical and intuitively written. If you are considering or involved in a divorce where there are children involved, then you need to give a careful reading to Diane Berry's *Child-Friendly Divorce*."

–Midwest Book Review

"Diane M. Berry has written an incredible title on how parents can help their children through a sometimes difficult and confusing divorce. Finally, there is a book that parents can use to help their children come through with flying colors. A highly recommended book!"
"*Child-Friendly Divorce* is packed with advice, resources and real world examples on how parents can navigate their children through a divorce. A must-read for every divorcing parent!"

–USA Book News

A Peace of

My Mind ~

A Therapist's Guide to Handling Anger and Other Difficult Emotions!

Diane M. Berry,
MSW, LCSW, JD
With
Terry J. Berry,
MSW, LCSW

First Edition
Blue Waters Publications,
Manitowoc, Wisconsin

A Peace of My Mind
A Therapist's Guide to Handling Anger and Other Difficult Emotions

© 2008 by Diane M. Berry, MSW, LCSW. JD with Terry J. Berry, MSW, LCSW

Blue Waters Publications, LLC
P. O. Box 411
Manitowoc, WI 54221-0411
Email: bluewaterspublications@lakefield.net
Website: www.bluewaterspublications.com

While the case studies and examples described in this book are based on interviews and situations experienced by real persons, the names, professions, locations and other biographical details have been changed to preserve their privacy and anonymity. Unless otherwise noted, examples provided in the text do not reflect actual persons, living or dead. Any resemblance to actual persons is purely coincidental.

Printed in the United States of America
ISBN, print ed. 9780974207858
First Printing 2007

Cover Design by Dunn+Associates   *Back Cover Photo by Heilmann*

Publisher's Cataloging-in-Publication
(Provided by Quality Books, Inc.)

Berry, Diane M.
    A peace of my mind : a therapist's guide to handling anger and other difficult emotions! / Diane M. Berry ; with Terry J. Berry.
1st ed.
        p. cm.
    Includes bibliographical references and index.
    LCCN 2007900179
    ISBN-13: 9780974207858
    ISBN-10: 0974207853

    1. Anger.   I. Berry, Terry J. II. Title.
    III. Title: Handling anger and other difficult emotions!

    BF575.A5B47 2008   152.4'7
                              QBI07-600061

Dedication

This book is dedicated to the hundreds of men who have come through our anger management and family violence groups over the past 14 years. Know that you have taught us much about anger and its effects on your lives and relationships. You have made it possible for us to learn much and share it now with a wider audience. For this, as well as your curiosity and your humor, we are grateful.

*"Anyone can become angry — that is easy.
But to be angry with the right person, to the right degree,
at the right time, for the right purpose,
and in the right way —
this is not easy."*

~Aristotle

Contents

About the Authors

A native of Manitowoc, WI, **Diane Berry**, MSW, LCSW, JD started her professional career as a divorce attorney in 1983. She quickly realized that she preferred dealing with the emotional aspects of a breakup to the legal issues involved and headed back to graduate school for her Master's Degree in Social Work. In 1995, Berry completed her schooling and began working as a therapist with clients struggling with the issues of depression, anxiety, stress management and life change adjustments. Divorce, step family adjustment, court ordered anger management and family violence treatment became areas of expertise for her as she was able to combine her experience in the areas of law and social work.

In May of 2000, Berry opened a small mental health clinic, Blue Waters Family Counseling. Acting as Director of the clinic, Berry continues her therapy practice, in addition to facilitating Parenting Through Divorce, Divorce Adjustment and the Men's Family Violence groups discussed in this book.

In 2004, Berry penned her first book, *Child Friendly Divorce: A Divorce(d) Therapist's Guide to Helping Your Children Thrive*, using materials she had written for the court ordered class she teaches for divorcing parents. In 2005 Berry wrote *Romancing the Web: A Therapist's Guide to the Finer Points of Online Dating* after finding herself advising one single client after another regarding the practice of online dating. *A Peace of My Mind* is her third book.

Berry has been married for 18 years to **Terry Berry**, MSW, LCSW, who works as a therapist for Manitowoc County Human Services. He also co-facilitates the Family Violence groups with Diane and sees individual clients on a limited basis at Blue Waters Family Counseling.

A Peace of My Mind is the Berrys' first collaborative published work but they have plans for books on the subjects of parenting and stepfamily adjustment.

Preface

A Note to the Reader

Whether you are picking up this book out of curiosity about this most troubling of emotions or because you believe you need to make immediate changes in how you handle your anger or risk losing those most important to you, you will find help here. Take the time to read through the chapters and the techniques outlined in the book, paying particular attention to the examples provided. Then practice the techniques on a regular basis and before long, you will have made remarkable changes in your life and relationships.

Anger is one of the most difficult emotions to express appropriately and most people could benefit from reading a book like this one. This is not a skill we are taught in school; most of what we know we have learned from what was modeled for us by other persons in our life, for better or for worse. As a result, many of us have learned some destructive ways of handling and expressing anger that we now need to unlearn. You are taking the first step by opening this book.

There is not enough room in one volume to cover everything there is to know about handling anger successfully. Further, this book is not meant to take the place of a certified treatment program. If your anger has led to police or court involvement in your life, or physical harm to your partner, you will find this book helpful and supportive, but will also probably want to contact a therapist who specializes in those issues to work with you on learning these new skills.

If you are willing to share your insights and experiences, we would be honored to hear about them. Remember, the most important thing you can do to make a marked change in how anger affects your life is to practice the skills we explore in this book.

Good luck. We wish you happy, fulfilling relationships.

Terry and Diane Berry
Manitowoc, Wisconsin

Acknowledgments

We have not attempted to cite in this volume all of the authorities and resources consulted in the preparation of this material. To do so would require more space than is available. This list would include government agencies, libraries, periodicals, Web sources and many individuals.

Scores of people contributed to this text, including the hundreds of men attending our family violence and anger management groups and to whom this book is dedicated. You have taught us much and we have enjoyed (almost) every minute of our work with you.

Special thanks also go to Dr. Robert A. Dickens and Don Vogt, Former Unit Supervisor of the State of Wisconsin Division of Corrections, Department of Probation and Parole for their kind words about this work. Thank you also to Hobie and Kathi of Dunn+Design for another terrific book cover in two of our favorite colors, Nate Lyman and Ryan Berry, computer consultants extraordinaire, Heilman Photographers for the back cover photo, Dan Poynter for his continued wisdom and inspiration and to our friend and right arm, Lisa Klein, for *all* she did to make this book possible. We could not have done it without your help!

We would also like to express a heart-felt thanks to our children who cared for themselves remarkably well on Tuesday nights when Mom and Dad were doing group and at other times when we were working on the book. You are exceptional people and we are honored to have you in our lives.

A Note on Gender

To avoid long and awkward phrasing within sentences, the publisher has chosen to randomly alternate the use of male and female pronouns in referring to individuals within this work to give acknowledgment to persons of both genders.

Disclaimer

This book is designed to provide information about the subject matter covered. It is sold with the understanding that the publisher and authors are not engaged in rendering legal, accounting, therapy or other professional services. If legal, therapeutic or other expert assistance is required, the services of a competent professional should be sought.

It is not the purpose of this manual to reprint all the information that is otherwise available to persons on this subject matter, but to complement, amplify and supplement other texts. For more information, please see the many references in the Appendices.

Every effort has been made to make this book as complete and accurate as possible. However, it may contain mistakes, both typographical and in content. Therefore, this text should only be used as a general guide and not as the ultimate source of dating information. Further, this manual contains information on anger management that is current only up to the printing date.

The purpose of this manual is to educated, inform and entertain. The authors and Blue Waters Publications shall have neither liability nor the responsibility to any person or entity with respect to any loss or damage caused or alleged to be caused directly or indirectly by the information contained in this book.

If you do not wish to be bound by the above disclaimer, you may return this book to the publisher for a full refund.

Introduction

Twelve Angry Men

Why Anger Management?

Dale clenched his jaw tightly as I turned to him and said, "So, tell us how you come to join our group." In the few seconds it took for him to formulate his response, you could see the muscles of his face tensing and releasing as he concentrated, struggling to come up with a good story that would get him off the "hot seat". Like most of them, Dale had no desire to be sitting in this group of twelve men, myself the only woman among them, and was quite certain he didn't need to learn anything we could teach him.

"Well we were out drinking and got into an argument and here I am!" Dale stated, somewhat defiantly.

"No, give us some detail," I persisted gently, "Who's we?" The rest of the group smiled, knowing full well I wasn't about to accept a response like that as an introduction.

"The wife and I, and she was flirting with another guy. I got mad and told her to knock it off. When she didn't, I grabbed her by the arm and pulled her out of the bar. Someone called the cops and here I am. They have to take somebody and it's always the guy." Several of the *newer members of the group nodded, slightly. Other group members just smiled knowingly again.*

Anger management treatment? I was a little surprised and not at all excited at the prospect facing me. I was interviewing for a field placement position at one of the few mental health clinics in my small town that accepted student placements. I hoped to be spending twenty hours a week during my final year in graduate school at the clinic, seeing clients as a student therapist, work that I could not wait to begin.

About halfway through the interview, Monica, the therapist who would be supervising my work, explained to me that she and a male co-therapist ran a weekly Anger Management Group for men who were referred either by their probation agents or the district attorney's office due to some type of domestic violence offense of which they had been charged or convicted. It was customary at this agency for all field placement students to participate in the group for the length of their time at the clinic as it was "good experience" for them.

This was not music to my ears. While I had no experience with domestic violence, I was quite certain I did not want to spend one night each week for the next nine months in the company of men considered by our "civilized society" as batterers. Over my thirty five years of living, I had formed more than a few opinions about what such persons might be like and to say I was less than thrilled at this "opportunity" would be an understatement.

However, I was also a realist. A field placement at this agency would be the best opportunity near my home to get a wealth of practical experience in a private practice mental health setting with people I respected and from whom I knew I could learn much. I agreed enthusiastically.

A month later, I was seated around a large table on a Tuesday night on the lower level of the agency with a group of men, one a co-facilitator, and one other woman, Monica, getting my first taste of domestic violence treatment.

That experience has been a life-changing one. Far from meeting men who were beasts and bullies, I met men who were loving and caring people and who had often been victims of violence themselves. In fact, the Tuesday night "Peaceful Alternatives to Family Violence" Groups that Terry and I now enthusiastically run at our own clinic is typically a high point of our week. While we have changed the format in several significant ways, as we will explain in just a moment, it is still a group largely made up of men who are court ordered to attend following some violent incident with a wife, child or loved one, that has come to the attention of local authorities in some fashion. Most hate the idea of being there when they first arrive.

We do at times have volunteers join the group; men who have not been arrested, but perhaps on their own or with the help of a partner have identified anger as an issue they need to work on. As I write this, we currently have three such volunteers in our group of ten participants. They are a nice addition because their attitude is a little more accepting coming in and they balance the group nicely. But we have done many a group made up only of court ordered men, angry and resentful at being there.

"Aren't there easier ways to make a living?" you may be asking yourself. As a therapist, my work is about helping my clients to make changes; being a facilitator of change, as it were. Whether the change is acceptance of oneself or a partner's habits and idiosyncrasies, focusing on the positive instead of the negative in any situation, adjusting to a divorce or other life change or managing negative emotions in a more positive manner, I am all about change. Much of the time, I must content myself with "planting the seeds" that will lead to change down the road and which I will never see. Most often I do not see the end result of my efforts, as it happens slowly and over a period of years. Many of my clients present themselves willingly for counseling, eager to learn and grow, but I only see them for a brief period of time. Thus, the end results remain a mystery.

With the anger management group, the situation is reversed. The typical group member comes in angry, frustrated and resentful with a huge chip on his shoulder. While our group is an open one, meaning that people start at different times, it is also a twenty week group, so we have contact with these men for five months. In most cases that is long enough to begin seeing some real change happen. When we see a man who started the group hostile and resentful, come in early so he can spend an extra fifteen minutes talking with other group members or with Terry and me, and talking about handling his current frustration with his wife or child in a positive manner, that's our reward. That makes all of the orientation nights of grumbling and bitterness and negativity worthwhile!

Terry came to domestic violence treatment in a completely different manner, but is no less enamored of it. Terry was married for ten years to Barb, the mother of his two older sons. Barb had a sister named Anne who was married to John, a military man. The family liked John and thought he complemented Anne nicely. She had always been a bit disorganized and now Anne's life had become more orderly, her house was clean and her children were well-disciplined.

The family was saddened but not alarmed when John wanted to move Anne and the kids to Utah, far away from the rest of the family. About six months after the move, they received a call from Anne that she was thinking of leaving John; she just wasn't happy. The next telephone call was from the Utah police—hearing of her impending departure, and desperate to hold onto his prize, John had taken a shotgun and killed first Anne and then himself.

As a therapist working with troubled families, Terry began to learn more about domestic violence. Recognizing it as a problem in his northwoods community, he helped to organize an informational program for the community. This led to the development of a domestic violence task force comprised of various community agencies working to eradicate domestic violence on a local level.

In late 1999, I was co-facilitating an anger management group at the same clinic at which I had done my field placement. This group was largely based on the original model of domestic violence treatment, which will be explained later in greater detail. In November of 1999, my male co-facilitator became seriously ill and was unable to work for a lengthy period of time. The treatment model requires a male and female team, for some very good reasons. This is a requirement which we have continued to maintain. As he was the only male at the clinic, our choices were to discontinue the group or find a replacement. Terry was a practicing therapist with a pretty significant background in domestic violence treatment so he was a natural for the role. The rest, as they say, is history.

Six months later we opened Blue Waters Family Counseling and offered the group as one of the services we provided. It has gradually continued to evolve, over the past seven years, into the product we have today and upon which this book is based. We have "evolved together" in this group, changing both individually and in our relationship, growing even as we encourage others to do so.

I want to give you a few other specifics about our "Peaceful Alternatives" group for purposes of perspective and to give you some history of how and why the ideas we will share with you have developed over the past fifteen years. As any professional will tell you, there is a distinct difference between domestic violence and anger management treatment. The former explores power and control, values and beliefs, relationship and coping skills in addition to the regulation of emotion. While this book uses the terms somewhat interchangeably, it contains all of these concepts in an attempt to give you a complete picture of how they are interrelated.

We do **not** mean to imply that anyone picking up a book on anger management is in need of family violence treatment. Indeed, we applaud you for identifying anger as an issue you would like to work on without being told to do so by an outside entity. Nor do we want to give the impression that if one has a serious problem with domestic violence, merely picking up a book can solve it. But it can be a starting point.

We also believe that the family violence treatment we provide is as much a resource for learning life and relationship skills as it is an anger management group. Most of these are skills that we should, but unfortunately do not, learn in high school or in our families of origin. It is far broader than a mere discussion of anger. This book is as well.

You will likely find yourself incorporating ideas and skills suggested in this book into all of your relationships: with partner, children, friends, coworkers, clients.

Nor do these ideas only apply to men. Our group is gender specific for some therapeutic and referral-source related reasons that will be discussed later. But the skills taught in this book are universal. For a satisfying relationship, both parties would ideally be practicing these ideas and behaviors. Indeed these skills are crucial for persons of both genders and all ages to learn and practice.

As previously stated, ours is a twenty week group that meets weekly for two hours on Tuesday evenings. It runs year-round, with the exception of our vacations and holidays. We usually hold an orientation one Tuesday per month, at which new members arrive a half hour before the group normally begins to hear about our mutual objectives and expectations of them during the time they are in the group.

After the orientation, the rest of the group members join us and new members are asked to introduce themselves to the remainder of the group, as indicated in the example at the beginning of this chapter. We ask them to discuss the incident that brings them into the group. For court ordered members, it is obviously the "arrest incident." For volunteers, there is often an "ah-ha" moment, at which they decided they needed to do something about their anger. That is the event we are looking for. This is essential for Terry and me to know where these gentlemen are at and how best to work with them.

After the new members introduce themselves, it is time for the veterans to do so. This is an especially telling moment for them as Terry and I use what they say and how they say it to assess their progress in group up to that moment. We will typically ask questions in an attempt to encourage them to take responsibility for their role in what led to their arrest or attending the group. We are also quick to praise the taking of responsibility with few or no questions and a simple, "Good job" or "Nicely done." Through the years, it is sad to see how many of these men have rarely, if ever, heard comments such as these. In many ways, we are re-parenting them, and helping them learn to re-parent and affirm themselves.

After the introductions, we go right into "Check-in" which is how we typically start each week. We use approximately the first half hour of group each week to talk about situations and events that have happened in our lives that week and how we handled them. Group members are typically questioned about their own opinions of how a situation went, given feedback from facilitators and other group members, and helped to focus on future aspects of the issue at hand to prepare them to handle the situation in a positive manner.

On orientation nights, this is about all we accomplish, but often "Check-in" can be the most important time of the group. In fact, many of our group members find themselves gathering in the group room 15-20 minutes before group starts doing their own informal check-in. If I happen to walk in or through at the time, I am excused as they are just, "doing the guy thing." What a wonderful event! Many of these men have never connected with another person, certainly another man, in this way before. They are informally learning and practicing their relationship and communication skills, voluntarily, and before the group actually even begins!

While we do not have a set agenda for the group, we do rotate through a set of topics, making sure to hit on each topic every twenty weeks. In this way, we can tailor the material to the needs of the particular group members. For instance, right now we have several group members experiencing divorce. (You may assume this is typical, but it is not. The majority of these men enter the group still involved with the wife or partner who was involved in "the incident" with them, making it even more crucial that we teach relationship skills!) As a result, we are adding in components of divorce adjustment that all the men benefit from; everyone has ended a relationship at one time or another and can benefit from some additional understanding of that experience.

We have been quite amazed at the amount of caring and support the men provide to one another in this setting, in addition to feedback about abusive behavior. That is the most powerful part of the group! Terry and I can talk until we are blue in the face. But often what really hits home, and what the men take with them, is what they hear from a peer.

We also celebrate a group member's graduation from his twentieth group. Terry usually picks up some chewy chocolate chunk cookies on his way over to the agency and we make a point of mentioning who will be graduating the week before and several times that night and giving out a Certificate of Completion of the program. Finally, we save ten minutes at the end of the group for the "Graduation Speech," during which we ask the graduate to answer three questions: a) how were you feeling about coming into the group; b) what was the first thing you heard here that started to make sense to you and c) what's the one thing you will take with you that will prevent you from ever being ordered to attend a group like this again.

Most admit they hated the idea of coming into the group and thought they didn't need any help. In response to the last two questions, group members typically cite one or more of the skills and techniques discussed in this book that have made a difference for them. Very occasionally, in response to the last question, we hear, "Next time I'll let them throw me in jail instead!" Well, you can't win them all!

The final component of the graduation "ceremony" is the offer we make to all graduating group members: because he is now a graduate of the group, he may attend **free of charge** as long as he is not ordered to attend again or charged with another violent offense. While most do not take advantage of this offer, we have had a number do so over the years. This serves to provide a life time support group for the changes these men are making. One man I can recall practically completed a second 20 week group! Most that do come back, stop in for a few sessions, or show up when something has happened in their lives that they feel it would be helpful to process with the group, such as an argument with their partner, a job loss or difficulties with a child. As I said, most do not take advantage of this offer, but it is a part of every graduation ritual that we hold.

I mentioned previously that Terry and I had made some changes to the program I was originally taught. These changes are also important in understanding the context and philosophy of this book.

The group I did during my field placement was based on the original model in the domestic violence treatment field. Back in the 1970's a group of social workers in the Midwest were interested in developing a comprehensive format for domestic violence treatment. They designed a twenty week program, done in a group format, which would identify abusive attitudes and behaviors and teach healthier, more egalitarian relationship and self-care skills with which to replace them. It was the first major treatment work done with this population and groundbreaking in its day.

However, this treatment model had a major flaw, with which both Terry and I were uncomfortable. We have been relieved and excited to hear other therapists and researchers in recent years express this concern as well. While the initial model identified the imbalance of power and control in any relationship as an abusive behavior, it was heavy on the power and control it **exerted over** group members. It was, in effect, condoning and exercising over group members, exactly the principles it condemned in them. What a confusing message!

In my early years of doing the group, I became aware that this exercise of "power over" group members often led to frustration, resentment and defensiveness and prevented them from being open to making the changes that would have truly improved their lives and relationships. They stayed locked in a power struggle with the system and facilitators and, thus, could not hear or exercise the ideas the system had to offer them. Of course, if it was acceptable for "the system" to exercise an abuse of power, why was it not alright for them to do so? The approach of this model often acted to prevent the very changes it sought to elicit in participants. I will outline as we explore the issues and exercises how our approach varies from the more typical domestic violence treatment programs, most of which are based to at least some extent on that original model.

We view this approach as exercising "power over" an individual, who often subsequently feels overpowered. Our group is more akin to a shared power or a "power with" approach. We look at ourselves as sharing the power of the change process with the individual members of the group who are free to question, challenge, accept, and reject varying aspects of the program.

While we do have some power over group members in that it is our duty to report to probation agents, the district attorney and other referral sources if they do not attend the group, we limit the information that will be shared and this is made clear at the orientation session. Further, we will not share specific comments with referral sources, but do provide general feedback as to an individual's participation and progress. Group members are entitled to the same protection and confidentiality as all other clients. In this way, we find in participants a greater openness and receptivity to ideas presented.

We also attempt to make it safe for group members to challenge ideas being presented and ask them to let us know if a particular skill or technique that we are teaching them is not working for them. That, again, gives us the opportunity to "fine-tune" the approach to make it work for each client. We want group members to feel "safe" raising issues and challenging authority in a way that perhaps they do not feel safe doing in other areas in their lives. You, also, will have a greater likelihood of making lasting changes if you feel safe to experiment with new behaviors.

The other issue we have with the original treatment model and many of the current domestic violence treatment programs is that they can be extremely punitive and shaming. It is difficult, if not impossible, to encourage acceptance and openness of new strategies and ideas in a client by beating him up and punishing him. This only serves to make him defensive and to stubbornly refuse to look at this opportunity for change. We strive to provide information to stimulate thinking that may lead group members to make better choices in the future. We seek to impart this knowledge while speaking and listening with the utmost respect for them as individuals and what they know, challenging and confronting in a gentle, respectful manner.

We have struggled to create a kinder, gentler family violence treatment group, but one which still holds persons accountable for their behavior. There is some basis for this shift in approach from people who have researched this phenomenon. However, the majority of these treatment programs still use the older approach. Perhaps this work will challenge them to look at the outcomes of their programs in a different way. In evaluating outcomes with our program, less than 15% of persons completing our group re-offend. While there is some inconsistency regarding the recidivism rates reported by studies of standard domestic violence treatment programs, these seem to vary between 34 and 60%. As an aside, recidivism rates are up to 75% in persons who fail to complete our group, eliminating potential speculation that we are somehow dealing with less serious or violent offenders.

We did not arrive at our approach overnight. Much of it came gradually over a period of years, almost unconsciously as we met and worked with the various men who have taught us so much over these last ten years. Initially it was almost an unconscious thing, as we would hear a story and empathize or respond to a group member much as we do to an individual client alone in our offices. We observed the positive reaction to this softer, more accepting approach and noted the subsequent change this individual was able to achieve. Other changes were more momentous, such as sitting in domestic violence and anger management workshops with other treatment providers and hearing them echo the very same ideas and cite research that has been done out east that verifies the ideas we had arrived at intuitively! We learned some important things from those workshops that have greatly strengthened our program.

There are a number of other teachers, therapists, speakers, researchers and group members that have significantly influenced this book. We do not see our "Peaceful Alternatives" program as something of our own creation, but rather as a culmination of life and work experiences that have led us to this point in time. The snapshot of our approach, with which we have seen some positive results, is what we hope to share with you in these pages.

We expect as we continue to have experiences, similar to those that have shaped this text thus far, our program will continue to evolve. We will do our best to share that progress with you in future editions of this work. If you are interested in receiving updates as they arise, please send us an email at the address at the end of the book. We look forward to hearing from you. In addition, if you have experiences to add to our work, please let us know those as well. We would enjoy learning about them and may want to incorporate them into our program and future editions of this book.

We'd like to say a brief word here about the organization of this book. Each chapter begins with a real life example from our experience of working with persons with anger problems, either as part of the group or through our work with individuals or couples. While many of the examples used do come from the group members, and may seem a bit extreme to some readers, it is often easier to identify the problematic belief or behaviors in a more extreme example than in something more subtle. These are given for the purposes of illustrating one of the points made in the chapter.

It is our hope that readers are able to see themselves in these experiences and can find something to identify with. Only when we are aware of our issues do we have the ability to change them. We hope to empower you to make the changes you need to achieve positive, healthy, respectful relationships. We also find through our work that learning by example often removes the shame from admitting to an issue or problem. If one can see that someone else has engaged in similar behaviors or struggled with similar problems, it is safer to admit to their own transgressions. It is only when we acknowledge a problem that we are in a position to actually achieve lasting change. This is our hope for you. If you see yourself in these pages, you will be empowered to see that, though you may feel out of control, you actually have the ability to choose how you will handle most any situation.

Each of the chapters to follow will focus on a problem area related to the handling of anger. These chapters roughly parallel the topic areas we introduce in our group. Examples are included of how some of our group members identified with or responded to the teaching. Readers will learn why the issue is problematic and how it can affect relationships. Information will be shared as to how to deal with issue differently and changes that can be made.

The chapter will then end with a summary or checklist to determine whether you have more work to do in the area of that issue. In my therapy work, I tell my clients in the first session that I like to give homework. In spite of occasional groans and eye rolls, this is where real change happens. True change cannot happen in my office in an hour every other week. A client and I can sit in my office and have a pleasant conversation for an hour, and, without further efforts on their part, nothing about their lives may change. I consider this a waste of a client's time and money.

The same is true for progress in anger management or emotional regulation work. That's the reason for homework. Most often it is not something that needs to be written down, but often it is helpful to do so. The assigned task is typically to try a new skill or pay attention to when you feel a certain way. This will help you to take the teaching out into your lives and start using it, rather than merely reading about it. This is the challenge I make to you: you've invested in this book; now invest in yourself in terms of actually doing the exercises included in it. Aren't you and your relationships with those you love worth the time and money?

Before continuing on with the rest of the book, please take a look at the chart on the following page for a self-assessment of anger-related issues. This can help focus your progress through the book.

Anger Issue Self-Assessment

Before you continue, glance over the issues listed below that roughly correspond to the chapters in this book. Mark in the first column, the issues which you identify as areas in which you may have some work to do. Then, proceed to read through the chapters that follow. As you complete each chapter, flip back to this page and check the issue if you discover that, once you have read the chapter on that issue, you feel you do have some changes you could make with regard to that topic. Additionally, if you have ever heard from a partner, friend, co-worker or supervisor that you have trouble with any of these issues, please note that in the "Others" column as well.

Issues	Myself	Others
I experience anger more often than others	___	___
I have experienced intense feelings of rage	___	___
I have been angry in reaction to stress	___	___
I have been violent when angry	___	___
I have difficulty walking away from conflict	___	___
It is difficult for me to calm myself down	___	___
I have experienced communication problems due to my anger	___	___
It is hard for me to negotiate without getting angry	___	___
I have trouble taking responsibility for my behavior or actions	___	___
I have become angry when jealous	___	___
When I experience anger, my anger seems more intense than most others'	___	___
My anger seems to last longer than others'	___	___
Due to my anger I have experienced:		
Damage to relationships	___	___
Problems at work	___	___
Health problems	___	___
Worrying or dwelling on problems	___	___
Guilt or shame	___	___
Inability to handle difficult situations	___	___
Contact with police or court system	___	___

Chapter 1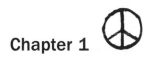

The Rage Within

All About Anger (or, So What Is Anger, Anyway?)

Walking *into the group room, the first thing I notice is a young man sitting at the table with his head down, clearly a new member of our group.*

Later, still struck by his earlier demeanor, I invite him to tell us his story. "Well it happened on New Year's Eve," he begins. "My wife and I were at a party and I noticed her flirting with another guy. I told her to knock it off, but she wouldn't. After watching for awhile, I told her we were leaving and as we were getting in the car to go home, I just went ballistic. I grabbed her by the neck and strangled her. She almost passed out. I don't know what came over me. I've never done anything like that before."

What is this mysterious demon we call anger. Is it a feeling? Is it a behavior? Or is it both? There is a common misconception that anger can be either a feeling or a behavior.

We have had men come into our group introducing themselves with comments such as "My anger is hitting people," and "I have no control over my anger."

However, anger is a feeling, an emotion. It is not an action. And the feeling is not good or bad; it just *is*. The feeling must be accepted and dealt with. The same is not true of the behavior.

The Issue of Control

We do have control over our emotions. Even when feeling out of control, there are situations when we each exercise an extreme amount of control over our feelings and, especially, our actions.

For instance, even someone who reports he has no control over the anger causing him to strangle a partner or punch her in the face, would not treat an employer or a police officer the same way. For whatever reason, he is able to exercise sufficient control over his emotions, even when extremely upset with his boss, not to hit him. And he typically will not punch a police officer who performs a routine traffic stop, even when the officer is sarcastic and provocative in his demeanor. Our angry man knows there will be extremely negative consequences if he becomes violent with his boss or the "law."

Additionally, we set limits on our behavior. For example, a man who has strangled his partner, when asked why he didn't stab her or throw her to the floor and kick her in the stomach, often becomes appalled. He may respond with, "Well I would never do that!" He has set internal limits on his behavior and that which he views as acceptable treatment of a partner.

Where Does Anger Come From?

Anger is useful to us as it is a signal that something is wrong. Anger identifies dissatisfaction, unhappiness, an unresolved conflict, an issue we must deal with. It can be a trigger for us to undertake to change a situation that is causing some trouble in our lives. It can be a catalyst, spurring us to action, enabling us to take actions we may not consider otherwise. It can be a motivator for action and change. It can lead to many positive changes for us.

Who among us has not become angry about a situation in our lives, taken action and experienced changed circumstances as a result? We do this personally, in families and also in larger groups. All of the major changes in law and social policy that we have experienced in our country, the women's movement, civil rights legislation, the slogan "No taxation without representation!" just to name a few have all been motivated by anger about the existing situation and conditions. Our country has become what it is because of the anger of various groups of people.

As a catalyst for change, anger can be an extremely useful emotion. The key is control. We must be able the control and channel this emotion into useful action and results. If we merely run around shouting and swearing about what's not fair or just, we accomplish little, other than perhaps irritating the powers that be.

Our goal, therefore, is not to rid ourselves of all anger, but to channel it in ways it can do us the greatest good. Once we can make our anger work for us, it becomes a useful element in our lives. But, how do we do this? And where do we learn it?

A Model of Anger

Of all the men who have attended our group on a voluntary basis, those not ordered to attend by a District Attorney, probation agent or court, the majority have chosen to do so because of the modeling effect. Many were the product of abusive parenting, i.e. mom or dad blasting around expressing anger like a two year old and taking it out on them or were concerned about the effect of their anger on their own children. As one recent group recruit stated, "When I saw my six year old son acting like me, I knew I had to do something." Others have said, "I saw myself acting like my father; I had always told myself I would never do that."

But this is where we learn. When we are in intimate relationships as adults, most of us act toward our partner as we have observed our parents behave in their relationship. This is where we form our ideas about what it means to be a husband, wife or partner. This, also, is where we get our judgments of what is a "good" husband, wife, mother and father. When our partner does not measure up, problems ensue.

It's a set-up for conflict in all actuality. We take two partners from completely (or at least somewhat) different backgrounds and families, because no two families are alike. There will be at least minor differences, even if we can avoid major ones. We put these two persons with dissimilar expectations together and expect them to share a home, family and their lives. No wonder they get into trouble!

As you can see, conflict is inevitable. How they deal with it makes the difference between those couples that can weather the storm and those that will choose divorce. In more extreme situations, it can lead to violence, often when that has been a pattern in the family of origin, but even at times when it has not. That is when anger and conflict becomes a problem that must be addressed. Most people can use some work on their emotional regulation and anger management skills. When violence results, intervention and change is imperative, both for the individuals involved as well as for the relationship.

A Secondary Emotion

Anger is what we call a secondary emotion. This means that whenever we feel anger, we have felt something else first; most typically some variation of hurt, fear or frustration. Often all three emotions combine to lead to our anger. In most cases, however, if you deal with the underlying and primary emotion, the anger will take care of itself.

For example, assume you are driving down the road, minding your own business, when suddenly a big black car swerves in front of you and cuts you off. You are enraged, incensed. "How dare he?" you shout to yourself, shaking your fist at the offending driver. You are aware of your anger, but you may not be aware of what preceded it.

If you let yourself think back, you begin to discover that your first thought was one of fear, "Oh my gosh, he's going to hit me. I'm going to get into an accident!" Then, before you knew it, the anger kicked in and that's what you are aware of.

In our society, it is easier, safer and more socially acceptable to express anger, than it is to express fear or hurt. Rather than saying, "I was scared," it is far easier to say "What a jerk!" or "What an outrage!" We can picture the people nodding and agreeing with us in our rage, making us feel vindicated in our vengefulness.

Yet, this outcome is not working for us. As a society we tend to be very angry. We have more road rage than most other countries, in addition to higher rates of murder and many other violent crimes than most other "civilized" countries. Not to mention the multitude of school shootings, from Columbine to Virginia Tech. Yet we are supposedly a world leader, a super-power. As a society, we resemble a bully more than a role model or a peace maker.

Why, then, are we so angry and defensive? Is it making us feel any better? Is it leading to more positive choices? Better relationships? We think not. It's keeping us stuck and miserable.

What's a person to do? First of all, identify and accept the underlying emotion. Then, ultimately, deal with it!

If you are the driver who has been cut off, there is much you can do to temper your reaction to this incident. This will be discussed in great detail in Chapter Seven. But the first job is to identify the problem. If you are having this type of reaction to situations in your life with which you routinely come into contact, you are creating a great deal of unhappiness for yourself. First of all, these situations are almost always out of your control. Getting upset about them just keeps you at the mercy of everything and everyone with whom you come into contact. What a nightmare!

You need to take back the power you are giving away. Identify yourself as someone who has this problem. Then think of trigger situations that you routinely react to. Some of the more typical ones include: standing in line (i.e. at the bank, gas station or grocery store), being cut off in traffic, being reprimanded at work, a partner or children not doing what you want or expect them to do. You may need to walk yourself through the past few months of your life and think of the times you were most upset. What do these various situations have in common: was there a loss of control, a surprise, an unexpected turn of events, damage to your pride, etc.

Once you have taken the time to come up with your own list of situations, take a look at page 74 for a list of some of the more common Triggers and Hot Buttons that people find themselves reacting to. With a few additions, this list was compiled by our group. Feel free to add your items to the list, but read it through to see if there are any others you can identify for yourself.

With this information, you will be able to then list some of the more typical events you are likely to experience that will be troubling for you and be on the lookout for them. Carry your list with you and read it over often. In Chapter Seven we will discuss a new way of handling these situations. This list will be helpful in identifying some of the best times to practice these new skills.

The Iceberg

Another helpful way to think about this issue is to imagine an iceberg. Close your eyes for just a minute and picture it in your mind's eye. See it there all frozen and white, jagged and cold. Picture also the water level about two thirds of the way up the iceberg.

The anger you express to the public is the top third of the iceberg; the part that is exposed and out of the water. Underlying the anger, just under the water-level so you (and others) can't quite see them lay a multitude of other negative emotions: hurt, fear, frustration, jealousy, insecurity, loneliness, guilt, shame and the like. When we are talking to someone who is hurt, we are more accepting and behave differently than when we are dealing with someone who is enraged and screaming at us.

Many times I have been in session with an extremely angry client, who is quite upset. Often this occurs in the context of a couple's session. The angry client is often blasting the other partner about some imagined insult or indiscretion. How easy it is to take the wind out of their sails by identifying the true emotion that is getting to them by making a comment such as, "Have you even told your wife how hurt you are because she refuses to go bowling with you?" Immediately the enraged partner feels heard and understood and the other partner's eyes are opened to the hurt little child that is feeling unimportant to his partner. The whole discussion shifts into something workable, solvable and often tears are present and change, inevitable. Often the angriest person in the room is merely the one with the greatest hurt.

If we can only get into the habit of looking for the true negative emotion underlying our partner's (or our boss's, employee's, co-workers', child's, friend's or our own) anger, we are in a position to identify and deal with it. We can also help them to identify this as well, thereby introducing a change that can occur in later conversations and troublesome situations. We are helping them and ourselves to learn a life skill.

Why this is so difficult to uncover has to do with our socialization. As enlightened a society as we think we are, it is still safer and more acceptable to express the feeling of anger, than those of fear or hurt. We accept anger more easily from others and are more comfortable expressing it ourselves. Expressing the more painful, less acceptable and difficult emotions is something we all can learn. But, often men struggle with this more than women.

Men are socialized to be tough and not to let adversaries see them as vulnerable. For this reason, men are trained to show anger rather than hurt or fear. Their role models are John Wayne and Rambo—be tough, don't show pain (even when the arrow pierces your body and your have to pull it out yourself!) Never let them see you sweat.

Women often have a very different experience. Little girls that are caught expressing anger and frustration, through shouting or some type of physical behavior are often given a message such as, "That's not ladylike," or "Nice girls don't do that." Then, when still frustrated, she bursts into tears, she quickly gets an arm around her shoulder and a, "That's alright honey."

I cannot count the number of women in their thirties, forties and fifties who come into my office and ask, "Why is it that when I am frustrated or angry, I burst into tears." The answer, my dear, is that you've been trained to do that. You were given the message that that was the only socially acceptable way to express those emotions. Now, however, as adults in relationships and in the workplace, this isn't working very well for them anymore. So I help them learn a new style of expressing those feelings.

Often male partners see tears as a manipulation. While there are isolated cases when this does occur, by far the vast majority of situations in which women cry are true expressions of genuine emotion, rather than manipulation. If their partners can learn to respect these tears and the emotions they represent, the relationship can only benefit.

Hidden Anger

Anger that is openly shared is easily recognized. However, persons who have been taught that it is not acceptable to show anger may be very adept at hiding it. Others who come in contact with them may be unaware they are angry, but confused about their own personal reaction to those who hide their anger. Often we can have strong emotional reactions to these persons without completely understanding why. Let me explain.

Some examples of hidden anger include the following:

- Procrastination
- Perpetual or habitual lateness
- Sarcasm or cynicism
- Over-politeness, constant cheerfulness
- Silence or withdrawal
- Belittling
- Manipulative or controlling behaviors
- Over-controlled or monotone voice
- Slow movements
- Drowsy at inappropriate times
- Other behaviors consciously or subconsciously having the effect of interrupting another's plans or arrangements.

If you are dealing with a partner or friend who is adept at hiding her anger, she may be unable to get to a lunch date with you on time, or may be yawning through your meal together or her movements while on a romantic walk may be so slow as to ruin the mood and cause her to be dragging behind. All of these can be efforts, conscious or not, to express her anger about something in your relationship that she is not comfortable expressing with you directly. If there has been a pattern of abuse or excessive anger in your relationship, she may not be comfortable expressing these feelings more overtly. Or, if she grew up in an abusive environment or where anger was unacceptable, she may have learned early on to hide her anger.

One woman we know, Julie, grew up in a family where anger was not permitted in any form. Her father was a highly religious man and expected his children to behave appropriately at all times. Anger and sadness were not permissible emotions. One was always expected to maintain composure. As an adult, Julie presented a flat, calm affect. She denied that she ever felt anger, but even though she was a college graduate, she suffered from such severe Depression that she was unable to function or to maintain employment.

Other signs and symptoms of hidden anger can include frequent sighing, disturbing dreams and other sleep problems, irritability, headaches, fatigue, increased irritability, ulcers and a depressed mood. An attraction to sadistic or ironic humor and a habit of smiling when hurt or upset can also indicate hidden anger.

When you become aware of these symptoms in a partner or friend, it can be helpful to note them and inquire whether there is something wrong. While the individual may deny the upset, you will at least have put her on notice that you are aware of the change in her. Perhaps in time, she will become more adept at identifying her true emotions and more comfortable sharing them with you.

Summary

Take some time to think about the ideas this chapter has presented about anger. Give them a chance to sink in. You have probably been presented here with some ideas that vary a great deal from what you were taught about anger growing up, so don't be surprised if they feel foreign and unfamiliar to you.

A common response upon hearing ideas foreign to us is to doubt and try to contradict them. If you are having this reaction, take a little more time; give them a chance to start making sense to you and see if they don't strike a chord of truth deep down inside. When you are ready, take a look at the chapter summary on the following pages and see how you respond to some common ideas about anger.

Thoughts About Anger

	True	False

⊕ I must never feel angry. ____ ____

⊕ I am a bad person if I feel angry. ____ ____

⊕ People will not love me if I get angry. ____ ____

⊕ People will reject me if I express anger. ____ ____

⊕ If I'm angry I must be out of control. ____ ____

⊕ Other people make me angry. ____ ____

⊕ People should know that I'm angry
without my having to tell them. ____ ____

⊕ If I'm angry, people should do things
to make me feel less angry. ____ ____

⊕ People will like me better if I never
express anger. ____ ____

⊕ I must never show anger toward my
family. ____ ____

⊕ If I become angry, I might stay
angry forever. ____ ____

⊕ I must be right about an issue before
I can be angry. ____ ____

⊕ I need to have logical reasons before
I can be angry. ____ ____

⊕ My angry feelings should always make
sense. ____ ____

⊕ My anger will always hurt other people. ____ ____

⊕ Anger is evil. ____ ____

⊕ I have no control over my actions
when I'm angry. ____ ____

⊕ I am not responsible for my actions
when someone makes me angry. ____ ____

⊕ People should know **why** I'm angry
without me having to tell them. ____ ____

⊕ People should take care not to get me
angry. ____ ____

⊕ People just have to accept my anger; I
can't do anything about it. ____ ____

The appropriate response to each of the above statements is "False", for reasons that should be obvious after reading the preceding chapter. If you responded "True" to any of the above items, please review Chapter One for a greater understanding of this powerful emotion.

If you did believe some of the thoughts in our summary to be true, you are in good company. Anger is the most misunderstood of our emotions. And remember, that's why you're reading this book after all — to learn more about it. So, don't be too hard on yourself.

Read on!

Chapter 2

How Anger Hurts

The Concept of Violence

The big man seemed to be epitome of meekness, a true gentle giant, as I turned to him and asked, "So how do you come to join us?"

"I gave the wife a bear hug and here I am," he replied, a little sheepishly.

"What?" protested others in the group, "They don't arrest you for hugging your wife now, do they?"

"They do when you're drunk and angry and it cuts off her air so she can't breathe!"

"OK, I think we'd better hear the whole story," I stated, eager to avoid another protest against the system that would convict a man for showing his wife a little affection.

"Well, we were arguing. She was upset because I'm always working. I had stopped for a few with the guys after work and just didn't want to listen to her bitching. So to shut her up, I walked over and gave her a big hug. It worked! Until the cops came!"

We are an extremely violent society. From the outset, it seemed that our culture was based on violence and valued the ability to prevail at all costs over most other skills. We obtained this land that is now America by cheating the Native people out of it and, when that didn't work, taking it by outright force.

We also encourage and accept competition, even when it becomes brutal and damaging to participants, valuing survival of the fittest over success and acceptance for all. We seek to win at the expense of others, vying with friends, acquaintances, co-workers, even family for money, jobs, and possessions. And we set our children up to do the same. These ideas are the very basis of our capitalist society and the economy of which we are so proud.

It should come as no surprise, then, that we have a higher murder rate and more violent crimes than most other civilized countries. We also, however, have more prisons and more child abuse than most and certainly more than we can or want to afford.

And we are a nation of people who have problems with anger, violence and aggression. We hear daily about incidents of road rage and violent attacks on neighbors and school children. Most recently the extreme violence at Virginia Tech devastated the nation. We should not be surprised at this. We have created a culture that expects and supports this violence and the only way to reduce these incidents is to change that culture and the values that make it acceptable to hurt someone to get what we want.

What is Violence?

In addressing the issue of anger, we believe it is helpful to spend some time actually trying to arrive at a definition of violence because when we are angry, most of us act in habitual ways, often learned in childhood from our parents or primary caregivers. Many of these lessons, these behaviors we visit upon our own loved ones when angry or upset, are violent ones. When our emotional response is triggered, we act as if on automatic pilot, going though our damaging behaviors without giving them much of a thought. If we are to truly get a handle on anger we will, therefore, also need to look at our violent beliefs and actions.

Everyone whose anger has ever caused a problem for him, whether in an intimate or family relationship, friendship, work or other setting, can benefit from taking a good hard look at his angry behavior and comparing it to behavior he views as acceptable. This is necessary to determine what behavior he would like to see himself doing differently. When making this comparison, most angry people typically find that they become quite violent, either in the words or actions they use, when they are angry. But to many of us, our violent culture is so ingrained, that it is difficult to see what is violent and hurtful to another without taking a step back and holding our own actions up to the light for a good hard look. When we do this exercise with our anger management group, it is often several weeks into the group before the concept of violence is truly understood.

We would like to spend some time now outlining a number of ways we can be violent in relationship to others. Often we may be causing pain without realizing we are doing so. Other times, we know exactly what we are doing and are looking to gain something from it. Remember, one true goal of violent behavior is most often "to get what I want when I want it!"

Violence in Relationships

Just as anger and violence damage our society, they damage relationships as well. There are a number of ways in which this occurs and a number of different, often seemingly harmless behaviors that occur in the course of our relationships with others that can cause them harm or exercise an inappropriate amount of power or control over them. While we will look at a healthy balance of power and control in a relationship in Chapter Eight, what we will be exploring here is an excess or abuse of power and control in relationships.

Most people come to a group, or pick up a book like this one, assuming we are talking about anger that leads to actual physical violence. However, much of the time anger does not lead to physical contact, but is just as damaging to a relationship as if it were used. There are also cases in which non-physical power and control can be more damaging than physical violence as it is more pervasive and repetitive and can take longer to recover from than a hit or a slap.

Even when there is physical violence in a relationship, it usually occurs relatively rarely. What does happen, typically on a daily or at least weekly basis, is a pattern of one partner exerting power and control over the other in hundreds of subtle and insidious ways that work to destroy her confidence and, eventually, her feelings for him. We will be discussing here the myriad ways of being violent in a relationship with a partner or loved one, some of which have nothing to do with raising your hand to her.

In our group, Terry and I find it is often easier to work with persons who have actually been physically violent with a partner or child because the problem is much clearer and easier to identify. Non-physical forms of power and violence are much more subtle and easier to justify to oneself than actually punching someone in the face. Even if they disagree with us, anyone walking into our group can understand why someone might have a problem with that behavior. But most of us can find a multitude of reasons why it is acceptable to prevent our partner from going out with her friends (it takes away from our family time, we don't have the money, I don't like her friend and so on) so it becomes easier to delude yourself that she is the problem and you have nothing to change. See Chapter Eleven for a further discussion of justifications we use for our behavior. But know that attempting to control her behavior, either with or because of your anger at her, will damage your relationship, even if you never physically hurt her.

Strategies of Power and Control

There are a number of different techniques that lead to an abuse of power and control in a relationship. Most persons who are violent do not engage in all of these behaviors but typically have one or several "favorites" that they resort to on a regular basis. Just as we all get into habits of how we behave in relationships and how we interact with our partners, persons who become abusive and controlling have habits as well. Identifying your own habitual ways of relating to a partner gives you the power to change them if you find they are not getting you the result you desire. See Chapter Seven for a more extensive discussion of outcomes of our behaviors.

Let's take a look at some of the innumerable ways we can exert power and control over a partner, perhaps without realizing it. As an aside, control is not necessarily a bad thing— it is only the abuse of control, an inappropriate amount of it creating an imbalance in a relationship, that is harmful.

Intimidation

Intimidation is inducing fear or anxiety in a partner to get what you want. It is more specifically defined as the use of looks, actions, and gestures that are meant to frighten or bully another person. Prior use of physical violence enhances the impact of intimidation on most people. Therefore, if when angry in the past you have punched your partner and now you merely give her an angry glare, you are likely to get more mileage out of your glare than if she had never been hit. The message will be clear and you will be more likely to get what you want.

There are a number of ways to do this with a partner that are easy to justify and rationalize. Giving angry looks and stares that send the message, "You're going to be sorry for this," can be very effective. Slamming doors, throwing things, punching or kicking walls or furniture can send the messages, "You're next," or "Give me what I want or else." Using intoxication or giving the "silent treatment" is effective as well.

Standing in a way to crowd her, preventing her from leaving a room, getting in her face or standing above, looking down at her can have an extremely intimidating effect. The more obvious techniques of yelling and screaming are intimidating, as is walking around acting like you are about to blow up so everyone, including the dog, gets the message they have to walk on eggshells around you. Tearing up or ruining things she gave you or you gave her is intimidating behavior, as are smashing things, harming pets, driving recklessly, acting "crazy," invincible or like you have nothing to lose. Stalking and threatening suicide are also extremely intimidating.

Each of these acts sends the message, "Do what I want, or else..." Even when the threat is nonspecific, it is very effective. The message is clear.

We want to add a couple of examples from our group that will clarify this concept as well. One of our group members, Jeremiah, who we will meet more fully at the beginning of Chapter Nine, got into the habit of sitting down and very calmly cleaning his gun whenever he and his partner would argue. He never overtly threatened to shoot her, just very calmly and quietly got the gun down and started taking it apart. His message was clear to his partner. She learned to shut up and eventually left the relationship.

We live in a town of about 34,000 persons and everyone knows much about everyone else. Several years ago, we had a murder that shocked the community when an 82 year old man, during an argument with his wife of some 60 years, calmly took out his gun and shot her twice in the head, killing her in their backyard. When police came and questioned him, he quickly admitted, "Sure I did it," and made some comment to the effect of, "I just couldn't take it anymore." One of our group members, Dan, told us he cut out the newspaper clipping of this event and hung it on the refrigerator in his kitchen, saying to his wife, "See, that's what happens..." I'm sure she understood his message. She filed for divorce shortly thereafter.

Emotional Abuse

There are a number of different ways to be emotionally abusive as well. Some of the more common include putting her down and saying things to make her feel bad about herself. Any name-calling is emotionally abusive. The same is true with playing mind games and doing or saying things to make her think she's crazy, such as, "Look at you, yelling and screaming," or "You should be on medication."

Humiliating her or making comments designed to induce guilt, such as "A good mother would stay home with her children rather than going out with friends," are emotionally abusive. Negatively comparing her to others, making unreasonable demands of her or expecting perfectionism is abusive. Any type of behavior designed to manipulate her, such as honeymooning her by buying flowers after an abuse incident, or the opposite, using things that matter to her against her, such as refusing to participate in a planned event like a family reunion or vacation unless she gives in to you, is an abuse of power.

Isolation

While emotionally abusive comments are relatively easy to hear and identify, isolating behaviors are often difficult to recognize from the outside of a relationship. Though they can be quite overt, more often they take a very subtle form. An isolating partner often does most of his work in the privacy of his home when others are not present.

Isolation is accomplished by controlling a partner's access to friends and family, and also to resources such as money, education, employment opportunities, transportation, telephone use, and reproductive choices, such as birth control. Jealousy is often used to justify these actions. An angry controlling partner may say, "I don't like it when you go out with her; she goes to bars and picks up men," or "You don't want to go back to school and take all that time and money away from our family and the nice things we could have, do you?"

Notice that in neither of these cases, has he said, "You can't do this," but the intent is clear. While it may not happen the first time his wish is challenged, over a period of time, a partner becomes aware that there is a price to pay for going against his wishes. Often these discussions include the words that whatever she wants to do, see family or friends, go back to school, get a job, etc. is or will be "harmful to our relationship."

Additionally, an isolated yet assertive person may attempt to reassure her partner and still make the choice to go out with the friend he doesn't like. However, when she returns home, the price is often 20 questions:

☮ Where did you go?
☮ Who did you talk to?
☮ Why did you get home so late?
☮ Did you flirt with anyone?
☮ Did she take anyone home?
☮ Did you see anyone you knew?
☮ And so on…

The next time the opportunity to spend time with this friend arises, she will remember this exchange and many women eventually just stop making the choice to see the friend. Or go on to school. Or whatever it is she wants to do that displeases him. So she becomes isolated, in part by her own choice. But the seeds of isolation are planted by his responses to her before she ever turns down her first invitation.

Other, more overt ways of inducing isolation include embarrassing her in front of others, kidnapping her or coming right out and telling her she can't do what she wants, often accompanied by the words, "I forbid it!" For a wonderful example of this type of behavior, take a look at the movie, *"This Boy's Life"* starring Robert de Niro, Leonardo di Caprio and Ellen Barkin. The scene in which Ellen tells her husband, Robert, that she is planning to volunteer for John Kennedy's presidential campaign is an excellent example of this more overt type of isolation. The movie also contains terrific examples of a number of other control techniques, so we highly recommend watching it in its entirety.

Minimizing, Denying and Blaming

This encompasses any technique used to avoid taking responsibility for one's actions, which can also be called obfuscation. Typically when we don't feel good about our actions, we will come up with some defense or excuse to rationalize or feel better about them.

While we cover this more fully in Chapter Eleven, which focuses on this subject, we wanted to briefly define this concept here to give you a basic idea of what we mean in this area. Any attempt to deny or minimize the existence, severity or impact of abusive behavior, or blame or otherwise shift responsibility for abusive behavior is considered obfuscation. In the real world, comments such as, "I just pushed you a little," or "If you would know when to shut up I wouldn't have to hit you," would qualify.

Other types of obfuscation would include omitting or concealing information in order to gain an advantage or playing the victim to gain sympathy or support. Using intoxication to excuse abusive behavior is a denial of responsibility as well.

Using Others

Using children to relay messages or using visitation to harass or control a partner is abusive. A common technique is to agree to a change in the placement schedule for a given week, then to call an hour before the relied-upon change to tell her it isn't going to work out and you want to go back to the original plans. She is then left to scramble to change plans or find child care at the last minute. Often, a cleverly manipulative ex-spouse can also arrange for the placement order to require partners to ask if the other parent would like to provide child care for children if it is needed for a specified number of hours, rather than having the children taken to a sitter. He can then use this tactic to maintain control over a former spouse for a year or more by changing plans at the last minute.

Threatening to take children away, to take her back to court, to report her to human services or actually abusing children to get her to do what you want are obviously abusive. The tactic here is to blatantly hurt whoever is most important to her to exert control over her behavior.

Using Male or Female Privilege

A controlling partner often takes the initiative to define what men's and women's roles should be and attempts to justify his opinion by some authority, such as, "The bible says..." or "That's the way we do things in my family." We typically see this more from controlling men than controlling women, but it can cut both ways. She can be helpless and unable or unwilling to do many of the day to day tasks she finds more disagreeable with the excuse that, "It's the man's job."

By the same token, he may also define what is and isn't important or valid and control the decision-making process in the household, walking out or becoming intimidating when a discussion is not going his way. He may make and enforce self-serving rules, treat her as an inferior ("You don't have as much education, make as much money, know as much about the world, have as many years living on your own, etc. as I do") or act like the "Master of the Castle." Again, the movie *"This Boy's Life"* contains some wonderful examples of this tactic. He may come right out and state, "It's my right as a man to make these decisions," or, as Robert de Niro quips so eloquently in the movie, "My house, my rules."

This behavior was justified in the past by the belief that a man should be the head of the household. For most relationships today, where both parties work outside the household, that belief is not accepted, validated or workable.

Economic Abuse

Economic abuse involves behaviors such as concealing or denying access to information about resources, using assets, hers or the family's, without her knowledge, preventing her from getting or keeping a job, damaging her credit rating, giving her an allowance, making her ask for money or destroying or denying her access to checkbooks, credit cards, money or property.

This technique is often closely associated with the Male Privilege tactic. The ways in which they are enforced are often inextricably linked. For example, he may make the rule that each is to pay one half of the family's bills or expenses (male privilege). He may argue, "That sounds fair, doesn't it?" On its face it does, but when, as is often the case, his income is three times what hers is, the picture changes. The family expenses then take up every penny of her income, while he has two thirds of his paycheck to blow (economic abuse).

We then need to address both issues: that of male privilege issue (Who gets to make the rules and how are they made?) as well as the economic issue (strapping her with so many expenses she has no money to spend going out with friends, buying clothes that may make her attractive to others or give her access to resources).

Threats and Coercion

This technique is closely associated with the Intimidation issue. Often a behavior can be both intimidating and threatening or coercive at the same time.

Threats are statements which promise negative consequences for certain behaviors or actions. For example, "I'll kill you if you ever leave me." Often abusive partners also threaten suicide if she leaves or divorce if she doesn't do what he wants.

Coercion can be statements or actions which imply, indirectly, negative or positive consequences for pursuing a certain course of action. An example of this might be cleaning the house the day after an incident of physical abuse. Coercion is often more subtle than threats. She is typically left to draw the conclusions on her own, but the message is still clear. In this case, "Don't press charges; I'll be good and help out."

Physical Contact

Not all abusive physical contact takes the form of hits, slaps or punches. Often it is much more subtle than that. It may be something as simple as preventing someone from leaving the room or leaving the house; it may be simply standing in your partner's way as he is trying to accomplish something, such as making dinner or working on the car, in such a way that physical contact ensues. Other times, it may be actually holding him so that he cannot leave, look away or move his body or holding onto him or forcing affection when he does not want it.

Sometimes couples engage in mutual playful slaps or aggressive play that leads to one overpowering the other. Usually the male is the overpowering partner. Sometimes this aggressive play leads to anger and additional violence.

Any form of physical contact that attempts to control another person's movements so that you get what you want is an abuse of control even though it does not leave a mark. I have heard from group members the excuse that, "I just wanted her to hear what I had to say!" That doesn't matter; you have no right to make her stay or to make her listen. Communication requires two willing participants. If either is forced, it is an abuse of power.

Physical Violence

This one is obvious. Physical violence in the form of hitting, slapping, punching, kicking, shoving, etc. is an abuse of power and control in the relationship. This is the easiest form of abuse to identify so I won't belabor the point by going into great detail listing all of the different ways of causing physical harm to the one we love.

It is easy to see that there is some overlap between these various categories of behavior. The important concept is not what category a behavior correctly fits in, but the goal or intent of the action. The most common intent of a controlling behavior is "to get what I want when I want it!" If the goal fits, the behavior is an abuse of power and control in the relationship.

Gandhi

In introducing the concept of violence to our groups, we often start with a quote from Mahatma Gandhi that reads as follows:

*"Any attempt to impose your will on another
is an act of violence."*

This usually provides fodder for a lively discussion as we typically write it on the grease board before group members arrive so they have some time to read and think about it before we begin. In addition, we don't tell them, "This is the way it is." We direct their attention to the quote and ask, "What do you think about this idea?"

Read over the quote now and ask yourself intuitively how you feel about it. Does it ring true? Do you agree? Do you find yourself looking for exceptions? Whatever your reaction was, read on.

In this text, we will pose questions to you that we typically ask in our group. The intent of the questions is not to shame or belittle, but to encourage you to think about issues that, by and large, most of us have never thought about until participating in a group or reading a book like this one. Pay close attention to your reactions as you read; they will help to develop your choices and values later on.

What exactly does it mean to "impose your will?" What most people come up with is something like, "To try to make someone do what you want." How does this happen? Well, one way is to ask, but does that qualify as "imposing" your will? Probably not. So, we are probably looking for something more than simply asking, "Honey, could you please wash my jeans tonight?" We would probably look for a comment that made your partner feel obligated to wash the jeans, either out of fear, guilt, shame or some other negative emotion.

A comment such as, "If you were a decent housekeeper (partner, mother, etc.) I wouldn't even have to ask to get my clothes washed." Notice this is not an out and out fear-inducing threat, but a comment designed to motivate through guilt and embarrassment. This is much more subtle than inducing fear, but also much more effective in achieving the desired outcome and keeping a loved one in her place. And notice we have not been talking about physical violence at all.

What about the phrase "on another?" Well, clearly you need to be directing your demands or complaints at someone else. Do we include pets in this discussion? It is certainly possible to use violence with a pet and to induce sufficient fear to get the reaction you want. How does the pet (or, by comparison, a partner) react to you afterwards? Have you ever seen a dog that's been beaten? It typically reacts with fear, suspicion and contempt, right? The same is true with a partner or child.

Is Violence Ever Justified?

After spending some time on a lively discussion about what qualifies as violence, we turn our focus to whether it is ever justified. We are typically asked, "What about self-defense?" "What about kids? Aren't we supposed to have control over them?" is another common question. "What about war?" is often heard as well.

Remember, we have not accepted Gandhi's definition yet. But if we do, are there exceptions? Probably. Let's take a look at a few of them.

Self-Defense

What is self defense? Webster's New World Dictionary defines it as "the right to defend oneself with whatever force is reasonably necessary against actual or threatened violence." (Prentice Hall, 1986). What if someone comes up and punches you in the face and walks away. Is it self defense if you punch him back? No — he's no longer a threat to you. Now it becomes retaliation, not defense. If you do punch him back you do so to vindicate and soothe your injured pride, not to defend yourself.

You have other options for how to handle this situation than physical violence. Pick up the phone and call police. He will likely be charged with assault or battery, depending on the extent of the injury. This is the process our social structure has established for handling an incident of this type. Even our very violent culture would not condone punching someone in the face (or the back of his head) if he was not an immediate threat to you.

What if someone walks up to you and spits in your face. Is it self-defense if you punch him? Absolutely not, although it may be tempting to do so. Again, this is an instance of retaliation.

What if someone walks up to you and says, "You are the ugliest SOB I have ever seen!" Is it OK to punch him in the face? Not under this definition because he has not physically hurt you. He may have hurt your feelings, but there is no threat of physical danger unless and until he raises his hand to you.

In the event someone does walk up to you and raise his fist, you would probably be legally safe to punch him, but is that your only option? Or, if he punched you and then raised his hand to do so again, you could most likely justify punching him, especially if you have witnesses, but, again, is this what you want? Probably not.

War

War is another commonly mentioned exception to our prohibition on violence. In a war we have a government sanction to go out and, not only hurt, but kill the enemy. Whether we are willing to put ourselves in this situation, however, depends on our values.

Interestingly enough, many of us accept and understand being physically or verbally violent with a partner, but would never dream of enlisting in the armed forces or participating in a war, at least voluntarily. Why is it OK to hurt those closest to us? What is the value operating here?

Parenting

It is also commonly accepted that parents are expected in this and many other societies to exert some control over their children. We are expected to feed, clothe and care for them and send them to school. We are expected to make sure they don't break the law, and if they do, we are responsible for the consequences. This may be a true exception to the Gandhi definition of violence.

As our children get older, however, we must gradually allow our control to recede into the background, until they reach the age of majority and are able to have control of their own lives as well as the responsibility for those choices. If parents have exerted complete control over the child until that point, the child has no experience in making choices for himself and often struggles to learn this after the fact.

Even when children are younger, there are certain types of control that are acceptable and others that are not. While it used to be acceptable to hit children with a belt or switch as punishment for "bad behavior" it is no longer acceptable to do so. While spanking children is still legal in this country, a movement to end all corporal punishment is gaining momentum as nation after nation passes laws to outlaw this practice in schools and homes. The United States, with our culture and attachment to violence to solve problems, still lags behind other developed nations in this movement.

For anyone struggling with anger, it can be difficult to keep himself under control if he chooses to use such a technique, especially when upset. While therapists used to recommend hitting a punching bag or other inanimate object to express anger when upset, more recent research is finding that often this leads to a greater degree of aggression and violence, rather than a decreased amount. For the same reasons, spanking a child when angry and upset, can lead to an accidental crossing of the line of acceptable behavior.

Anyone who struggles with his anger would be well advised to learn and exercise other child management techniques than physical punishment for this reason. If you had used physical punishment before reading this book and are not familiar with other non-violent techniques of child management, please look in your community for a parenting class that can assist you in learning some healthier alternatives or consult some of the websites listed in Appendix J.

We are not recommending giving your child free reign or suggesting there should be no limits on them, just that they should not be parented with violence. We have quite a number of men in our group that are there due to altercations with their children, rather than a partner, and often due to the disastrous results of giving free reign to your anger by using violence.

How Does Violence Affect Relationships?

Relationships are profoundly affected by violence. As we will discuss in greater detail in Chapter Four on Basic Needs, we get into relationships in the first place to get our needs met. If we end up in a violent relationship, not only are our needs not getting met, we are not even accepted for who we are. Someone is trying to control and change us, to meet their needs, while causing us to suppress our own.

It is natural in such a situation for fear and caution to develop, and a distinct mistrust. This can lead to resentment and a continued withdrawal of the controlled partner. When she has had enough or becomes strong enough, she often leaves the relationship, so the violent partner's needs go unmet as well and nobody wins.

In explaining the effect of violence or overpowering on a relationship, we like to use the analogy of an overpowering abusive employer. Imagine yourself at the bottom of the totem pole or power pyramid and working for such a person. Your boss is tyrannical and unfair, making arbitrary rules that make no sense to you and expecting you to follow them with unquestioning obedience.   The diagram below is an example of this type of relationship.

What feelings do you have about this boss? All power is centralized in this person. He makes all the decisions about your work and the conditions of the job. He, alone, determines what you are paid and whether you will have a job tomorrow. How do the persons on the bottom rung of the ladder typically feel about a dictator such as this?

In most cases, they are afraid of him. They are afraid he will abuse his power and make their lives miserable. Typically they do not trust him and rarely do they respect him. In addition, there is typically a resentment that builds in the employees that is directed toward the boss that poisons any remaining positive feelings they may once have had for him.

How does the boss feel toward the employees? Typically, starting in nearly reverse order, he doesn't trust them to do an honest day of work for an honest day's wage. In addition, he doesn't respect their ability to do the job or to make decisions, even if they had the right to do so. He often views them as children, needing to be told what to do "for their own good." He may feel they could not function if he was not there pulling the strings. He typically begins to resent them and is often afraid that one of them will eventually work his way up the ladder to take his job and replace him.

The same feelings result in both positions when you are in a situation of having power **over** another. This is true in intimate relationships as well. Violence imposes such a power structure in intimate relationships and families. What we frequently hear is that the entire family is afraid, mistrustful, disrespectful and resentful of the violent member, who in turn harbors those feelings toward them. Nobody wins and everyone is unhappy and afraid. We will look at a different way to handle power in relationships when we take on the concept of Control in Chapter Eight.

Legal Ramifications of Violent Behavior

Aside from the effects it has on our relationships, there are a number of other negative consequences that can arise from the use of violence toward others. It is helpful to split these out into categories to get a complete picture of the effect of violence in our lives.

Arrest

In Wisconsin, persons who come to the attention of law enforcement due to relationship violence can be arrested on several different charges, depending on the severity of the offense. Disorderly Conduct is the most common charge we see among group members. In Wisconsin, this is defined as "... in a public place, engag[ing] in violent, abusive, indecent, profane, boisterous, unreasonably loud or otherwise disorderly conduct under circumstances in which the conduct tends to cause or provoke a disturbance..." according to Section 947.01, Wis. Stats. This statute provides that persons engaging in any or all of these behaviors may be arrested and, if convicted, fined not more than $1000 or imprisoned not more than 90 days, or both. Other states have laws with similar provisions.

It is clear to see that even engaging in a vigorous argument, whether with a partner, a child or a co-worker, in which voices become raised and perhaps profanity is used can lead to a disorderly conduct arrest and some pretty serious consequences. Verbal violence alone is sufficient to trigger all of these consequences.

Wisconsin law also provides that when the parties to an altercation are, or have in the past, been married and/or shared a residence, or have a child in common, the arrest can be for Disorderly Conduct, Domestic Abuse. A conviction on the charge of DC/DA carries certain other penalties, such as the inability to own or use firearms, including hunting rifles. Living in a part of the country in which hunting is a common pastime, this is a pretty serious consideration for many members of our community. Even if the emotional effect of violence on a relationship doesn't get their attention, the inability to hunt often will.

Further, in addition to the Disorderly Conduct penalties, additional consequences can be imposed on individuals convicted of DC/DA, such as an additional domestic abuse fine, participation in a treatment group such as ours and limits on the contact one may have with the victim or children. Sections 939.51(1)(b) and (3)(b), 968.075(1)(a), Wis. Stats.

If there are physical injuries resulting from the altercation, or a weapon was used, charges of Battery, Substantial Battery or Aggravated Battery may be used. These felony charges raise the penalties to a fine not to exceed $50,000 or imprisonment not to exceed 15 years or both. Sections 939.51(3) and 940.19, Wis. Stats. Quite a substantial price to pay to make a point!

Custody and Placement Laws

In March of 2004, Wisconsin added a law to address violent behavior in divorced families. Specifically, it provides that if the court finds that "there has been a pattern or a serious incident of interspousal battery or domestic abuse," the court must provide for the safety and well-being of the child and the safety of the parent who was the victim of the battery or abuse by ordering at least one of several conditions. Section 767.41(6)(g),Wis. Stats. Two of the conditions a Wisconsin court may order include completion of a certified treatment program for batterers and supervision of placement time, among others. The court is entitled to withhold placement from a parent who does not or has not yet completed the conditions it determines appropriate.

The issue of domestic violence is getting increasing attention in many jurisdictions and a number of states have enacted laws such as this. I would expect more such laws to be cropping up in the future as well.

Additional Financial Considerations

Aside from the legal ramifications of an arrest associated with violence, there are a number of financial consequences as well. First of all, as previously discussed, there is a fine associated with most charges, even the most innocuous. In Wisconsin, this can range from a municipal citation in the amount of approximately $200 to a State Disorderly Conduct charge amount of up to $1000 to a Substantial Battery charge of up to $50,000. These costs alone are no laughing matter.

In addition to the fine, many persons arrested for such an offense incur attorney fees when seeking assistance and advocacy. Most attorneys in our area charge between $150 and $250 per hour and keep close track of any time spent on your case, including making telephone calls and reviewing correspondence from other attorneys. These fees can add up quickly.

A period of probation is often ordered, either in addition to or instead of a jail term. The State of Wisconsin, and most other jurisdictions, imposes a fee to cover the cost of supervision by the probation agent. A typical fee is $30-$60 for each month of probation, in addition to any restitution ordered paid to the victim. A common probation term for such an offense is typically 18 months.

Often, and I would add, ideally, in an offense such as this, treatment is ordered. Many individuals arrested on these charges are ordered to participate in an Anger Management or Family Violence Treatment Program. An intake session is required of each participant prior to participation in the group. This is billed at $150.00. Ours is a 20 week program; others are 40-52 weeks long. Our group fee is $150 per week and we have learned to require that a participant's co-pay be paid each week. Therefore, even if you have health insurance coverage, there will be a payment required each week you are in group. We do have a sliding fee scale available in cases of financial hardship, but there are costs associated with attending group each week. We receive no grant funding for the services we provide.

Additionally, if alcohol was a factor in the arrest incident, an Alcohol and Other Drug Assessment (AODA) may be ordered. In our county, an individual must produce $200 in order to schedule the appointment. This is in addition to the cost of any treatment ordered, which may include either individual counseling or, more often, an AODA treatment group.

A number of group members end up experiencing a divorce as a result of their violence as well. This multiplies the financial costs exponentially. But you can see, even without the divorce variable, the legal and financial ramifications of violent behavior can be significant!

A number of individuals are required to attend group due to altercations at work. Even in the absence of physical violence, a threat to a co-worker can lead to ramifications such as these. In addition, certain employees have lost their jobs as a result of their violent or abusive behavior. Others, in positions such as security requiring them to carry weapons, may lose the ability to even perform the job if convicted of certain domestic violence charges as they are unable to carry a firearm. This takes the financial consequences to an entirely different level.

Emotional Costs

Aside from the legal and financial ramifications of a violence-related arrest, there are emotional costs as well. Most of the men arrested and ordered into our group speak of the shame and embarrassment of being labeled and forced to participate in treatment. Court documents are a matter of public record and, in most communities, convictions are published in the local newspaper as well, increasing the likelihood that friends, co-workers and acquaintances will become aware of the situation.

Loss of self-respect is another matter to deal with. For most persons, it is difficult to reconcile positive feelings about themselves with the idea that they were arrested, booked, charged and put through the court process like any other criminal. Your self-esteem will take a hit from an experience such as this.

You may also lose the respect of your family. If children have been on the receiving end of your temper, or have at least witnessed it, they may view you differently as a parent. You may instill fear in them, but lose something much more valuable than their obedience — their trust.

As you can see, there are many consequences that occur when we use violence with those we are in relationship with. You are reading this book because you have either accepted that you could use some help with your anger, or are at least wondering if you need it. Now that you are aware of all of these potential consequences, what do you have to lose by trying some of the ideas presented in this book and taking the risk of improving your most important relationships?

Why Do We Use It?

So, if it doesn't work, is damaging to our relationships and has negative legal, financial and emotional consequences, why do we use violence? Well, it **does** work, for the short term. Inducing fear in a partner or a child can be the fastest way to get them to do what you want. The cost comes later and is longer lasting. Persons using these techniques may win the battle, but lose the war.

Many parents learn this lesson the hard way. Instilling fear of punishment in a child is one effective way to get them to do the right thing while you are watching. However, unless children learn to do the right thing because it is the right thing to do, they will be the first to act out or step out of line the minute your back is turned. Think about it. If you only obey because you don't want to get caught, as soon as there is no danger of that, why behave?

Also, it is often the only thing we know. Many persons who are violent in relationships grew up witnessing violence either from or between their parents. When we are in intimate relationships, we typically repeat what was modeled for us by our parents and others who we've observed as we were growing up, such as grandparents, aunts and uncles, neighbors and the like. Even when we didn't enjoy that experience, the most natural thing in the world for us is to develop habits of being in a relationship that duplicates our parents' relationship. Additionally, in times of stress, we will most likely resort to the automatic behaviors that we observed, even if we told ourselves we would never, ever use them.

Any of us who are parents have had the experience, in a moment of stress, of having words come out of our mouths that are our mother or father's. We think at the time, "Where did that come from?" or, perhaps, "What am I saying?" But it is the most natural thing in the world for this to occur. Those old tapes are still running in our heads. The same is true for our intimate relationships as well.

This is why it is so common in our group to have an entire session or two devoted to the abusive discipline members received as a child, or to discuss the violence group members observed between their parents. Understanding how influential this is on our development, we have incorporated these discussions regularly into our group material and inquire about them routinely in our intake sessions.

So how do you change this pattern? By reading a book like the one in your hands. We can tell and show you by the examples we have what to do differently. We can teach you techniques that will change how you think about various events that happen in your life and techniques that help you to handle them and to manage your anger in a different way. In addition, we will also try to let you know where the difficulties lie in making these changes and how to overcome them. That's our commitment to you.

The rest is up to you. The hard work will be yours. While these techniques are not hard to do, to be effective they do require practice. If you skim through this book and never look at it again, and don't practice the skills we can teach you, nothing about your life or your anger will change. You will get out of this book what you put into the experience. The most important predictors of change are an open mind, a commitment and a willingness to try something new.

We can promise you that if you work at this program and practice these techniques your life and your relationship will change. Expect to feel closer to your partner and to your children if you have them, and expect to find more peace of mind in the process.

Whatever you do, don't lose hope—everyone can make these changes. We have seen some individuals in which these patterns were so ingrained that even we wondered if there was any hope. Often-times these were the individuals that were able to make the most amazing changes. All it takes is practice. Doing this work over the past 14 years, we have both learned never to say never and to believe in the possibility of change in everyone.

What About Mutual Violence?

As explained in the Introduction, the way our group is run, one of the first experiences a new member has, following an intake session with one of us, is "telling their story" by way of introducing themselves to the rest of the group. One of the most common phrases uttered during these introductions is, "She hit me too." It seems to be a universally held belief that this justifies his battering her to a pulp, or that this equalizes the fault in the situation. If you have ever used this excuse yourself, please read on as we will give you some food for thought and another way to look at this situation. No, it is not OK for her to hit you first, or at all, but that is her issue to address. In dealing with your issues, ask yourself if she is truly a threat to you. Then think about the following ideas.

Often people indicate that because a woman used violence, too, the case should have been viewed as one of mutual battery or mutual abuse and both parties should have been arrested. While it is true that some women use violence in intimate relationships, the term mutual implies equality. Obviously, violence is not an acceptable conflict resolution tactic, regardless of who is using it. However, when violence occurs in relationships between men and women, there is nothing mutual or equal about it. Consider the following factors which generally apply:

☮ **Inequality in Physical Size** — Most often men are taller and bigger than the women they are involved with. This fact alone makes him much more lethal than she will be in any altercation involving violence.

☮ **Inequality in Physical Strength** — Even when partners are of equal size, or even if the woman is taller or bigger than her male partner, his physical strength is far superior to hers. Men have a different build and musculature than women that gives them greater physical strength. This is why women can lift weights like a man and still not develop the same look or muscle tone.

⊕ **Inequality in Severity of Injury Produced** — Except
when a weapon is used, a man is generally able and
likely to produce a more severe injury than a woman
when using violence with a partner. Of the evaluations
we have done, even when the woman was larger, the
most severe injury from a woman to a man that we can
recall was a scratch on the face or neck, often defensive
wounds. On the other hand, we are aware of a number
of severe beatings imposed on women by men, even
when a severe result was unintended.

When a weapon is used, the danger is more
equalized. I remember one man in our group whose
partner had sneaked up and hit him over the head
with a large rock, causing a concussion. But this was
the only situation I have come across in all of the years
I have been dealing with this issue in which the female
partner caused greater injury than the male and she
had to utilize both stealth and the weapon to achieve
that result. Further, while the injury could have been
worse, even in this case it was not as severe as a
number of injuries I have observed women receiving
from men.

⊕ **Inequality in Terms of Resources** — In many, but not
all, cases, men have a greater income and an increased
ability to take care of themselves, even in the case of an
arrest. Many of the women we see are either un- or
under-employed, especially in this economy, and often
have no health care coverage to seek treatment, no
transportation to get to services and they are often
responsible for childcare as well.

⊕ **Different Intent/Purpose of Violence** — Often what we
see is that men have used violence to get their way and
most of the women we have been aware of who were
arrested for violence toward a partner, have been
defending themselves. Most typically, these women
have a long history of being victimized, making them

more susceptible to getting together with violent partners and, at some point, have either had enough abuse and lash out or hook up with a partner smart and cunning enough to call police the minute she steps out of line the slightest bit.

I am reminded of a wonderful Hispanic woman who was ordered to see me by her probation agent as she had been arrested for domestic violence toward her husband. Rosie had been married to Jose for 30 years; they had both children and grandchildren together. This year he had become involved in yet another affair and finally told her he was leaving her and filing for divorce. She was hurt and afraid, not to mention incensed that after all this time, he would leave her for someone else. She slapped his face. He picked up the phone, called police and she was arrested. It was only during her intake that I learned from Rosie that she had been hospitalized several times during her marriage due to the beatings Jose had visited upon her. It would have happened more often, but there were also a number of times he refused to allow her to seek medical treatment. Jose has never been arrested or received any treatment for his violence.

☮ **Difference in Fear Factor** — Our first response when a new group member uses the mutual violence excuse to justify his abuse incident is to look him directly in the eye and ask, "Were you afraid of her? Were you afraid she would hurt you?" They have never failed me. Invariably the men respond with a laugh and a comment such as, "What, are you kidding? She couldn't hurt a fly." End of argument. In all of our years of doing this work, we have never heard a man admit he was physically frightened of his partner, even when these partners seemed to be some pretty scary people. We have heard, however, through our contact with both female partners and women arrested for violence to a partner, some very genuine and chilling descriptions of the fear these women have felt for their male partners. Descriptions such as "I hid in the bushes in front of a neighbor's house with no clothes on because I was afraid he would kill me if he found me" and "I keep a cell phone in the bathroom at all times because I know he will let me go to use the toilet even when he's beating me" we have heard on more than one occasion. How frightened does someone have to be to hide naked in front of a neighbor's house so her husband doesn't find her?   That sounds like genuine terror to us. Something to think about.

Who Needs to Change?

Due to their socialization, men often have a more difficult time than women admitting they have a need to change how they are in a relationship. Much of this is due to our socialization. Men are conditioned to look for solutions to problems outside of themselves and to competitively find fault in others, rather than looking at their own behavior. Messages such as, "Never admit you're wrong," "Don't let 'em see you sweat," "Never give an inch" and "Don't let them see weakness" are powerful examples of the ideas that little boys grow up hearing.

A person who uses controlling abusive behaviors in relationships can't fix the problems that this behavior creates by doing more of the same or expecting others to change. He must choose different behaviors.

Accepting personal responsibility to change ourselves is all that is within our control. In fact, no matter what our partner, or anyone else for that matter, does, we always have choices in how we respond. Even if our partner comes up and slaps us in the face, we have a number of options. We can:

☮ Slap her back
☮ Turn and walk away
☮ Call the police
☮ Call her a name
☮ Engage in a respectful discussion with her
☮ Do nothing.

There are probably a number of other choices we have as well. These are just the most obvious. There is no right choice here, just several wrong ones. You want to think about what kind of an outcome you want to have. See Chapter Seven for a complete discussion of outcome and how it is determined by our choices.

But one of the most important concepts we want to teach you in this book is the concept of choice. So many of us tell ourselves we are at the mercy of others (my partner, my boss, society, etc.). This kind of thinking is extremely disempowering and serves no helpful purpose. It is self-defeating.

You will get much further if you can acknowledge that you have made some choices to get to the point that you are reading this book, or to get to where you are in your relationship. If those choices are not getting you the outcome you want, it would be in your best interest to change them. Admitting this can be a sign of strength and very empowering. The bottom line is it takes two people to make a relationship good or bad. Blaming your partner for everything bad in the relationship just gives her all the power and doesn't change anything.

The only person you can control is yourself. The person you can most influence is yourself. It is most important that you care for yourself and take charge of yourself. It is a waste of energy for you to upset yourself because others are not the way you think they should be. It simply frustrates you and it accomplishes nothing in the way of change.

Accepting the Anger of Others

Resentment, anger and rage smolders within any group of persons that has experienced significant oppression. Women, persons of color and the poor have a long history of being controlled by our male-dominated white culture.

The anger of a group or person who is dominated or under the power of another is always powerful and frightening to the group in control. Persons of Caucasian descent are afraid of the anger of persons of color: African-Americans, Native

Americans, Hmong, the list goes on. Management is afraid of the anger of labor. Parents are afraid of the teenager's anger. Men are afraid of women's anger.

In family and intimate relationships, women have long been oppressed in our male-dominated culture. Their anger reveals outrage, resentment, resistance and defiance. Anger is also one emotion that women are discouraged from showing, while it is often the only feeling that men are encouraged to express.

A group or person in power often attempts to minimize or block the anger of the oppressed in order to maintain the status quo. There are different ways we attempt block another person's anger. Some of the more common techniques for doing so include:

⊕ **Denial**—"I don't know what you're talking about; I don't understand" or simply walking out of the room.

⊕ **Accusation**—Accusing the angry person of attacking; "You deserve better; you should leave me, I'm a horrible person; You're right; I'm no good."

⊕ **Attack**—"What about when you do this; You are even worse than me; You're the one who's crazy, hysterical, shouting..."

⊕ **Trivializing**—Laughing at a partner; making fun of her; "So what's the big deal? Are you on the rag? You're so cute when you're mad."

⊕ **Invalidation**—Putting a hand on her head, holding her at arm's length as if she was threatening to him, then laughing at her while she yells at him.

⊕ **Intimidation**—Stopping her physically, putting a hand over her mouth, hitting her, choking her, or otherwise forcing her to stop showing her anger, escalating until she stops.

⊕ **Patronizing**—Pretending to go along, but only paying lip service to the requested change so no true change occurs.

Both our society and persons they are in relationship with tell women not to be angry. This has a destructive effect on the women, themselves, damages their relationships and leads to a repressed anger. Again, this is the repetition of the message she received in childhood about not showing her anger.

Why do we want to stop our partner's anger? What would happen if we didn't stop it? How does keeping one partner from being angry keep the other powerful? Or the other, powerless? What would be different in our relationship with our partners if, when our partner is angry, we responded in a respectful way? When a partner is angry and the anger is blocked in one of the ways listed above, what happens to that anger? What is the effect on the relationship when the anger is blocked?

As frightening as our partner's anger can be to us, we must remember that her anger is an expression of herself and of her desire to influence a situation. If we reject the desire to stop or deflect the anger, we may be in a position where we have to do something new and different and change is threatening to most of us. We are not sure we want to take on any major changes, especially if we are pretty comfortable with the way things are going right now. And, if we have a significant amount of control in our relationship, and get our way much of the time, what investment do we have in changing it?

When anger gets blocked, however, it doesn't just go away. It often gets directed in another way or stuffed down so deep so that it will either come out later or in another direction. Anger that is not respected can take the form of a brick that starts building a huge wall between you and your partner; a wall of emotional distance that can be difficult to break down and move beyond. This often leads to an increased silence between partners. Each is afraid to bring up any subject for fear it will lead to this or that unresolved issue or argument. Gradually these two people have less and less to say to each other and the relationship often ends as they continue to drift apart.

Anger that is blocked also leads to a partner feeling controlled and not accepted. The partner in control often takes on almost a parental role in the relationship, making most of the decisions and directing the behavior of the "child." The biggest problem with a parent-child type of intimate relationship is that the partner in the child role eventually has to rebel, as any good adolescent would do. This rebellion can be physical, as in just leaving the relationship outright, emotional, as in withdrawing and shutting herself away from her partner, or sexual, as in the case of an affair. She may engage in all three forms of rebellion. In any case, blocking this anger can have a very negative effect on the relationship.

Many people are surprised to read that violence can be verbal and emotional as well as physical. Our society tends not to think of aggressive communication as hurtful, yet every day we find ourselves damaged by it.

After you read this chapter the first time, it is a good idea to put this book down and give this new way of thinking some time to sink in. Let it stew for awhile; sleep on it for a day or two. Then, when you are ready, review the chapter again before moving on. It really sets the tone for the remainder of the book, so be sure to give it some time to set up before rushing ahead. It can lead to profound changes in your belief system and in your relationship.

As we have in each chapter, on the following page we have summarized the ideas and concepts covered in this chapter in the form of a worksheet. Look it over to identify some of the key problem areas in your own anger management process and your relationship. It would also be helpful to ask your partner to look over the sheet and give you some feedback about what she sees as the key problem areas. Reassure her that you want her feedback and that it will be safe for her to be open and honest with you.

If you find yourself beginning to react as she is talking or responding to the sheet, quickly read over Chapter Six on the Time-Out Process and put it into practice. Getting yourself away from whatever is upsetting you buys you some time to determine how you want to handle a situation.

"Why Anger Hurts" Summary

☮ Identify each of the ways you have been violent in your relationships, past or present:

___Intimidation   ___Emotional/Verbal Abuse
___Isolating Behaviors   ___Obfuscation
___Using Children   ___Using Male Privilege
___Financial Abuse   ___Threats & Coercion
___Physical Violence   ___Sexual Violence

☮ What messages did you get about violence as a child? _____
_____

☮ How did you see your parents resolve conflict?
_____
_____
_____

☮ Have you ever been in a relationship (employment, intimate, friendship) in which the other party had more power in the relationship than you did? Describe the relationship and your feelings toward that person:
_____
_____
_____

☮ What techniques or defenses have you used to block your partner's anger?

___ Denial   ___Accusation
___Attack   ___Trivialization
___Intimidation   ___Patronizing
___Invalidation   ___Other:_____

"He who laughs, lasts."

~Unknown

Chapter 3

Fight, Flight or Freeze

Exploring the Stress Response

Afger spending some time explaining the body's physical reaction to an increase in adrenaline, I asked, "Can anyone tell me the first reaction you notice in yourself when your adrenaline increases?"

Travis calmly raised his hand, "Well, I feel this sort of rushing in my head. Then my face feels all hot and my heart feels like it's going to jump out of my chest."

"That's wonderful! How is it you are so aware of those physical responses in yourself? Most people haven't paid that much attention to them prior to being in a group like this."

"I just know that that's how I've felt and the next thing I know, my wife is crying and telling me I've hurt her, but I never remember doing what it is she says I did. And it's always different. Sometimes I hit her; sometimes I've called her some really awful names. The only things these times have in common is that I feel that way before and I don't remember what I did to make her cry."

We are busier today than at any other period in our existence. Our time is spent attending to one obligation or another for many of our waking hours each day. Research done recently showed that for all of our time saving devices, such as dishwashers, automobiles, clothes washers and dryers, grocery stores and the like, the average person has fewer hours of free time in each 24 hour period than when all of these activities were non-mechanized.

Additionally, everything is moving at a faster pace today than in the past due in large part to the mechanization of these routine tasks; the expectation is that persons will move faster and accomplish more as well. All of these factors lead to a higher level of stress than at any other time in our history. This has a significant impact on our lives and our relationships with those most important to us.

What is Stress?

But what is this mysterious intruder in our contentment we call stress? By definition, stress is nothing more than "the way we respond to change." Any change in our lives, even a positive one, causes stress. Stress, then, is the physical response by the body to any demand, or change, made upon it.

The body responds in many ways to stress or change. These effects, or responses, have remained the same since the beginning of time. In fact, they helped pre-historic humans, our ancestors, survive.

It was in 1900 that Harvard physiologist Walter Cannon first identified the Fight or Flight Response. This was the name he coined for the series of biochemical changes that helps prepare us to deal with threats or danger. Continuing with our example of our cave dwelling ancestors, primitive men and women needed quick bursts of energy to fight or flee predators, such as dinosaurs or saber-toothed tigers.

In recent years, researchers have also discovered and noted that, rather than fight or flee, the adrenaline and other hormones released during the stress response cause some individuals to freeze, even in the face of danger. In terms of the cave dwellers, these were probably those who didn't survive encounters with predators, so escaped notice by earlier researchers. But the very hormones that cause some of us to become activated and vigilant, cause others of us to become virtually paralyzed.

How Does Stress Affect Us?

Cannon, and later, Hans Selye, the first noteworthy researcher on stress, were able to identify exactly what happens in the body during the Fight or Flight response. Selye discovered that any problem, real or imagined, can cause the cerebral cortex (the thinking part of the brain) to send an alarm to the hypothalamus (the main switch for the stress response, located in the midbrain) which stimulates the sympathetic nervous system to make a series of changes in your body.

And notice, it does not have to be a true, real or lasting threat for this reaction to occur; it can exist solely in our imagination. Therefore, if you are a person who perceives threats easily, or you hold onto a threatening experience for a lasting period of time, you may find yourself regularly and significantly affected by the stress response.

One of the first changes we may notice in our bodies is that our heart rate, breathing rate, muscle tension, metabolism and blood pressure all automatically increase. Our hands and feet may feel cold as blood is directed away from the extremities, such as our hands and feet, and into the larger muscles of our arms and legs, preparing us to fight or flee. We may experience butterflies or nausea in our stomach as blood is directed away from the digestive system which is not viewed as essential for survival at this moment. If you have just eaten a large meal, then become stressed, your meal may sit undigested in your stomach for a significant period of time, causing irritation or an upset stomach in the process.

Continuing our stress response, our diaphragm locks; our pupils dilate to sharpen our vision and our hearing becomes more acute, again preparing us for battle. The adrenal glands begin to secrete hormones which prevent digestion, reproduction, growth and tissue repair as well as the responses of our immune and inflammatory systems. Thus, some of these very important functions that keep our body healthy begin to shut down.

What does this mean for the average person? A great deal! For example, we all come into contact with millions of germs and viruses each day, but are able to fight off most of these due to these systems normally operating in our bodies. If we frequently perceiving stress in our lives, our immune and inflammatory systems shut down, making us more likely to succumb to some, or many, of these germs. Thus, we may become ill on a more frequent basis.

Having many of our essential systems inactivated can have long-term negative effects if left unchecked. We do not need, nor can we easily endure, a constant or prolonged stress response.

Again, the stress response makes sense in view of the world in which we humans first appeared on the earth; in a violent, "survival of the fittest" climate. However, in this day and age, when stress is likely to be invoked by traffic on the road, our boss pushing up a deadline or our partner being unhappy with us for forgetting to pick up milk on the way home, this extreme response is, perhaps, not the most practical or functional. We will see in a moment how this can even be harmful to us.

It is true there are a few occasions we face today in which the stress response may prove helpful: if we hear footsteps following us down a dark street at night, if we observe a heavy object fall onto a loved one or when we are participating in sports requiring fast, rigorous activity. At these times we are grateful for our trigger responses. At most times, however, this response is not helpful to us today.

How Stress is Harmful

Chronic or persistent stress can occur when the stressors in our lives are, or seem to be, unrelenting. Perhaps we have a stressful job or we are a caregiver at work or at home for a loved one. We may be undergoing a major reorganization or downsizing at work, so our job description changes from one day to the next and we are never quite sure it will be there when we arrive the next day. Perhaps we are experiencing a messy divorce and are never quite sure what each day will bring: contact with our former partner, a letter from the attorney or other problems related to the children's adjustment. This can be like living in a war zone for the six to twelve to eighteen months a divorce can take.

Some people must endure the stress of living with a chronic or life threatening illness; their own or that of a loved one, which can be worse and more difficult to tolerate. I have also worked with clients that have lives that just seem to involve many, continuing changes, or have changes in many of the major areas of their life at once: job, home, relationship, etc.

The stress response also occurs when the little stressors that all of us are faced with on nearly a daily basis, accumulate and you are unable to recuperate from any one of them. Some days it seems there is just one thing happening after another. When we can't process or work through these small frustrations, they can feel overwhelming. Current research is showing that it isn't so much the big problems in life that really take a toll on people, but all the little irritations or frustrations that do seem to build up to really get us down. So it's normal to feel overwhelmed when you're having one of those days when everything seems to be going wrong.

Many adults are surprised to hear this, but this happens for children as well, just with different stressors involved. As a wonderful and enlightening example of a children's version of stress, that adults will also enjoy, I highly recommend Judith Viorst's book, *Alexander and the Terrible, Horrible, No-Good, Very Bad Day* (Atheneum, 1972). To give you a flavor of the story, the book starts out, "I went to bed with gum in my mouth and now I have gum in my hair." You can just imagine where it goes from there!

As long as your mind perceives a threat, your body will remain aroused, even long after the event precipitating the arousal has passed. If you have ever had a close call while driving, you understand what this is like. Your heart is often still pounding long after the incident is over and the other vehicle is long gone. Your mind still perceives a potential threat, perhaps in the form of the other 100,000 vehicles on the road, so you continue to react for a period of time.

As long as your body remains aroused, all of those important systems remain shut down. If this occurs on a regular basis, you are greatly increasing your chances of a stress related illness.

In 1972 two researchers, Holmes & Rahe, developed a stressful life events scale, assigning a numerical rating to various events that we will or may experience in the course of a year. Asking subjects to identify each of the events they had experienced over the preceding twelve months, the researchers then assigned a numeric value to each event and were able to determine the likelihood that a subject would succumb to a stress related illness within the next year of his life. We have included an updated version of this scale as Appendix B

In scoring the events, total scores of under 150 typically lead to a 37% chance of developing some stress related illness within the succeeding two years. A score of 150-300 leads to a 51% chance of stress-related illness. Scoring over 300, which many of our clients have done, typically indicates an 80% chance of becoming ill within the next two years. Notice that "Christmas" and "vacation" both appear on this scale.

Stress Related Illnesses

Researchers have been examining the relationship between stress and disease for more than fifty years. They have discovered that people suffering from stress-related disorders tend to show hyperactivity in one or several preferred systems of the body and that stress shows up differently in different persons. In other words, people typically show or exhibit stress in one system of their body or another, wherever they are most vulnerable. But almost any system in your body can be damaged by stress. Just look at the wide variety of over the counter medications and remedies for ulcers, upset stomachs and headaches we have available to us.

A less obvious example that many may be unaware of is that stress-triggered changes in the lungs can increase symptoms of asthma, bronchitis and other respiratory conditions. I have a friend who develops bronchitis whenever she is faced with a significant stressor in her life, such as a job change, relationship issues or concern about a family member. Her upper respiratory system is how her body exhibits stress; hyperactivity in that system, for her, is triggered by stress, leading to serious illness.

Loss of insulin during a stress response may be a factor in the development of adult-onset of diabetes. Perhaps you have a genetic predisposition for this illness and are then faced with a stressful life-change, such as a job loss or a divorce. You are more likely to develop symptoms or be diagnosed with this ailment during or immediately after these stressors than at any other time in your life.

Stress suspends tissue repair and remodeling which causes decalcifications of bones, osteoporosis and susceptibility to fractures. An individual experiencing a long period of stress in her life may be more likely to break her hip when she falls due to the damage to her body caused by the stress in her life.

A prolonged stress response can also worsen conditions such as arthritis, chronic pain and diabetes. There is also evidence that chronic stress can cause or contribute to depression.

Inhibition of the immune and inflammatory systems can make someone more susceptible to colds and flu and can exacerbate some diseases such as cancer and AIDS. This is my own personal system of hyperactivity. When I am in a period of stress, I typically contract the common cold or, occasionally, the flu, whereas normally I am healthy as a horse.

Back in 1989, Terry and I were about to marry. It was the second marriage for both of us and I would become a stepmother to two teenage boys and he, a stepfather to my young daughter. In addition, we were purchasing a home, on which we were scheduled to close two weeks before the wedding so we could be married in our new home. I had also transferred to a new position at work, which I was greatly looking forward to, but was a stressor just the same. In fact, each of the events described above was positive and something I had chosen and was looking forward to. But, remember our definition of stress, "the physical response of the body to any demand, any change, made upon it."

Well, here I was making multiple demands for change on my body and it let me know it was not happy. For about a week between the closing and the wedding I was sick with the worst cold and flu I had ever experienced in my life. The flu rivaled that I had experienced my first semester in college, another major life change. It was my body's way of saying, "Enough already!!! Give me a break!"

If you take a few minutes and think about it, you, too, can probably come up with your own weakest link; the system in your body that first succumbs to stress and disease. It is helpful to be aware of this in yourself, because when you are not paying attention, your body can point the way to times in your life when you are overly stressed.

To this day, even though my own "Aha!" moment in the year of my wedding was eighteen years ago, when I catch a cold or feel a bit of flu coming on, I do a mental check of what I have been subjecting myself to that could be causing me stress. Also, having experienced this misery, I am careful to space stressful events in my life, whenever I can, to give myself some time to deal with one stressor prior to taking on another.

Current research is exploring stress as the cause of some of the maladies listed above, rather than just being a contributing factor. Researchers are looking at the role of stress in the emergence of a number of degenerative disorders, such as cardiovascular disease, cancer, arthritis, respiratory disorders, such as asthma and emphysema and depression.

Further, there is a substantial body of evidence that long-lasting, unresolved anger can lead to an inability to manage day-to-day stress effectively and can cause serious mental and physical health problems. If you are having difficulty letting go of some deeply buried anger, and believe this is affecting your ability to deal with current stressors, it would be worth your time to see a counselor or therapist to work through it.

Positive "Stressors"

I want to come back to this issue of stressors being both positive and negative for a moment. Most people think of stress as negative. Issues such as traffic, job difficulties, divorce and relationship or parenting issues come to mind. We may be aware of muscle tension, headaches or stomach aches before, during and after such situations.

As we said before, and as occurred in my own most stressful experience, stressors can also be positive experiences that we are choosing for ourselves and truly want to happen. Developments such as actually getting that new job, having a baby, getting married and moving into that brand new home can be incredibly stressful. Each of these changes activates your body's stress response.

Your body cannot tell the difference between positive and negative stressors. It secretes the same hormones in each case and goes into survival mode, experiencing the same effects in both. In both situations, your body is merely responding to the changes.

What Stress Looks Like

Individuals respond quite differently to episodes and periods of stress. How you react may be quite different from how your partner and children react to stress. Unless you know how someone typically responds to stress, it may be difficult to recognize and you may be inclined to take the individual's behavior personally, assuming you have done something to upset them. You are especially likely to misinterpret a situation if the individual's stress reaction is very different from your own.

To give you an example, when I am stressed, my tendency is to get quiet, to sigh frequently, to forget things and feel disoriented. Unless someone knows me well, it may be difficult to determine when I am stressed. Terry knows when I am quiet or if he hears me sigh that I am stressed. He will often ask "What's wrong?" thereby encouraging me to talk about what's bothering me.

His reaction to stress is quite different, however. When Terry is stressed or upset, he engages in busy-work to burn off his excess energy. What this often looks like is cleaning the house, especially the kitchen: washing dishes, wiping off countertops, cleaning out sinks, etc. There is often a flurry of activity that spurs me to ask him, "Is something on your mind?" I will admit, I have been tempted to start a minor argument when the kitchen is in need of a good cleaning, but have thus far restrained myself.

Each of our children responds differently to stress as well. Katie, the oldest, often explodes, much as I used to do when I was her age, blasting anyone or anything in her path, until it's over. And with Katie, when it's over, it's over and she's her old self again. The target of her assault, however, may not be. We need to work on this with her.

Ryan, our son, can react one of two ways when stressed or upset. If he's feeling safe to do so, as with his younger sister, he is likely to lash out like Katie. When he is not feeling it is safe to do so, he withdraws, internalizing the stress like his dad, and can either retreat to his bedroom or begin organizing things. A favorite of his is lining his shoes up in his bedroom. When I see this, I know he is upset and something must have happened that day. To be perfectly honest, I prefer this response to his other choice and find it much easier to deal with.

Meghan, our youngest child, is the most unusual when it comes to stress reactions. Meghan was born with clubfoot and received her first cast the day she was born. She was fitted with one cast after another until, at the ripe old age of seven months, she underwent surgery to permanently correct the problem that casting alone could not solve.

Terry and I were both terrified at the prospect of our infant daughter undergoing surgery, much less receiving general anesthesia. Being therapists and concerned about what her emotional reaction to the surgery might be, we inquired about this issue of her surgeon, a man at the top of his field. His response did not reassure us. He replied with absolute certainty, "It won't affect her at all; she won't even remember it." Knowing as therapists that memory is not the key to being affected emotionally by an event, we continued to be concerned. Needless to say, she survived the surgery just fine and the problem was corrected, but Meghan was forever changed.

She was a calm, cheerful and contented baby from the first and I found that by getting very close to her face, looking into her eyes and talking or singing calmly and softly to her, she would lay calmly and quietly while her cast was removed. Her local doctor, an orthopedic specialist who would cast many children in the course of any given week, was astounded at her reaction. Week after week we endured this ritual, with me looking into her eyes and talking softly to her and Meghan calmly looking into my eyes while they removed her cast with a small circular saw!

During her hospitalization after the surgery, I was allowed to sleep in her room with her, while Terry stayed at the Ronald MacDonald house across the street. We would spend our days in her room with her and made it a point to always be with her for emotional support when she was examined. On the day she was to be discharged, we inquired as to what time "the team", as it was a teaching hospital, would be in to give her her final examination. We were given a time, several hours in the future, and, as we had had nothing to eat that day and Meg was asleep, decided to stop at a nearby restaurant for a quick meal before heading home with her.

When we returned, I knew from my first glance at Meghan that something was wrong. She was awake, laying still and silent in her crib, staring at the ceiling. I tried to engage her attention, but she would barely look in my direction; she would not meet my eyes.

I went immediately to the nurse's station and asked whether anyone had been to her room while we were out. I was cheerfully informed that "Yes, the team" of approximately six doctors and residents, all strangers to her, had arrived earlier than expected and surrounded her crib to give her the final exam. We were now free to take her home.

This explained the change in Meghan. My sense of her reaction was that she had been overwhelmed and virtually traumatized by the strangers who examined her.

To this day, when Meghan is stressed, she goes into her "freeze" as I call it. If she is called on in class and doesn't know the answer or if I scold her unexpectedly for something, she will virtually freeze up and be unable to respond. I attribute this reaction to the traumatic events (for her) surrounding her surgery and examination. I have learned to be gentler with her as a result of this experience, probably something I needed to learn and from which my husband and all of my children benefit.

I think some children would have handled that situation a lot more easily than Meghan. I believe Katie, for example, would have just "rolled with it" and not reacted much at all. But this confirms the point I am trying to illustrate: that different people respond differently to the same stimulus or stressor. There are other situations to which Katie reacts, but which leave Meghan unflustered.

This is true for adults as well. What you react to may be very different from what pushes your partner's buttons. We had one man in group who drove truck for a living and he found himself enraged by relatively normal traffic patterns. One woman I know gets extremely upset when she must stand in line at the bank or the grocery store.

The more you can become aware of what typically upsets you (and your partner, your children, your boss), the more power you have to modify the result. You can prepare yourself for times when you know you will be facing a stressful experience. And, after reading Chapter Seven on Emotional Regulation you will be able to prepare a list of Replacement Thoughts especially for your uniquely stressful experiences.

Behavioral Signs of Stress and Tension

It is a valuable experience to take a look at our own response to stress and assess how we typically react when tense or angry. Similar to what I have done in the descriptions of my family and myself above, think back to several occasions when you were experiencing negative emotions and identify the various behaviors you have exhibited at those times. To assist you with this, we have developed a worksheet in Appendix C, entitled **Behavioral Signs of Stress**, which outlines some of the more typical problematic responses to stress.

If you are uncertain how you react, invite your partner to provide some input on this issue. However, before you do so, read over Chapter Ten on Communication Skills so this can be a positive experience which enhances your closeness, rather than a negative one which leads to defensiveness and conflict. Spend some time preparing yourself to potentially hear some unflattering descriptions of your behavior. Remember, this exercise, if done in a positive, receptive and caring manner, can enhance your relationship and bring the two of you closer together.

Long Term vs. Short Term Stress

I want to differentiate between long and short term stressors. Some events in our lives affect us very briefly and for a short period of time. These might include our child acting out on a given day, the boss getting on our back about a work issue, a driver on the road cutting us off today or our partner spending too much money on an "unnecessary" item.

Short Term Stressors

In our lives these events happen, we react to them in some fashion and it's over. We go on about our day and week and may not give it another thought.

We can, however, do some damage to our relationships by our reaction to these triggering events. Just because the event is over for us, does not mean it's over for others involved, especially because our reaction may have been their initiating stressful event. We will talk more about these reactions and the effect of our reaction on others in succeeding chapters, but for now, I would like to identify these short-term stressors as "triggers" or "hot buttons."

"Triggers" and "Hot Buttons"

Triggers and Hot Buttons are events and circumstances, most often beyond our control, that we automatically respond do with negative emotion. These are behaviors or events that upset, anger or disturb us in some way. Each of us has different triggers or hot buttons; what upsets me, may have little or no effect on you. Some typical hot buttons are listed below. It is important to identify these for yourself and to divide them into major, average and minor upsets. This helps you develop insight into your reaction to these events and also to plan how you would like to respond when next faced with this provocative situation. Remember triggers can be very individual, depending on your own life, relationship and family history experience.

For example, if **you** know you react negatively to someone singing the song, "Hello Pussycat" this fact doesn't have to make sense to anyone else. You will want to do some soul searching to find out what this means to you, but you will also want to control your environment and if you are out singing Karaoke one night and you hear them announce "Hello Pussycat" as the next song, **LEAVE** the club!

Some common examples of triggers and hot buttons include:

- ☮ Observing your partner flirting with another person,
- ☮ A child being disrespectful in public,
- ☮ Being stopped by police,
- ☮ Finding the house messy when you come home,
- ☮ Having to wait for someone who is late,
- ☮ Having your car break down,
- ☮ Getting fired,
- ☮ Being lied to,
- ☮ Your team losing a big game,
- ☮ Being robbed,

☮ Being accused of something you didn't do,
☮ Being ignored.

As a rule of thumb, unless you have progressed to the point where you are fairly certain you can positively mange your reaction to these triggers, **AVOID THEM** whenever you can! It only makes sense to take care of yourself in this way; it avoids trouble (legal, financial, etc.) and prevents further damage to your relationships. Give yourself permission to act in ways to avoid your triggers; it doesn't mean you are a wimp or a coward—just too smart to get caught up in the same problematic situation over and over again.

That's one definition of insanity: doing the same thing over and over again and expecting a different result! You are smarter than that. Protect yourself by acting in ways to prevent this reaction.

Dealing With Short Term Stressors

We can deal with these stressors by becoming aware of them as suggested previously. Knowing what we react to gives us the power to prepare for them and be on the lookout for situations in which they arise so we can maintain better control of our response. Long term stressors need to be handled a bit differently.

Know yourself, also, so that when you are unable to avoid a short term stressor, you are aware of its likely effect on you and can take steps to minimize the damage. Let me give you an example from the past week for me.

Ironically enough, doctor's appointments are stressful for me. Whenever I am in town, rather than at the cabin relaxing and writing as I am right now, my time is not my own. It is committed; typically over-committed, but I am working on this. My typical day is booked with back to back sessions with clients, 7-9 each day, and perhaps a group or class, in addition to 10-15 phone calls which must be responded to in one form or another, a letter or two to write and send off, paperwork for each client session I do, not to mention doing my part to nurture, feed, clothe and raise three children and attend to my relationship with my husband. I have little time for myself.

When I do have a doctor's appointment, as we all do from time to time, something has to give. I rearrange my appointments, make special arrangements for my children, make plans for my husband to drop off a bite for me in the middle of my twelve hour workday so I will get to eat, make arrangements with my secretary to have crisis and business matters handled in my absence. I am stressed, but handling things.

Then the doctor's office calls, minutes before the appointment, to tell me she is held up in surgery and we will have to re-schedule the appointment. This is inconvenient, but understandable. I am not happy; I am stressed, but I cooperate, understanding what they are dealing with on their end. My replacement thoughts are: "Now I will have an hour and a half free to catch up or take some time for me!" and the like (see Chapter Seven for a discussion of Replacement Thoughts).

However, there is still the matter of the rescheduled appointment. It must be set up and all of these arrangements made again. We do this and it is manageable.

The difficulty comes when I am scheduled for my appointment for four weeks in a row before it finally materializes! Three times I am called and asked to reschedule due to an emergency. Now I am really stressed! In fact, when I am called in week three, I am a bit less pleasant than I was the first time I was called. I still understand, and I am struggling with my frustration and with my sense of being overwhelmed due to all the details I have to, again, rearrange. However, now I am thinking and talking, I hope respectfully and politely with the doctor's office, about finding a new physician. I inquire whether there is someone else I can see and whether all of their physicians are this busy. These are, I believe, legitimate questions. This is a short term stressor (the initial appointment) which became a long term stressor due to the repeated cancellations.

In truth I really struggled with this situation because of the level of difficulty it presented in my life. By the end of the month, my clients were feeling bounced around, themselves because of all of our rearranging, my office manager was about ready to quit and my family just wanted it all to stop so I could be there for them again.

This was also a situation in which I believe my anger worked for me because I was able to access it and use it appropriately and constructively. See Chapter One for a greater discussion of how anger can motivate and help us. Finally in week three I explained to the woman calling me how my own practice worked and the level of difficulty these repeated cancellations presented in my professional as well as personal life. If not for my great frustration, I would have said little or nothing, as in weeks prior. I don't know whether or not this made a difference, but they called me back soon after and offered me an appointment time that worked with my schedule, which they kept and the doctor apologized at the appointment saying, "I'm sorry about last week," apparently having no knowledge of the three weeks prior. I chose to let it drop with that.

I do know that my office manager, my family and I, as well as, to an extent, my clients, paid a price for all of that stress. I am tied to a schedule when I am in town, not by my own choosing, but by the nature of my life and business. This started out as a short term stressor that became a long term one, initially affecting only one week but ending up affecting my life for an entire month. Especially when this is unexpected, its effect can be cumulative. It was much easier for me to accept and think positively about the cancellation in week one than in week three when I actually voiced my frustration (productively and effectively I hope!).

Long Term Stressors

Some events are in our lives on a long term basis and affect us over a period of weeks, months or years. These may take the form of a painful divorce, a loved-one's lingering illness or a difficult downsizing at work where the result is uncertain for a period of time. These are long term stressors and the type of stress that can lead to the stress-related illnesses that we were talking about earlier in this chapter.

When you are experiencing one of these stressors, it is almost like living in a war zone for as long as the stress continues. Your adrenaline levels and other powerful hormones remain at unnaturally high levels for an extended period of time. This is what does the physical damage to your body and causes the illness we discussed previously.

Take, for example, someone going through a divorce. Everyday might bring a new stressful experience related to the major stress: an upsetting contact with the former partner, a letter from your attorney, kids acting out, a bill you didn't expect, a rumor shared by a "friend" who thinks he's doing you a favor. It doesn't take long before you start looking for and expecting these experiences, keeping your adrenaline high even when nothing new is happening. Thus, for the 12-18 months you are going through the experience, you are never at rest. This is what takes the toll on you, physically and emotionally, and leads to stress-related illness.

In the situation regarding my doctor's appointment described above, albeit relatively minor in comparison with a chronic illness or a divorce, I was careful to take better care of myself. I kept to a regular schedule as far as rest and exercise was concerned, I made more of a point to schedule "down-time" for me, ate food with good nutritional value and checked myself before I opened my mouth. I also made a regular habit of talking with my husband about my feelings to try to release them rather than bottling them up. Compare these ideas with those suggested later in this chapter as recommendations for dealing with long term stressors.

And, remember, it isn't only negative life events that cause us stress. As we have said before, actually getting that new job, getting married and having that baby all will cause long term stress in our lives, but they will also hopefully make it richer and more rewarding as well.

Further, stress is not all bad. Like body temperature, your stress level can be too high OR too low. If it is too low, you will be bored, lethargic and unchallenged; not living up to your potential.

In either case you won't thrive. It is the right balance that can keep you happy, healthy and going strong. When you are aware that your stress level is too high, the key is to pay attention to the symptoms and stressors you're experiencing and take some action to moderate your stress.

Dealing With Long Term Stressors

This "short" chapter on stress and how it affects anger has continued to grow as I have been writing this book. I feel compelled to spend a bit of time giving you some information about how to handle long term stressors, but this area will be explored in much greater depth in a later book focusing primarily on stress and stress management. But I don't feel it would be fair to give you so much information about stress and how to identify it and not give you some ideas of what to do about it. Just be aware, this is only the "tip of the iceberg," so to speak in terms of stress management techniques.

The TEAM Approach to Stress

I like to talk about stress management in terms of the TEAM approach:

- ☮ **Take time** for yourself,
- ☮ **Eliminate** what you can,
- ☮ **Accept** the changes you cannot or don't want to eliminate and
- ☮ **Manage** your stressors with positive coping skills.

Take Time for Yourself

Most people groan when I talk about time because we are all so busy in this day and age that it's hard to fit one more thing into our lives. When this happens, I like to tell my favorite "time" story to help with a little change in perspective.

In January of 2001, Terry and I took our first vacation without children in over ten years. We were headed out to Santa Fe, NM, an area we had visited very briefly the year before and had fallen in love with, so we wanted to investigate it further. We were planning to fly into Albuquerque, because fares were cheaper, and had reserved a four wheel drive Jeep for the week in which we would drive the 60 or so miles to Santa Fe.

As we neared the Albuquerque airport, the pilot announced that, as the city was experiencing a blizzard, we would be unable to land until the snow and winds died down. Our plan was to circle the airport for a time to wait for conditions to improve. After approximately one half hour, he announced that we would be re-routed to Phoenix, AZ to refuel, and then head back to Albuquerque to see if it was safe to land, but he was making no promises.

As we landed in Phoenix, an announcement was made that passengers should stay on the plane as the refueling would only take fifteen minutes and the plane would not wait for persons who had deplaned and returned late. I had been worried about our car rental as, having been the person to make the arrangements for the flight and the vehicle, I knew there were only four Jeeps available at the Albuquerque Airport. Knowing they were experiencing a blizzard, and that they would only hold our reservation for limited time, I was concerned that when we finally arrived our Jeep would be gone, leaving us with no transportation to Santa Fe that evening.

For this reason, Terry and I decided to leave the plane only long enough to place a phone call to the car rental agency at the Albuquerque Airport to explain what had happened and ask them to hold the Jeep for us. While Terry was placing the call, I used the restroom, then, hand in hand, we ran back through the airport so as not to be late to the plane. As we were running past the various shops and restaurants, I remember remarking that it would be nice if we had the time to have a bite to eat; the southwestern food smelled wonderful and we had been on a plane for, perhaps six hours at that point, with nothing but a meager bag of peanuts to eat.

We made it back to the plane in plenty of time and settled ourselves in for the return flight to Santa Fe. As we were doing so, the third person in our row of three seats, a college student headed back to school for the Spring Semester at NMU, boarded the plane just as they were closing the doors.

As she sat down, I smelled the most delicious aroma and, looking over, discovered she had stopped at one of the small restaurants and purchased a plate of burritos and nachos which she proceeded to eat.

Three women in the row ahead of us, who had chosen to remain on the plane during refueling, were aghast! As each turned and watched her eat, one of them snapped, "You're not just going to eat that in front of us, are you?"

The young woman looked up cheerfully and confidently and said, "I sure am. We all had the same fifteen minutes!"

What a wonderful message about time! We were struck by this at the time and have since shared it with many individuals and groups. It is so true. We each start out the day with the same 24 hours and continuously make choices about how to spend them. As we finish the day, without having accomplished what we'd hoped, or spent time with loved ones or activities that are important to us, we are all choosing how to spend our precious minutes and hours. If we were as conscious about how we spend our time as our money, we would probably be a much happier, more contented nation!

Think about it: we monitor our bank accounts, keeping track of where our money has gone, we meet with a financial planner to think about how we will spend our money in the future. If we put one quarter of that thought and planning into how we spend our time, would we be spending it the way were are now? Or would we be making some different choices?

Even though I've used that example to teach others about time, that flight to Albuquerque was a life-changing experience for me as well. Since that time (no pun intended!), I have been more conscious about choices I make about how to spend my minutes. I am doing a better job at setting aside time in my day for people and activities that are important to me. And I am doing a better job eliminating time-wasters that used to eat up my precious minutes: excessive TV watching, looking at junk mail, engaging in activities that I don't enjoy.

Know that we have to nurture and give back to ourselves, because we can't give to others, such as partners, children and friends, when our own cup is empty. We must fill up our own cup, so that we can give to others from our overflow.

So here are some quick ideas about how to take more time for yourself. Remember this is just a beginning; again, the tip of the iceberg, as it were. Use these to start setting aside more time for yourself, but don't be afraid to branch out from here.   Just get in the habit of asking yourself, "Is this how I choose to be spending my next fifteen minutes?" Your gut reaction to this question is your best guide.

If you get a chance, drop us an email about some of your favorite self-care solutions so we can include those that may be helpful to others in the next edition of this work.

⊕   **Let the answering machine pick up your phone calls.** Who says you have to drop everything and answer the phone just because someone decides to call you at a given moment? It will interrupt what you are doing and it will take you twice as long to get back into your project, costing you even more time. Set aside a time for returning all your messages that is convenient to you. You will be more efficient at it, doing it all at once, and will also resent it less.

Think also of the activities that are interrupted by the phone and the message that sends to people important to you. We have stopped answering the phone during dinner, unless a member of our immediate family is calling. How do you think your children and partner feel if you sit down to dinner and, rather than talking with each other, spend a half hour talking to a friend on the phone. It sends the message they are not very important to you.

⊕   **Limit the news broadcasts you watch.** Many people watch the news when they wake up at 6 a.m., then again at 6:30, 7 and 7:30 before heading in to work. Often these same people are in front of the television again at noon, watching the news and at 5, 6 and 10 p.m. When you add it up, at a half hour per broadcast, this costs four hours of time, to hear information that has most likely been repetitive after the first half hour. Think about it. Have they really told you anything new? Couldn't you be just as informed by limiting yourself to one hour (total) of news each day? You have just saved yourself three hours of time which you may spend as you wish!

The second aspect of watching the news that disturbs me is that most of it is negative. It is very easy to become depressed when bombarded with one negative report after another. Why subject yourself to this? Do something fun instead.

⊕ **Subscribe to only one newspaper.** Those of you watching several news broadcasts are often also reading several newspapers each day. Is the information that different in each? Choose the paper that you most enjoy and cancel all the others. At a half hour per paper, surely you can find a better use for that time.

The negativity aspect applies here as well. Most of what is "newsworthy" is negative and we can become depressed, cynical and jaded on a constant diet of bad news.

⊕ **Limit television watching.** Have you ever found yourself sitting in your living room watching a television show and wondering, "Why am I watching this? I don't even like this show!" Most of us have. The answer is habit. When we come home from work, it is far easier to flop down on the sofa and get absorbed in some mindless program than to put ourselves to the task of coming up with something more interesting to do. This costs us, and our children who learn this habit from us, many hours during the course of the average week or month.

Make a conscious effort to choose the programs you enjoy watching and limit your viewing to those. When the program is over, get up and turn the television off before you get absorbed in the next program and lose another half hour of your precious time. Spend a few minutes thinking about what you would like to be doing instead of wasting this time and point yourself in that direction after you turn off the set.

⊕ **Schedule time for yourself right in your calendar.** After our discussion about how crucial it is to take care of yourself and all the harm caused by stress, surely you can see that you deserve time for yourself. Most of us today carry around a calendar of some kind in which we write all of our most important commitments. Understanding how damaging stress and not taking the time for yourself can be, isn't your commitment to yourself at least as important as all of the others written in your book? I'm sure those who depend on you would think so. Schedule "me time" right in your calendar for activities you enjoy and find helpful in relieving your stress.

Eliminate What You Can

As we have established, we all make choices about how we spend our time and the obligations we choose to take on and commit our time to. Make wise choices to let go of those time users that do not give back to you by practicing the following:

⊕ **Be gentle with yourself.** Watch how much you take on at a given time. Whenever possible, give yourself time to adjust to one stress before adding another. A good rule of thumb is to allow at least six months between major stressors in your life, even happy ones. Don't choose to move at the same time you are changing jobs and getting married (like I did in 1989) unless you absolutely cannot avoid it.

⊕ **Also keep an eye on your expectations of yourself.** Don't attempt to conquer the world in times of stress. Do what you have to, but don't be afraid to let some things go, or do a less than perfect job, if they add stress rather than pleasure to your life.

For example, if you are in college or have recently gone back to school, temper the expectations you have of yourself in this experience. You can get a degree with B's just as easily as with A's and it may cost you less in the long run. If you are a person who has always driven yourself to be the best, and find yourself back in college, but now also managing a job and a family, you may want to work on accepting slightly lower grades, understanding that you have more responsibilities now than when you were in school in the past.

I will share with you my own experience with this issue. I attended law school in 1983, just out of college and before I had any children. I attended graduate school to obtain my Master's Degree in Social Work some ten years later, the mother of three children ranging in age from six years to three months.

As difficult as law school was, it was a cake walk compared to attending graduate school with three children and a job. When I was in law school, there were only my husband and me to think about. He was pretty self-sufficient, so if I wanted to study through a mealtime or for an entire weekend, it was no problem. In graduate school, I had to write most of my papers during my youngest daughter's two hour naptime each afternoon, before I ran off to work several evenings a week. It was no picnic. But it eased up once I stopped pressuring my self to be the best and holding myself to the same standards I had met before I added all of those wonderful responsibilities to my life.

Give yourself a break! You're only human. Remember, "B's get degrees!"

⊕ **Schedule some down time as well.** Make time to relax and do nothing. Time to let your mind wander. Don't push yourself to be busy all the time. Give yourself permission just to "be."

⊕ **Treat yourself well and reward yourself amply.** That new haircut, massage, good book or just the gift of time can be just what you need at the moment. Give yourself whatever you find yourself wanting the most!

⊕ **Sleep is nature's medicine.** Make sure you are getting enough. Also, during times when you are under stress, make sure you are operating on a relatively regular schedule, going to bed about the same time each night and waking at about the same time each morning. This helps your body to predict when to wind down, so you will find yourself starting to relax somewhat automatically as your regular bedtime nears.

⊕ **Shut out worries at night.** If troublesome thoughts keep you awake, keep a pen and paper at your bedside to write them down. Then you can put them out of your mind for the night and deal with them in the morning. If the thoughts keep bothering you, just imagine there is a light switch in your brain and turn it off when the thoughts start coming to you. You've already written them down; now reassure yourself you can deal with them tomorrow.

Accept What You Cannot Change

There are many variables in each of our lives that are not within our control. Traffic patterns, the weather, and moods and reactions of others are just a few of these. Even when faced with many changes or stressors over which we have little or no control, we typically have at least three choices of how to react:

⊕ We can fight it every step of the way, clawing and scratching tooth and nail, keeping ourselves continually in a state of stress with each little change;

⊕ We can resign ourselves to the change and go along half-heartedly, holding onto little resentments that eventually build up and overwhelm us; or

⊕ We can embrace change as an opportunity for person growth, working with it and using it to our best advantage.

Research is finding that people who choose the last option tend to be happier and healthier than those who choose either of the first two. Looking at our reaction to stress in general, it is easy to understand why this may be the case.

As a follow up to the stress research, we have also learned that the same mechanism that turned on the stress response can turn it off. First identified by Herbert Benson in 1975, this has been called the Relaxation Response. To paraphrase his philosophy, as soon as you decide that a situation is no longer dangerous, your brain stops sending emergency signals to the brain stem, which in turn ceases to send panic messages to your nervous system.

Thus, approximately three minutes after you turn off the danger signals, the fight, flight or freeze response fizzles. Blood pressure, metabolism, breathing rate, heart rate and muscle tension all return to normal levels. You can use this information to relax yourself in the face of stress or change. With a bit of deep breathing and openness to learning something new, all can be resolved. See also Chapter Seven on Emotional Regulation for a more complete description on how to achieve this effect.

I used to have a poster hanging in my office that expresses this last approach to change perfectly. It read:

Life is Change; Growth is Optional!

I was working for our county Child Protective Services agency at the time. Being a public agency, many decisions were made on a monthly and yearly basis that affected my job and working conditions, all of which were out of my control. This slogan helped keep me focused on doing my best and taking care of myself in the process.

As an aside, I had another stress-relieving poster hanging next to the first. I loved this one as well and have used it with many groups and clients since that time. It read:

Many things may be sad and unpleasant,
but the only thing that's the end of the world
is the end of the world!

Isn't that the truth? But how many of us are able to remember that in times of stress? With practice, we can get better at remembering to let go and accept the things that are out of our control.

But how do we do that? By making adjustments when appropriate. For example, when you experience a change, some of your old hobbies or habits or friends may no longer fit anymore. If you have recently retired or changed jobs, you may have lost the social network you had through your job. If you recently lost a spouse through death or divorce, some couple or individual friends may not fit as well with you now. If a friend with whom you shared a hobby has recently moved away, you may find yourself less interested in that activity now that you are doing it alone.

But our needs don't change because we have change in another part of our lives. See Chapter Four for a more complete discussion of our basic human needs.

We simply must find new ways of meeting those needs when the old ways no longer fit. If you used to do craft projects or gardening with a friend, you may want to take up something else, such as a painting class that meets your creative and social needs. If you and your friend used to walk or run together, you may want to take up rollerblading to meet this physical need.

The good news is that times of change are a wonderful time to explore and develop new interests. Go with your change! This is a wonderful time to:

⊕ Learn to play that musical instrument you always wanted to play,

⊕ Take a class in a subject that interests you,

⊕ Do the traveling you've always dreamed of doing,

⊕ Learn a foreign language,

⊕ Join a club or community organization,

⊕ Experiment with new foods and unfamiliar cooking styles or techniques,

⊕ Volunteer! Many organizations are just begging for help and will be thrilled for your time and talents.

Again, this list is just a starting point. Choose a direction and go from there. The world is your oyster and you are limited only by your imagination. Get out; meet new people and make new friends. The key is to use stress energy positively to meet the challenges and experiences life has in store for you. Enjoy!

Manage Your Stressors with Positive Coping Skills

Some people are unfamiliar with the term "coping skills," but these are nothing more than specific activities and helpful hints for dealing with daily and cumulative stress. Researchers have been looking at the effects of stress on individuals for a number of years now and are finding that it's not so much the major stressors of life that really get to people (with the exception of protracted periods of chronic stress as discussed earlier). It is the accumulation of day to day events, the little stresses that mount up and really take their toll on people. But the techniques discussed below will even help with this cumulative experience.

The coping skills are divided into two sections, **Relax Your Body** and **Relax Your Emotions**, but in many ways this is an artificial division. In reality, anything that affects your body affects your emotions as well, and vice versa. As you read through these techniques please keep in mind that both arenas are likely to be affected by any of the skills you attempt to use.

Relax Your Body

The next time you feel the effects of excessive stress, try some of the following ways to help your body relax:

1) **Deep Breathing** — While sitting, lying down or standing, close your eyes and breathe in slowly. Make sure you are breathing from deep in your diaphragm, not the shallow upper chest breathing that most of us do when we're stressed. Your tummy should move in and out when you breathe. That is how you determine you are breathing from the right place and relaxing yourself. Breathe in for a count of 5-10 seconds, then let your breath out just as slowly. Take ten of these relaxing breaths any time you feel tense. This is something you can easily do while sitting at your desk in your office or working in almost any capacity.

2) **Sighing** — Sighing can be a sign of stress, but it can also help us relieve stress. Make yourself sigh when you are aware of feeling tense and see if you don't feel better. Be sure to make some noise when you do so or it isn't as effective.

3) **Meditation** — Meditation seems strange or frightening to some people, but can be very relaxing. It helps to release creativity and energy in those who practice it regularly. Simply sitting for 5 or 10 minutes and keeping your mind free of distracting thoughts can be meditation. Focusing on a word you find calming or

relaxing, such as "Peace" is a form of meditation. Other people find it helpful to use guided imagery or visualization exercises that someone reads to them or they read into a tape recorder and play. A visualization exercise that I regularly use with clients entitled "My Favorite Room" is included in Appendix D.

4) **Stretching**—Practice simple stretches to relax, such as the "neck stretch." Stretch your neck by gently rolling your head in a half-circle, starting on one side, then dropping your chin to your chest and rolling your head over to the other side. Repeat in the opposite direction. Stretch each side five times. This is especially effective because so many of us hold our stress in our neck and shoulders and tighten those muscles accordingly. Loosening them in this manner can greatly relieve your physical stress. See also Appendix E for amore complete list of stress reducing stretches.

5) **Exercise**—Any kind of physical activity will help to reduce stress. This includes walking, running, biking, rollerblading, bowling, chopping wood, hiking, etc. Get yourself moving to alleviate some stress. If you can think about the source of your stress while engaging in the activity, it can be even more helpful. See Chapter Four for a more complete discussion of Exercise and its stress reduction properties.

6) **Take a Hot Bath**—Ask members of your household to allow you at least 30 minutes of uninterrupted soaking time. You can maximize this experience, by adding candle light, relaxing herbs from the garden, such as chamomile, soft lights and relaxing music.

7) **Get a Massage**—Massage is a wonderful way to get rid of physical tension. Professional massages generally take 30 minutes to an hour and will work on specific areas of tension, such as the lower back or neck. If your partner is willing, ask her/him to give you a massage. This can be a wonderful experience for both of you and you may end up returning the favor, and feeling very relaxed! A number of research studies

have demonstrated that positive touching can lead to a reduction in stress-related hormones.

8) **Eat Well**—Reduce caffeine (in coffee, black tea, soft drinks and chocolate) and alcohol intake. Make sure your diet is well balanced and take steps to eat nutritious foods to help reduce stress.

Relax Your Emotions

Relaxing your emotions can be just as important to relieving stress as relaxing your body. Here are a few suggestions:

1) **Talk**—Take the time to talk with a friend, partner or co-worker. Express feelings you might have been holding in. Listen carefully to the responses you receive. Walking in a quiet neighborhood or park while you talk can limit distractions and help you focus on the discussion, and work out some physical stress as well.

2) **Laugh**—Humor is a terrific stress reliever. Attend a comedy club, rent or see a funny movie, or spend time with a friend who makes you laugh.

3) **Cry**—Tears are a very honest expression of emotion and can be as good a release as laughing. If you haven't cried in a long time, try listening to mournful music, watching a sad movie or writing about a sad experience.

4) **Read**—A good book is a great escape. Reading a tear-jerker or a comedy can also help to release pent-up emotions.

5) **Do Something You Love**—When you enjoy yourself, whether it is while gardening, going to the beach, riding your motorcycle, spending time with friends or doing something else, you relax your emotions.

Create Your Own Stress Reducers

We have listed a few stress reducing ideas that commonly work for most people. These are just a few techniques you can try. You can create your own healthy stress reducers if you find something uniquely yours. You'll feel better and stay healthier if you do.

The first step in managing your own stress is to become aware of what it looks and feels like. To that end, we have created the Anger Cues worksheet on the following page to help you identify physical cues that indicate you are upset. Special thanks to the May, 2004 Men's Anger Management Group at Blue Waters for their assistance in developing this tool. You know who you are and your input is greatly appreciated!

Read through the Anger Cues thinking about what happens when you are upset. Circle all sensations that you can identify with. They all happen to each of us because it is a physical reaction; different people just notice different symptoms.

After you've gone through and circled all of the cues you can, read over the sheet one more time. What is the first physical sensation you are aware of that tells you, "Uh oh, I'm losing it." Put an asterisk or star by that symptom. That becomes your cue to use the Time-Out procedure that we will discuss in Chapter Six—the minute you feel your first sensation, take a time out! You will help yourself as well as your relationship!

On the final page of this chapter, we've also included a summary sheet on some of the other elements covered in this rather extensive chapter. Read it over, try some of the Stress Management techniques and, for future reference, record your results and reactions on this sheet. It is also helpful as a good summary of the information we've just covered.

Remember, stress is not all bad. It can stimulate and motivate us and prevent us from becoming bored. Our goal is not to have a stress- or change-free life but to be resilient and able to manage the difficulties we are faced with. The trick is to use stress and change to your advantage—to make it work for you. Positive stress can make your life both rich and satisfying.

Good Luck and Have Fun reducing your stress!

Stress & Anger Cues

Individuals have different ways that indicate to them that they are angry, tense, anxious or feeling some other negative emotion. Developing the ability to recognize these physical cues when they occur gives you the power to make conscious choices about how to handle them.

Circle the cues you are aware of when you are upset:

- ☮ You feel tension in your:
  1) Forehead
  2) Back of your neck
  3) Shoulders
  4) Chest
  5) Stomach
  6) Face
  7) Hands
  8) Legs
  9) Lower Back
  10) Another Part of Your Body:_____
- ☮ You have pain in your chest.
- ☮ You sweat.
- ☮ Your heart pounds or beats fast.
- ☮ You can feel or hear your heart pounding.
- ☮ You feel or hear a pounding in your head.
- ☮ Your face feels flushed or warm.
- ☮ Your skin feels cool and damp.
- ☮ You tremble or shake in your:
  1) Hands
  2) Legs
  3) Another Part of Your Body:_____
- ☮ Your stomach feels nauseous.
- ☮ Your eyes feel strained, dry or tired.
- ☮ You develop a skin rash or hives.
- ☮ You develop a headache or migraine.
- ☮ You develop twitches or tics (eyes, face, etc.)
- ☮ You experience diarrhea or constipation.
- ☮ You experience increased urination.

- You become impotent.
- You clench your jaw or grind your teeth.
- You have trouble with your speech, i.e. your words don't come out the way you want.
- You feel like you are going to choke.
- You are breathing heavily or quickly.
- You feel short of breath or can't get your air.
- You feel dizzy or lightheaded.
- You hear a ringing or feel a rushing in your ears.
- Your hands or palms sweat or feel clammy.
- You feel like you have a ball of bread dough in your stomach.
- You become sensitive to light.
- There is another symptom you are aware of: _____

Once you have complete this worksheet by circling **ALL** of the physical symptoms you have experienced during times of tension or anger, read over the list again and put an **asterisk (*)** by the symptom that usually occurs **first**, or is the first one you become aware of. This is powerful information and an effective tool for you in developing more positive methods of handling stress and anger. Once you are aware, from your physical sign(s) that tell you that you are upset, you are in a position to do something different to handle the situation in a more positive manner.

Remember:

"It's not stress that kills us,
it's our reaction to it."

Hans Selye, M.D.,
Stress Researcher

Stress Management Summary

⊕ Fight, Flight or Freeze
These are the ways I am most affected by stress:

___Flu   ___Ulcers
___Colds   ___Diarrhea/IBS
___Asthma   ___Headaches
___High Blood Pressure   ___Muscle Tension
___Diabetes   ___Allergies
___Bronchitis   ___Other:_____

⊕ My Own Behavioral Reactions to Stress include: ____
_____

⊕ My Triggers and Hot Buttons are: _____
_____

⊕ The TEAM Approach to Stress:
~I am taking TIME for myself by _____
_____

~I am ELIMINATING _____
_____ from my life in an effort to take better care of myself.

~I am working at ACCEPTING change by _____
_____

~I am MANAGING my stressors by using the following
Coping Skills: (Check all that apply)

___Deep Breathing   ___Talk
___Sighing   ___Laughter
___Meditation   ___Crying
___Stretching   ___Reading
___Exercise   ___Doing Things I Enjoy
___Hot Baths   ___Eating Well
___Massage   ___Other: _____

Chapter 4

No Man (or Woman) Is An Island

Why We <u>Must</u> Relate to Others

*A*fter explaining the importance of spending time with friends outside of the relationship to meet individual needs and avoid putting too much pressure on the intimate relationship to meet all of our needs, I am interrupted with a question.

*"But what if I can't trust them?" Kyle asks, "What if **they're** all whores?"*

"Who?" I ask, more than a little confused.

"Her friends. All they do is go to bars and pick up guys," comes the response.

"Do you trust your partner?"

"Not when she's with them," Kyle remarks, beginning to get agitated.

"Well, then you don't really trust her. Trust should not be conditional. You need to work on developing more trust in your

relationship so that you feel comfortable no matter who she's out with."

"But why does she have to hang out with them? Why can't she hang out with people who don't go to bars, women who are married and have kids and like to stay home?"

"Who do you think should choose your partner's friends?"

"Well, if she's hanging around with someone I don't like and I tell her I don't like them, she should stop."

"So you think you should be the one to decide who she gets to spend time with. Does that go both ways? Should she get to pick your friends, too?" I press him a little more.

"Well, all my friends are married. They're trustworthy. She has nothin' to worry about and she knows it!" Kyle retorts, completely missing my point. We have more work to do.

Every living creature has certain basic needs which must be met in order for it to survive. Some obvious needs include food, air, water and the like. As human beings, we are a slightly more sophisticated life form, so we have needs that can be a bit more complex than, say, a paramecium, and we would do well to pay some attention to how well we are meeting these needs.

When our needs are not being met on a regular basis, we feel out of balance and experience some of the stress we discussed in the previous chapter. If we are doing a good job meeting one or two needs, but virtually ignore the rest, or meet them half-heartedly, we are still out of balance and experiencing stress. We can be in top physical form, but if our social and emotional needs are not met, we are still in rough shape.

Understanding how harmful stress can be for us, we would like to spend some time now breaking down what these needs are and how you can meet them. Be thinking as you read about your partner's needs as well. After all, she is a human being with needs in her own right that must be met in order for her to be happy and content. Remember, if you want your partner to stay in the relationship with you, it is in your best interest to make sure she stays happy and content.

Basic Human Needs

There are many different ways to discuss the needs we humans share. One of our favorite is also one the easiest to remember. Using the image of a pie shape and a simple test-taking strategy, it can be transformed into an image virtually anyone can carry with him throughout his day or week without having to carry and refer to a piece of paper. This makes it more likely to be used and remembered, thus more effective.

SPICES

Notice the pie shape on the following page. Each piece of the pie represents one of our important human needs. As we said before, each must be met at about the same level in order for us to feel in balance and unstressed. Whenever we are not meeting each of these six needs, we become out of balance and more reactive to stress in our lives.

The best thing about this method, however, is that, beginning in the upper left hand corner with *Spiritual* needs, the first letter of each of these six needs spells the word SPICES. Thus, it is as easy to remember as it is to apply. If you can think of the word SPICES, several times each week you can run through in your mind what you are doing to meet each of these basic needs. Let's look at these needs a little more closely.

BASIC NEEDS

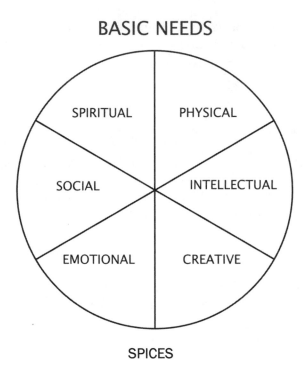

SPICES

Spiritual

All persons have the need to feel connected to something greater than ourselves. We need to feel we have a reason for being here, a purpose, a path or a mission that we are destined to achieve. And we have a need to believe that there is a force greater than us, or a higher power, that is out there for us.

Some people meet this need through participating in an organized religion of some kind. Attending mass on Thursday evenings or Sunday mornings, or synagogue on Saturdays, makes them feel connected to this greater life force. For some people, however, these services do not reach them.

Many of these persons are able to meet this need through some contact with nature. For many, walking through a forest, watching the waves crash onto the shore or marveling at the uniqueness of each snowflake in the middle of a raging blizzard is enough to awaken that appreciation of a higher power.

For some, it is a combination of both of these methods, and perhaps others, that assist them in meeting this need. I know for myself, I was raised Catholic and do belong to a Catholic church in the city in which I live, attending mass most Sundays we are in town. But I will also tell you that the weekends we are up north at our cabin in the middle of the forest or camping in Taos Canyon, in the very midst of nature, we do not even attempt to attend mass. I know there is at least one Catholic Church in Eagle River, the town nearest our cabin and there is a virtual plethora of Catholic churches in Taos, NM, but when I am immersed in nature I often feel more in touch with my higher power than when sitting inside a church.

Deep breathing, meditation, visualization, Tai Chi and similar techniques can also help us to experience the awe and appreciate the power that is outside of ourselves. Find some way to do this for yourself on at least a weekly basis to meet your own spiritual need. But remember, it doesn't have to be met in the same way each time. Often just sitting quietly and thinking or reading the Bible can be as powerful a spiritual experience as listening to what someone else has to say about this force.

Physical

Physical needs are usually pretty obvious. Nonetheless, we want to discuss them briefly to outline some simple ways they can be met.

The more obvious physical needs include air, water, food, clothing, shelter, and sleep. We all understand the needs for air, shelter and water, though may of us don't drink enough water on a regular basis. Each person should drink 6-8 eight ounce glasses of water every day. Failing to do so can lead to dehydration, which can cause all sorts of medical problems, including headaches, dizziness, nausea and worse. Keeping a glass or bottle of water with you at most times can insure you are meeting your quota. If you experience headaches regularly, before popping the pain reliever, try drinking a glass of water and see if that doesn't help.

Be careful of consuming too many caffeinated beverages. They are not a substitute for pure water and, something many people are not aware of, also tend to have a dehydrating effect, causing you to need more water than if you had not drunk anything to start with!

Food is a rather obvious human need of which most of us are aware. But what you eat can be as important as whether you do so. Be aware of the food you are putting into your body. I like to use the analogy that our body is like a vehicle that we count on to carry us from one place to another. If you put deficient or inadequate fuel in your car, it won't run as well or as efficiently. By the same token, if you put inadequate fuel in your body, in the form of junk food and processed foods, it, also, will not perform as well.

If, however, you fill your body with the premium fuel found in fresh fruits and vegetables and unprocessed items, it will run and perform at a much higher level. And it will feel better physically. The bottom line is, the better the fuel you put into your body, the better output you will get. The choice is yours.

To give you a bit of food for thought, so to speak, sugary foods may give you a temporary boost, but the high is followed one to two hours later by a chemically induced rebound, fatigue and sluggishness. This is too high a price to pay, in a time of stress, or otherwise, for the temporary high.

Eating adequate protein can maximize the body's ability to withstand stress. Protein, which contains essential amino acids, helps maintain healthy functioning of the body. Healthy sources of protein include fish, poultry (preferably with the skin removed), lean meats, peas, dried beans, nuts and seeds (sunflower, and the like), grains, tofu and skimmed milk products. Animal proteins should be kept to no more than 15% of your total diet.

Further, fatty fish, such as salmon, mackerel and herring, contain a high level of a compound called omega-3 fatty acids. They sound harmful, but eating them may help protect the body from the stress of heart disease by decreasing the formation of cholesterol clogs and blood clots.

There is a lot of information out there about how these vehicles that are our bodies are affected by the fuels we put into them. If you feel you are in the dark on this subject, educate yourself. Get more information by finding books that will inform you, meeting with a nutritionist or dietitian or just start reading labels at the grocery store. Because of the new government labeling requirements, there is a wealth of information at your fingertips. Use it to reduce your stress and improve your life.

Sleep is also a need many people think they can do without. However, sleep is crucial for both our physical and our emotional well-being. Not only do persons who are sleep-deprived have difficulty functioning physically due to tiredness, they have emotional problems as well.

Losing sleep at night, whether it is due to purposefully staying awake at night watching television, staying out late with friends or lying awake worrying about stressors, deprives us of rest that we require to function. We need to take steps to insure that we arrange our social activities so that we have adequate hours available to rest. At times, due to stress, anxiety or depression, we are unable to fall asleep when our head hits the pillow or we wake in the middle of the night or before the alarm goes off and are unable to fall back to sleep. In these situations, also, we are being deprived of our required rest and must take responsibility to provide proper care for our bodies to eliminate what stress we can and practice healthy coping skills so that the stress and tension we are unable to eliminate, does not overwhelm us. See Chapter Three for some ideas on how to do this.

It is also easier for our body to function, especially in a time of stress, if we have a reasonably predictable schedule as far as sleep and waking times go. If we go to bed at approximately the same time each night and wake at about the same time each morning, our body knows what to expect and can depend on this predictability. It can start relaxing and winding down as our bedtime nears and prepare itself to wake even before the alarm rings. We settle into a pattern and managing this whole waking/sleeping schedule becomes more automatic for us.

Emotionally, when we are deprived of sleep, we can expect to be more irritable, and, if the deprivation is significant enough, can even have trouble with balance, concentration and memory. Persons who have done without sleep for an extended period of time can even experience symptoms of various emotional and mental health disorders, such as depression, mania, hallucinations and delusions.

Recent research has indicated that sleep deprivation can prevent some individuals from losing weight, even when they were carefully watching their diets and activity levels. The study recommended that for the most successful weight loss, individuals looking to lose the greatest amount of weight should ensure that they are getting adequate sleep. Most likely the body was trying to conserve both food and energy when deprived of one or the other.

Two other very important physical needs are exercise and sex. While different individuals have differing needs and levels of desire for sex, it is an important human need that needs to be met on a somewhat regular basis.

Many people don't realize that we also have a need for exercise. We all know that our mothers and our doctors tells us we should get more exercise, but in the studies they are doing on persons living to be the ripe old age of 80, 90 and 100 or more, they find that one of the most important things these folks have in common is that they have **kept moving!** They tend to use their bodies regularly and are typically doing some form of physical workout on a regular basis.

I realized, also, from watching my mother-in-law how important this is. Born in 1912, she is from a generation in which many women never learned to drive an automobile. For approximately 35 years of her life, she lived in a second story apartment, which she would reach by climbing two relatively steep flights of stairs. In addition, as she lived relatively near the only grocery store in town, she would regularly walk the six blocks or so to the store and carry her groceries home several times a week, rather than call for a ride. In addition, she would walk to church twice a week, once to attend mass, the other time to perform volunteer duties. She was in terrific shape and never complained about the walking or the stairs.

When she was in her mid-eighties, a friend of hers died and her family was looking to sell Gladys' house, a one story two bedroom ranch style home, which was perfect for my mother in law. To make the situation even better, they were happy to sell it to a friend of their mother's so they offered her a terrific price. It seemed to be the perfect situation.

However, the house was a little further away from the church and the grocery store than her apartment had been. And as she was no longer on the second floor, there were no stairs to climb. In addition, probably due in part to the stress of the move, her vision began to fail. As a result, she walked less and less and her physical condition began to deteriorate rather quickly, leading to one health problem after another. Is it coincidence? Just a fact of aging? We think not. We believe it was directly connected to the change in her activity level.

Many of the men we work with tell us, "I'm moving all day at work. I get enough exercise there." But this is not true. Moving or not, you are not experiencing the sustained increase in your heart rate that your body needs and gets only from exercise. Your body needs you to raise your heart rate to a level over and above your resting heart rate, appropriate for your age and general level of fitness. Further, to achieve the full benefit, you need to sustain this level for a minimum of 20-30 minutes, three to five times per week. You can check with your doctor for the levels appropriate to your age and physical condition.

An even easier way to do this is to just start walking. Walk for a half hour three nights a week. Don't worry about how fast or how far you are going, just keep moving and you will be doing yourself a world of good. As you feel more fit and healthier, feel free to pick up the pace and even move into a jog or run.

Biking and rollerblading are two other forms of exercise that give you wonderful benefits at low cost. I used to feel I didn't get enough of a workout from rollerblading; it was just too easy! But once I strapped on my husband's heart rate monitor, I was surprised to learn that my heart rate was nearly as high as when I was running, at a much lower cost to my joints and my energy level.

A couple of other facts about exercise are important to mention here. Muscles burn more calories than fat. Regular exercise helps develop or at least maintain muscle mass, which tends to deteriorate as we age. This not only helps us feel more fit, but also can help prevent the weight gain that also tends to accompany added years.

Probably the most significant benefit of exercise, however, is emotional, rather than physical. When we exercise, our brain releases endorphins, which tend to have an effect similar to antidepressant medications. These chemicals give us the feeling the life is pretty good, our stress level is manageable and that most of those issues or problems we have are solvable.

I can tell you from personal experience that I have solved more of my own and the world's problems when out running than when engaged in any other activity that I do. Now, if I could only remember those terrific solutions when I stop... But seriously, my mood is greatly improved by exercise, even when it is lousy to begin with. I know that if I can just push myself to get out and go for a run when I am crabby or irritable, I will be much more pleasant, and I will feel better also, when I return! So, both my family and I benefit!

I also worked with a client who was in constant pain. She had a cyst on her spine that not only caused her discomfort of varying degrees every waking moment, it also greatly limited her movement and her activity level. She discovered that by riding 50 miles every day on a recumbent exercise bicycle on which her back could be supported, she could limit both her discomfort and the amount of pain medication she needed.

Further, she shared with me that the hours she spends "on the bike" are the most pleasant of her day. She has shown an incredible amount of courage in pushing herself, through the pain, to get back on the bike every day and I suspect that it is only her determination at continuing to "move" that enables her to function as well as she does. A less courageous person may have given in to the pain and stayed in the recliner long ago, causing her muscles to atrophy and decay. If she can do it, why not you?

Whatever you do, just do something. It's always a good idea to check with your doctor and get a complete physical before undertaking an exercise program, but virtually any of us should be able to do more walking than we are already doing and benefit from it. Forget the excuses. As the Nike commercial says, "Just do it!"

Intellectual

We also have the need to feel that our brain is engaged and that we are learning new things on a regular basis. There are many ways to do this that are easily accessible to each of us and which can be incorporated into our daily lives. Let's explore a few of them now.

Some people get this need met at work, learning new techniques or information associated with their jobs. Others engage in independent reading, picking up books on interesting subjects either at their local bookstore or library. Picking up this book would qualify as meeting your intellectual need.

Still other people prefer to meet this need in a more formal setting, taking classes at a local college or technical school to learn about subjects of interest to them. Others learn new things by watching programs on the History or Discovery Channels. And those in the right environment to do so learn new things by having interesting conversations with people they come in contact with.

My favorite example of this occurred when I was in college. A loosely constructed group of us would gather approximately once a week in the Student Union and discuss timely and controversial topics. We came from a variety of socio-economic backgrounds, religious persuasions, political beliefs, ages and life experiences. We had several from the Midwest, one from New York and one who'd lived in California. We had a number who were middle class, one who never knew where his next meal was coming from and one who lived off a trust fund from Daddy.

We had an atheist, several Catholics, a Lutheran and several lapsed practitioners of other religions. We were Democrats, Republicans and Independents. Several of us had been to Viet Nam; others of us were still living with our parents and had never left home. We ranged in age from 19 to nearly 50. And we debated every issue under the sun, depending on what the news and topic of the day was. I reflect on this as some of the best, though entirely informal, learning I experienced in college and believe it taught me tolerance and respect for others' opinions and experience, things I needed to learn coming from my white middle class small town upbringing.

No matter how we do it, we need to keep challenging our minds and learning new things. New research is finding the one of the best ways to ward off Alzheimer's and dementia is by life-long learning. Elderly persons, who challenge themselves to learn new things on a continual or regular basis, have a reduced likelihood of developing those illnesses. And, it makes life more interesting.

So, however you do it, keep learning.

Creative

We also have a need to be creative and to create things on a regular basis. The more obvious ways to meet this need are the typically creative activities such as watercolor painting, playing a musical instrument, sketching and the like.

As beneficial as these activities are, and I truly believe that everyone can benefit from engaging in activities such as these, not everyone can or will struggle to fit these into their already too busy schedule. There are, however, other ways of being creative that fit more easily into the average busy day.

Many women may be unaware of this, but they are meeting their need to create by putting thought and energy into decorating their homes or apartments, making or baking food for their families, buying or making clothing for themselves or their children and engaging in craft or needlework projects. Many men are very creative in woodworking projects they complete and in how they solve problems or things that need to be fixed around the house. Both men and women can meet this need, also, through gardening and landscaping activities. Also, any writing or journaling activities meet this need as well.

The bottom line, however, is that whatever you do, however you do it, you need to be creating something regularly in order to feel balanced and unstressed. Remember, you must be meeting all of your needs at about the same level and consistency in order for this to occur. And if you can find a way to work in the music or painting, by all means do so. It can only help!

Emotional

To meet our emotional needs, we need to be connecting with other living creatures. We don't just mean humans. Pets can contribute a great deal to our emotional well-being. After all, who else is just thrilled to see you walk in the door after a long day at work and has waited all day just to kiss your face?

To meet this need, we must be giving and receiving affection. Talking with others about feelings, giving and getting regular hugs, knowing we are important to someone or something and that we have emotional support from some source when we need it.

There is some interesting research documenting the need for the need for emotional connectedness with other humans. Two studies come to mind. One study was done with babies in an orphanage in Romania during World War I. The babies' physical needs were superbly met. They were contained in clean cribs and fed and changed meticulously, but they were never held. The only time they came in contact with humans and were touched was the few minutes when they were changed or bathed. They were fed by means of a bottle propped up near their heads. Even though the babies were clean, safe and adequately nourished, they were dying one by one, until someone figured out they were dying from the lack of human contact.

The other study involved chimpanzees. Baby chimps were removed from their mothers and put in cages with two surrogate mothers. One was a cold hard wire "mother" to which was strapped a bottle by which the babies were fed. The other "mother" offered no food, but was made of a soft cuddly material the chimps could snuggle up to. Overwhelmingly the chimps preferred the soft, cuddly mother and would only leave "her" to briefly feed from the cold metal "mother." Their need for emotional connection was not met by food, but by touch, just like the orphans.

Ideally, we get this emotional connection through a number of sources. We hope we have it with our partners if we are in an intimate relationship. We can get it from our children and pets, but must guard against depending too heavily on our children. Our parents can provide some of it, depending on our age and how available they are to us. Friends may provide a great deal of this support as well.

If you are finding yourself lacking in support, seek it out. Talk with persons you are comfortable deepening your relationship with to see if they are resources to meet this need. In the event the person you choose is unwilling or unable to provide what you need, don't take it personally. It most likely has nothing to do with you and everything to do with them and their life situation. Keep looking until you find the support you need.

Social

We human beings are social animals. We need to have contact with other human beings on a regular basis just for the sake of companionship. This also means without any other agenda than companionship, so the work meeting you were already thinking about doesn't count. But going out for coffee with a co-worker afterwards would meet this need very nicely.

Insure you have time on a regular basis to "just be" with others for the sake of enjoying their company. If you have many demands on your time, such as a full time job and young children, this can be tricky to arrange, but it is possible. It is also crucial to your happiness and well-being.

Schedule some social time for yourself right in your calendar, just like you do any other appointment. After all, with all the demands on you, aren't you at least as important as all of your other obligations and the appointments you keep? In order to keep doing what you are doing, and to minimize your stress, you must take this social time for yourself. If your partner objects, show her this section and encourage her to take time for herself as well!

These last two needs, social and emotional are a big reason we need relationships and partners in our lives. Most of us are happier and more fulfilled and feel that our lives are richer and more meaningful when we are in an intimate relationship. Even though there are some costs to being involved with another person (we don't always get to do things "our way" or perhaps don't get to do exactly what we want when we want to and have to compromise and negotiate with another) most of us find that we get enough back from the relationship that it is worth while. We are designed to live in relationship with others, so some of our very important needs are met in these closest relationships and are frequently denied if we are temporarily without a partner.

This is not to say that if your relationship ends you should run right out and find another. Take your time. Heal, recover and work through the baggage from the relationship before looking for another partner. But do understand you will most likely find yourself in another relationship in the not-too-distant future and that this is normal.

Again, when you are not meeting these needs at approximately the same level, you are out of balance and suffering from stress. If you are a marathon runner, paying exquisite attention to your training schedule and diet and rest patterns, all physical needs, but completely depriving yourself of human companionship and doing nothing to meet your intellectual or spiritual needs, you are still going to be severely stressed. If, however, you are running with a partner and, when running, you are talking about events in your life and sharing feelings and taking pains to meet your other needs, you can be in terrific health and suffering little to no stress. It's all up to you. You must be paying attention.

Get in the habit several times a week or even once a day, of asking yourself, "What am I doing to meet my spiritual need?" and so on down the **SPICES** line until you have them all met. The true benefit of this method of organizing basic needs is the ease of remembering them. As a therapist, I have had too many occasions where clients leave my office with the best of intentions, only to lose the piece of paper their assignment was on or to forget to take it with them where they are going. The technique is not very useful to them unless they are actually going to use it!

Reminding yourself to take stock of which needs you are meeting can be easy as well. You can set a timer each day for the time you want to give this issue some thought. You could also wear your watch on the opposite arm or a rubber band around your wrist. Or you could write a sticky note to yourself to remind yourself to do it or plan to do this with a partner and each of you remind the other.

But do pay attention to this important area of your life. Only when your needs are met in a balanced fashion are you capable of being your best. When anger is an issue, give yourself every chance to manage it successfully!

Supporting a Partner's Needs

We get involved in a relationship, in part, to get our needs met. Relationships tend to meet our emotional, social and physical needs. The right relationship can also help to meet our spiritual, creative and intellectual needs.

We will also have an investment in keeping our partner happy and getting her needs met, even if it is only so she continues in the relationship, because if her needs are not met, she will eventually leave. Therefore, it is in our best interest to make sure our partner gets what she needs from the relationship as well.

But how do we go about supporting a partner's needs? There are many ways to do this, most involving the exercise of empathy, or looking at a situation from her perspective. Ideally, you have the kind of relationship in which your partner will tell you what she needs. This makes it easy. When she does so, go out of your way as often as you can to support and make possible for her to do what she wants and needs. At times, this will be at a cost to yourself and, perhaps, your own needs. At other times, it will not.

What you want to remember is, the happier she is, the happier you will be in the relationship. And the more motivated she will be to help you get your needs met. It is a win-win situation for everyone.

In the event you do not have the kind of relationship in which your partner will tell you what she needs, please review Chapter Nine on Communication Skills for some ideas on how to change this. Chapter Ten on Negotiation and Compromise will be helpful as well.

The Seven Year Itch—Helen Fischer

Helen Fischer is a researcher who has been looking at relationships for a number of years. She proposes that, contrary to the relatively modern idea that relationships should last forever, if we look at a number of earlier societies, it is possible that human beings are programmed for only a four to seven year involvement. After that time, the theory proposes, we are biologically programmed to move on to another partner.

She finds the biological reasoning for this sound as well. In the first four to seven years of a relationship, there is typically the courtship and the mating. She has discovered that in these earlier societies, once a baby was born, the parents stayed together only long enough for the child to be able to navigate on its own, then broke up and moved on to new partners. Another relationship cycle then ensued. In this way, genes were shared in a number of different combinations, thereby ensuring survival of the species.

In some societies, the relationship often lasted closer to seven years. Typically in these cases, this was the length of time it took for the couple's second child to be old enough and self-sufficient enough to move around on its own, thereby enabling the mother to gather food.

The jury is still out on whether the high divorce rate in our society is the result of a biological predisposition to couple for shorter periods of time. But it is an interesting discussion worth having as we are talking about relationships, nonetheless.

What do Women Want—by Diane

While men and women enter relationships for some of the same reasons, there are some differences in how these needs are expressed. Women and men are socialized differently, even in this day and age, and this leads to some differences in what they expect from a relationship.

Women are still socialized to be caretakers, mediators and peacemakers in relationships and families. If someone in the relationship or family is unhappy, it is more often the female who will make it her mission to help turn that situation around. In many cases, she sees it as her duty, consciously or unconsciously, to keep the peace and make sure everyone is happy and contented. As an example, my work with a couple I am currently seeing was initiated by the young bride, not because she was unhappy in the relationship; in fact, she is quite pleased and content with their life together. But she initiated the counseling to make sure he was happy as well as he would occasionally appear sad or distant from her and she wanted to make sure he was getting what he needed from their relationship.

To that end, women tend to be better at talking about feelings and problems, and a woman will more likely need and want more of this than her male partner. She will look to that as a solution for unhappiness or discontent in the relationship. She will most like be the one to say, "We have to talk." Men often interpret this as the kiss of death and would rather have a root canal procedure than "talk," seeing this as an occasion of criticism, likely to focus on their failings in the relationship. They tend to take the situation described above, with a partner who reports things are fine, but who occasionally appears distant or sad, at face value and assume that if she was unhappy about something, she would let him know about it.

Men are also still socialized with the "macho" attitudes, such as "never admit you're vulnerable," "don't admit you're wrong," and "don't ever ask for help" or directions. With these contrary guiding principles, it's amazing men and women get together at all!

Some couples assume they can just ignore their partner's needs and still have the relationship last. The most typical scenario that I see, as a marriage counselor, is the couple that comes in after 15, 20 or 30 years of marriage. She, typically, has been attempting to get her needs met and often has been asking to go to couples' counseling for much of their time together.

He has refused and ridiculed that idea, again believing that "talk" is not necessary or important. Now, finally understanding that he will never talk and having spent years hoping things will change, her feelings have largely dissolved and she is ready to move on. She may already have contacted an attorney and filed papers or she may just have told him how she feels.

The couple appears in my office, now at his urging, because it is only when he is about to lose the most important relationship in his life, that some men will go along with what their partner has wanted all along. Unfortunately, for a number of these couples, it is too little, too late. She shows up in counseling for one session, often under protest, and refuses to come back because all feelings she had for him died over the many years he has denied her needs.

This is why it's important to pay attention to your partner's requests and needs. Whether you go to marriage counseling or figure out some way to meet her needs without doing so, she must get her needs met or she will eventually leave the relationship, one way or another. Some women do not leave physically, but leave emotionally or get involved in a series of affairs when their needs have not been heard or respected. The bottom line is, if the relationship is important to you, listen to your partner and make sure she's getting what she needs from the relationship.

When it comes to the physical aspects of a relationship, women and men approach this from different perspectives as well. After an argument, a man will often seek to be sexual with his partner as a way of getting emotionally closer to her. A woman, however, needs the emotional closeness first. A woman will want to "talk" to achieve the emotional closeness with her partner, before she will be ready to have sex with him. Therefore, when he approaches her for sex, without talking about the conflict first, she will likely feel used or taken for granted, often leading to a greater conflict in the relationship.

Understanding these principles, however, can go a long way toward helping couples negotiate their differing needs and expectations in a relationship. If you know your partner needs to feel close before she will want to have sex with you, you are more likely to be able to do or say something before making your move that will lead to emotional closeness. Further, understanding that it is not "just her" but something most women have in common, will make you less likely to take it personally or view it as a manipulation, also increasing your likelihood of a successful relationship.

What do Men Want—by Terry

While it is true that men and women seek some of the same things from a relationship, as Diane mentioned previously, often they are each looking for something a little different. Men are typically seeking companionship in a relationship, both in terms of having a partner to spend time with and also to share the workload.

While women seek emotional closeness with a partner by talking with them, men tend to feel emotionally close when doing something with a partner. It doesn't matter whether it is running, skiing, biking, rollerblading or having sex, men tend to feel closest to a partner when engaged in an activity together. No words need be spoken for men to feel close.

Additionally, men are often looking for someone to share the workload. A partner to help with the cooking, cleaning, dishes, childcare, laundry and the like is another incentive for getting involved in a relationship. While women may appreciate this assistance as well, it is not usually a motivating factor in committing initially to a relationship. Being aware of the different goals and objectives for a relationship can help us make sure our partner's needs are being met as well as our own.

Time alone or to spend with friends is important as well. It is important for both partners to take time away from the relationship in order to have more to bring to it. Most will appreciate understanding and support when seeking this time. All in all, these needs are not that different from what women are seeking from relationships.

As in previous chapters, we have included a summary on the next page on meeting basic needs. Look it over to assess how well you are meeting your own needs, and also how well your partner's needs are being met. We have left space at the end of each description for you to jot notes about how you feel you are doing at meeting the particular need in question, as well as notes regarding activities, persons and behaviors you are using to meet these needs.

You may want to copy the summary and complete one sheet for you and one for your partner. Check with her on her impressions as well. This can be a great way to begin that conversation about what you each can do to help the other feel happier and more fulfilled by your relationship. Enjoy!

Summary on Meeting Basic Needs

BASIC NEEDS

✌ Spiritual—To know that we are part of something greater than ourselves; that we have a personal mission. Met through organized religion, contact with nature, meditation, or other spiritual practices: _____

✌ Physical—Food, clothing, air, water, sleep, exercise, etc.: _____

✌ Intellectual—The need for intellectual stimulation, for thinking new thoughts, reading challenging books, learning something new: _____

✌ Creative—The need to create or make something: dance, write a poem, paint, draw, crafts, work with wood, make music: _____

✌ Emotional—The need to give and receive affection; need for love, praise, feeling worthwhile: _____

✌ Social—The need for friendship, companionship: _____
_____

Chapter 5

The Battle of the Sexes

More Differences Between Men and Women

I ntroducing the subject of roles in relationships, we ask the group, *"What are some of roles you play in your relationship with your partner."*

Roy, a relatively new member of the group who had been pretty quiet up to this point, spoke up quickly and with conviction, "The man is the head of the household. I handle all the finances and make all the final decisions in our home."

A bit surprised at the tone of his response, I ask him, "How does your wife feel about this arrangement?"

"It doesn't matter what she thinks. It says in the Bible that that's the way it should be. So that's the way it is."

They have since divorced.

In the previous chapter, we briefly explored several differences between the typical behavior of men and women in relationships, specifically in the context of meeting basic needs we all have. The needs are essentially the same; our styles of meeting them sometimes vary in accordance with our gender.

In this chapter, we will continue exploring some of the ways in which men and women differ and how this can complicate a relationship with a member of the opposite sex. Even though the ways in which we and our needs are similar are more significant and powerful than those in which we differ, there are several ways these differences can cause trouble in intimate relationships. Having an awareness of how this typically happens empowers us to deal with it in a more positive manner and allow each of us to complement our partner, rather than to battle her for control.

Our Minds Work Differently

Researchers have been spending an increasing amount of time of late researching brain function patterns. We have learned that our brains do not fully mature until we are between 18 and 25 years of age and, as a result, children and adolescents process events differently than adults do. This is useful information for parents assisting children in dealing with divorce and other life changes, and in just dealing with life. Knowing they will see things differently we can intervene to help them get a realistic view of what is happening to them.

One of the other results of this research is the discovery that men's and women's brains are wired differently. Men have an increased number of nerve endings that circulate and end up in the same hemisphere of the brain as they started, whereas women have an increased number of nerve endings beginning in one hemisphere of the brain and ending in the other.

What this means as a practical matter is that women have an easier time shifting back and forth between the logical and emotion hemispheres of the brain, while men have an easier time operating in one hemisphere or the other. Men do better at staying very logical and rational, if that's the part of the brain they are currently using, or reacting from pure emotion (often anger if in a heated discussion with a partner), while women are more easily able to bounce quite effectively back and forth, coloring their statements with both logic and emotion.

We do not represent that one way is better than the other; this is just the way it is. This is also why men are better at map reading, math skills and determining spatial relationships and women tend to have better short term memory and to be more verbally articulate, especially in discussions and arguments. Our brains are wired and structured differently. Awareness of these tendencies and strengths, however, can enable us to deal with them. For example, if you are having an argument with your wife and you start to feel anger or some other strong emotion, you would most likely be more effective negotiating a solution if you took a time out until you calmed down enough to shift back into your rational thinking. Knowing this prepares you to deal with it more effectively.

There is another major area in which men's and women's minds operate differently as well: the area of multi-tasking. Men are better at focusing intently on one, or maybe two, areas of thinking at a time, while women are better able to hold and access a variety of ideas at once, such as who in the family has what activities scheduled for this evening, what is in the refrigerator for dinner, what is on the grocery list, what are her current projects at work and which loads of laundry are waiting to be washed and dried at home. This difference was apparent even back in the days of the cave man.

Back in the cave, men had one primary function: to hunt. They typically went out together in a pack, following a lead hunter, to bring home food for their families. Women had many tasks: gathering food, tending the fire, minding the cave, caring for children. They were essentially keeping in mind back then the same myriad of things women do today. The one thing that is not certain is whether our brains developed differently due to our different functions, or whether our different functions followed our pre-existing strengths. This is the old chicken and egg question.

This difference in brain structure and function still affects us today and plays a part in what we are capable of accomplishing in a relationship. I know that my husband is an extremely intelligent man. However, I also know that if I give him a verbal list of four things to pick up from the grocery store, he will forget at least two of them. Errands and children's school events are another example of this. I can do my job and remain aware of the details of a school event scheduled for later that day. To get Terry there, I tell him two weeks ahead of time and post the notice on the fridge. I remind him a week before and the morning of the event. Still I get a call at work ten minutes before he is to meet me at school in which he tells my office manager, "I know she said something about a Parent-Teacher Conference, but I'm not sure where it is or for whom." While he was making this call, he was standing in front of the refrigerator on which the notice was posted. His focus, when I reminded him, was on something else and when he was calling, it was on getting dinner for the children. I promptly called him back with the details of the meeting.

In his defense, Terry is a person who can drive someplace one time five years in the past and, when looking for the same place, will find it without a map, directions or an address. That is something I can never hope to do. Even with a map, address and directions, I would struggle to find it if not familiar with the area. Our brains are wired differently. We have different abilities and strengths and can use these to complement each other and enhance our life together.

Differences in Problem-Solving—and Shopping!

This difference in brain structure and design helps lead us to different problem solving behaviors and differences in how we talk about solving problems. We tend to share in accordance with our gender related brain function and strengths.

When a man has had a problem at work during his day, if he mentions it at home at all, he is likely to say something like, "This happened today and this is what I did about it." When a woman has encountered a difficulty at work, she will quite likely come home ready to talk about it. She may start out by saying, "This is what happened and this is what led up to it." She may then go into what else was going on at the same time, reactions of others to the event, her feelings about it, what happened afterwards and the like.

Many good husbands choose that point to jump in and say, "Well, this is what you need to do about that!" at which point she gets angry at him and instructs him to "Stop telling me what to do!" He is then confused because he has heard her discussion as a request for advice.

To him, the only reason to say so much about a situation would be to ask for help. But she is not asking. She is processing the event out loud by talking to him about it. She is perfectly capable of solving the problem herself, she just isn't there yet. She can and will solve it when she is ready. But at this point, she is doing out loud and to him something he does, to some extent, internally, so he fails to recognize it for the part of the process it is. Many couples get into arguments just this way. He thinks he is being helpful and supportive; she finds his suggestions controlling and insulting. He then feels unappreciated when rebuked for trying to help. Both are hurt and frustrated.

What most couples need to do is, first, just to be aware of this process. Then, strike a balance between the number of words used. She needs to use enough words to process the event successfully, but not so much detail that he becomes completely overwhelmed with it. It takes time and repeated effort for couples to achieve this type of balance. I think it took Terry and me about five years to get to the point where we were both comfortable with our process. Just keep working at it; as with anything, the more you practice the easier it gets.

This same difference in process takes place when men and women shop. Men tend to be linear thinkers and shoppers. They go to a store, knowing what they are looking for. They find it, buy it and leave.

Women are circuitous shoppers. We perhaps have some ideas of what we are looking for, but can usually be persuaded by something else as well. We may go into a store and directly to what we need, but are just as likely to get sidetracked by the kids' lunch foods that are on sale, then walk over to check out the clearance items, oh, and then there was that blouse that I liked that may be on sale, etc. Again, he is focusing on (read "hunting) the item that brought him to the store, whereas she is gathering items she and her family could find useful.

For this reason, I rarely allow Terry to accompany me on shopping trips. Because his process is different than mine, it is very frustrating for him to accompany me and it takes the fun out of my excursions. If we do shop together, for example for children's back to school clothing, I try to give Terry a specific task or two, such as finding socks and underwear for Ryan. This gives him a purpose and is more comfortable for him than wandering around a store with three children heading in different directions.

Remember, it is not a "better than"/"less than" comparison that I am making here, nor is it a superior/inferior analysis. We are just different. The more we can be aware of the ways in which we truly are different and respect these qualities in each other, the happier and more positive our relationships will be.

Differences in Conversational Style

Allowing for individual differences in personality, men and women tend to have different speaking styles as well. Deborah Tannen does a wonderful job explaining this in her book, *You Just Don't Understand,* and if this is a subject that interests you, I strongly suggest you read her book. In brief, men tend to communicate more directly while women have a greater tendency to qualify their statements.

A good place to become aware of these differences is in a business meeting. In discussing strategy, a man is more likely to contribute something like, "Well, this is what we should do," or "We should handle it this way." A woman is more likely to qualify and modify her suggestions, by saying something like, "We could do this," or "Perhaps we could handle it this way."

These communication styles have their roots in our roles in society and the family. Women traditionally had the role of peacemaker and mediator, making sure everybody was happy and content. For that reason, we tend to state things in a softer, gentler manner. Men are socialized to take charge and make decisions. That is why they learn to make stronger statements of their opinions.

This stylistic difference is causing problems for some women in business. Men they work with and many of their superiors tend to disqualify what they are saying because it is not stated as strongly as the suggestions of their male counterparts. They are sometimes not advanced as quickly or denied promotions, even when they are as capable as the men with whom they are working because they seem less sure of their abilities and opinions. For this reason, many schools are adding classes to their curriculum for women to learn to speak more directly in a business setting.

In relationships as well, this can cause difficulties. If a man is looking for a strong direct statement from his wife when negotiating or making decisions together, such as where to go on vacation, he is in danger of invalidating her ideas or opinions if she comes across as hesitant or unsure. For example, in discussing the vacation issue, if he says, "I want to rent a cabin on a lake and go fishing," and she says, "Well, I might like to go to the Bahamas or someplace," she does not sound as definite about her suggestion. As a result, without an awareness of this stylistic difference, her opinion does not seem as powerful. He is in danger of walking over her ideas and, as the peacemaker, she is in danger of allowing him to do so. After a number of such experiences, she begins to feel she no longer exists.

Expressing Anger

Expression of anger is another way in which men and women tend to differ. As discussed in Chapter One, men tend to be more direct and to have an easier time expressing anger, whereas women often end up in tears when they are angry. In most cases they have been socialized to connect anger with tears and are, perhaps more in touch with the underlying emotions of hurt, fear and frustration, than men are. It is also more socially acceptable for women to express tears than anger while the opposite is true for men. All of these variables can contribute to a considerable amount of confusion about a partner's behavior. Awareness of these differences can help us to understand what is happening in our relationships.

This chapter was inserted at this point to provide background information, rather than to teach or introduce a new technique. It is important to understand some of these basic differences between the men and women before tackling the areas of communication styles and negotiation.

While in reality there are more similarities than differences between the sexes, in order to solve problems with a partner, it is important to understand how she is likely to communicate and problem solve, especially if, in that area she differs from you. In addition, it can be a wonderful negotiating technique to use the innate strengths you each bring to the situation to solve a dilemma you are facing as a couple. But to be able to do this you must first understand what these are.

Though we did not learn a new skill in this chapter, we have included a summary of the points and information covered here. It will be helpful to review this before tackling a negotiation or problem solving session with your partner to refresh your memory. Good luck!

"Avoiding danger is no safer in the long run
than outright exposure.
Life is either a daring adventure
or nothing."

~Helen Keller

Battle of the Sexes Summary

☮ ## Our Minds Work Differently:

~Men operate more effectively in one hemisphere of the brain at a time and can focus more intently on one subject.

~Women have an easier time bouncing between the logical and emotional parts of the brain and are better at multitasking, maintaining a lesser focus on a number of different areas at once, i.e. dinner, laundry, job, childcare, etc.

Become aware of these differences and use them to advantage in your relationship

☮ ## We Have Different Styles of Problem-Solving

~Men tend to be linear thinkers and want to jump right from problem to solution. This process usually involves few words.

~Women take a more circular approach to problem solving, considering a variety of factors and emotions and eventually arriving at a solution. She may do this verbally and it may overwhelm her partner.

Appreciate the difference in styles and work to find a balance between the number of words used so it is enough for her but not overwhelming for him.

☮ ## There are Differences in Our Conversational Styles

~Men tend to be more direct and absolute in their speech and value this approach as confident.

~Women tend to use more qualifiers and modifiers in their speech in their efforts at mediating and making peace in relationships (i.e. maybe, perhaps, etc).

This should not imply insecurity or indecision.

☮ ## We Express Anger Differently

~Men are taught to express anger aggressively.

~Women are socialized to express anger through tears.

Respect the emotion and take a break when it occurs.

*"A man who suffers before it is necessary
suffers more than is necessary."*

~ Seneca, A.D. 63

Chapter 6

Buying Some Time

Time-Outs Aren't Just for Children

S o, what's been happening with the two of you?" I asked the couple seated in my office.

Tearfully Rhonda sniffed, "Steve doesn't love me anymore."

"That's not true, Ronnie," her husband interrupted, "I didn't mean it; I was just exhausted!"

"Well you said it, didn't you?" Rhonda snapped back.

"Wellll, yes, but we had been arguing for 36 hours and I didn't know what I was saying. I just wanted it to stop and I couldn't make it stop."

"Wait a minute. You two had been arguing for 36 hours? What about sleep?"

"We wanted to get it settled. Who could sleep anyway?" responded Steve.

"What about work? Didn't you have to go to work?"

"Steve called in sick. After all, what's more important: our marriage or his job?"

As we discussed in Chapter Three, time is an important issue in our lives. We never have enough of it, it seems, and how we choose to use our time is always open to criticism. In this chapter, we will explore several ways in which time is a factor in our anger and how we handle the conflict in our lives.

Time Out from Conflict

The scene above truly did happen and this was not the first time this couple argued for an extensive period of time. Not only did these marathons do a substantial amount of damage to their relationship, they were harmful to them individually as well. Rhonda continued to hang onto the negative insults Steve hurled at her when exhausted and, feeling he had no way out, Steve eventually attempted suicide on the heels of one of these arguments. It was quite a serious attempt and only by fortunate accident was his life saved.

Still, they clung to this damaging pattern. Often, the unknown is still far more frightening than a destructive pattern, even when it damages the partners and the relationship. Because I would not condone their pattern of marathon sessions of verbal violence, Steve and Rhonda eventually stopped coming to see me, rationalizing that they really didn't need help after all.

The Theory

When disciplining children, we commonly use the concept of "time out from stimulation" or reinforcement to describe the act of removing a child from an upsetting situation to give him a chance to calm down. We physically remove an upset or acting out child from the source that is upsetting him and from any reinforcement for his inappropriate behavior. Unaffected by the upsetting stimulus, he can then calm himself down and behave more appropriately.

When we are upset as adults, we can use the same principle to buy ourselves some time to choose how to respond to a given event or stimulus. The goal in taking a time out from what is upsetting us is to completely remove ourselves from the stimulus, then use positive and healthy self-talk to make respectful choices about how to address the issue with our partner or others involved in the situation.

When we become upset, we are operating primarily with our emotional brain, which is by far, stronger and more powerful than our logical, rational, thinking brain. In a contest between the two, the emotional brain will always win. Therefore, we must take some time to shift into our thinking brain so that we can make more appropriate choices for ourselves. A time-out will buy us the time we need to make that shift.

We first heard the term "time-outs" as applied to adults by Dr. Anne Ganley who worked in a veteran's medical center in Tacoma, WA. Sometimes called "cool-downs," they are simply the tool to use to prevent yourself from doing or saying things that you will regret later, most often physically or emotionally abusive behaviors.

The process of actually using or taking a time out is quite simple, but preparation is an important component of success. It is important to prepare both yourself and your partner for this change. If this step is not done, this behavior can feel threatening to a partner and this can sabotage your successful use of a time out.

Preparation

Talk to your partner about time-outs as soon as you finish this chapter. Tell her that there will be times when you are together that you will be choosing to take a time out in order to relax. Let her know that you will tell her when this is occurring and that when you come back, you will set a time together, either later that day or in the next few days, to discuss the conflictual issue again. She may wish to use the process as well, but whether or not she does must be up to her.

As we tell our group, the only person's behavior you should be trying to control is your own and we will keep focusing on your behavior and the choices you have in relation to your partner and what she is doing. That does not mean she is right or perfect, but she is not reading this book any more than she is in our group. You must learn to focus on your behaviors and choices, not on her bad behavior. Therefore, while you can show her this book and this chapter and suggest that she use it as well, if she chooses not to, you have to let it go and make your own choices accordingly. No matter what she does, you can "take the high road" and continue to use time-outs. Don't let her choices dictate your behavior.

So, in preparation for using the time-out process, change your mind-set and your expectations, focus on your own behavior and have the talk with your partner. Explain the steps outlined below and prepare to use them. You may want to copy the checklist at the end of this chapter and either carry it with you or post it in a prominent location so that you (and, perhaps your partner) can keep it in mind for the upsetting times during which you will want to use it.

Why Time-Outs are Difficult

The time-out process is simple to learn but can be difficult to do. It is simple in that the concepts are easy and straightforward. It is difficult because, for most people, the push is to get conflict resolved as soon as it arises, once and for all, rather than to let it rest on the back burner for later discussion. The idea of letting something wait, unresolved, is very frightening to many people. They tend to feel that if they don't resolve it now, their partner will leave or the issue will never be discussed. Making the effort to push through these doubts and practice this technique, however, usually results in the knowledge that the issues **are** eventually worked out and often in a more positive manner than if we give in to the temptation to try to work them out now.

Another reason time outs are difficult to do is because of our socialization process. Men grow up to believe that only a coward will walk away from a fight. The impulse will be to stay and finish it, or at least get in the last word. Ask yourself what is most important to you: to maintain your image or to strengthen and improve your relationship? See Chapter Seven for a more extensive discussion of the potential outcomes we get in response to a relationship conflict.

Many men also fear that their partner will be gone when they return. This is part of the trust in a relationship. As each of you follows through with your part in taking a time-out and working on improving your relationship, the trust will grow that she will still be there when you return.

Although it is normal for taking time-outs to be very difficult and uncomfortable initially, they will get easier with time and practice. And the end result will be worth the effort.

The Process

Whenever you feel your anger rising, or are aware of the presence of your anger cues as discussed in Chapters Two and Three, say out loud to yourself and your partner, "I'm too upset to do this right now. I need to take a time out."

Use "I statements" so that you own the need to take a break from the action. Do not tell your partner, "YOU are too upset to talk about this now." All this will do is incite an argument about who is more upset than the other and whether the argument can continue. And then it will.

Notice also, this is not slamming out the door saying, "I'm out of here. I don't know when I'm coming back." That is intimidating behavior, designed to induce fear in a partner. That is not what time outs are about. The leaving statement should be said reassuringly and calmly.

Then leave. You **must** leave your home or whatever location you are at for a minimum of 20-30 minutes. For some, an hour is even better. You will need this amount of time to calm yourself down and reduce the chance of an eruption upon your return.

Ideally, you will want to do something physical or relaxing. Go for a walk or run, ride a bike, chop wood or lift weights. These behaviors help to express and reduce the adrenaline in your system. Relaxing behaviors might include deep breathing, stretching exercises, listening to music, meditation or prayer. You may go for a drive if you feel you can do so safely, but do not point your car down a freeway at 90 miles per hour. Do not drink alcohol or use any other substances. Both of these behaviors can cause more problems than they solve.

While you are out pay attention to your self-talk. If you tell yourself, "She is so unreasonable. We will never be able to agree on this issue," you will be continuing the argument and upsetting yourself even more, rather than taking a time out from the conflict. You need to be saying soothing things to yourself, such as, "I know we will find a way to work this out. We have a good relationship and we care about each other." See Chapter Seven for more positive self-talk and replacement thinking to use during a time out.

A time-out will not solve your disagreements or your difficulties, nor will it help you process painful events or negotiate solutions. What it will do is buy you some time so that you will be able to make more positive choices about your actions during the ensuing discussion. As many couples do, you may find that once discussed with a rational mind, many problems are quite easily resolved, the solutions seemingly apparent.

We have all had the experience of having a very upsetting disagreement with a partner that seems insurmountable. The situation seems so troublesome we fear the relationship will end. The discussion gets interrupted; perhaps one of you must leave for work, the kids come home or the telephone rings. When you finally get back to the discussion a day or so later, the solution seems obvious and the disagreement is easily resolved. What happened is that you were both reacting with strong emotion in the initial discussion and could not get past that to reason and negotiate a fair solution. After emotions cooled, reason prevailed and the situation was resolved. This is the principle upon which the idea of the time-out is based.

When you return after your 20 minutes or an hour, check in with your partner and decide together on a good time for discussion of the issue. Pay attention to what is going on internally for you and whether or not you are feeling ready and able to discuss the issue. If you feel capable of doing so rationally, ask whether she feels ready to do so as well. If you are not ready, or feel you are likely to erupt again, say something like, "I'm back, but I'm still not ready to do this. Let's talk about it tonight after dinner (or over the weekend, etc.)"

Do set a time to talk about the issue as, for most couples, topics leading to strong disagreements, even if they seem unimportant looking back, often represent bigger issues, such as trust or control that will rear their ugly heads again if not positively resolved. Even if the discussion is not very lengthy, set a time to talk about it and soothe any ruffled or hurt feelings.

When your discussion does occur, if you find yourself starting to feel angry or frustrated again, or are aware of the presence of your anger cues, take another time-out. This is important for a healthy and positive relationship.

Some topics of conversation may still be too charged to talk about, such as a partner's affair or another significant betrayal. If this is true in your situation, put those issues on the shelf for awhile, acknowledging that they are too difficult for the two of you to discuss alone. Take these issues to a counselor or therapist to get some help working through them. Often a neutral third party, especially one with training in working with these difficult issues, can make a world of difference in the discussion that ensues and the results you can reach.

We have included a summary of the Time Out process at the end of this chapter that will be easy to copy and make available wherever you need it. Most people find they are more likely to remember, practice and use this technique if they copy these ideas and carry them around in their wallet or post them inside a bathroom mirror or under the visor on their car. Make several copies and post them in various places you will see and use them. Remember, this will make a difference in your life and your relationship.

Practice Time Outs

It is a good idea to practice the time out process before you need it. Tell your partner, "This is a practice time-out. I'm too upset to talk about this now. I need to take a time out." Then leave and walk through the entire process.

It may feel silly to do and say these things when you are not actually in need of them, but the more we can rehearse new behaviors, the more these new options will be available to us when we are in danger of falling into old (read "bad") habits. You are rehearsing your success.

Follow Through

Then, use them! The more you do time-outs, the easier and the more automatic they will get to be.

A good practice is to do several practice time-outs, when you are feeling fine, then do one whenever you are feeling irritated, annoyed or upset for any reason. If you can't take a time-out when you don't need it, you will not be able to take one when you do. In addition, when those little irritations are not communicated and are allowed to build up, they do lead to full scale angers and rages. Think of a pressure cooker. When the pressure builds and builds, if there is no release valve, the pot would eventually explode. The same is true for you. Think of time outs as your pressure valve. Use them wisely.

The Need for a Time Limit

Time comes into practice in another way in dealing with conflict. Recall the example of Steve and Rhonda arguing for 36 hours at the beginning of this chapter.

When couples have difficulty stopping an argument or disagreement once it gets started, a time limit may need to be set for their discussions. I recommend to couples I work with to discuss a conflictual situation for no more than 30-60 minutes at a time. After an hour, everything that can be said has already been said. Further, after that amount of time, emotions start taking over, eliminating the effectiveness of the discussion. It is much better to stop after a short period of time, let it rest and then pick it up after you are refreshed to make further progress.

We will discuss negotiation and compromise further in Chapter Ten, but this point of a time limit cannot be stressed too much. We are at our worst and end up hurting ourselves, our partner and our relationship if we continue a discussion of emotionally upsetting issues when we are exhausted, as Steve and Rhonda did. The most common results are saying hurtful things out of frustration or the feelings of hopelessness and worthlessness that led to Steve's attempt at taking his life. Obviously, neither of these is healthy or positive for your relationship and they are to be avoided at all costs.

For further recommendations regarding discussing and working through a disagreement or conflict, please read over Chapter Ten. Devoted to the issues of negotiation and compromise, it contains more specific ideas about conflict resolution.

Time remains an important concept in relationships. Use it wisely. Take a few minutes and read over the summary on the next page and re-read any sections of this chapter that you are not feeling comfortable putting into practice.

As previously stated, we have included a complete summary of the time out process so you can copy the summary page and post it in a convenient place or carry it in your wallet.

Find a system that works to remind you what to do when you are stressed or upset.

When learning a new behavior, it is often helpful for most people to read through the procedures and the theory several times to get completely familiar with them. Then talk with your partner about the time out and time limit practice; you may even want to give her this chapter to read. Then, as the Nike commercials say, "Just do it!" Good luck!

"The best cure for anger is delay.

~Seneca, A.D. 63

"Buying Some Time" Summary

The Time-Out Process:

☮ Talk with your partner about the time out process. Prepare her and yourself for this behavior change.

☮ Practice time outs several times before the need arises.

☮ Assess your Anger Cues with the assistance of the Stress and Anger Cues Summary from Chapter Three, pp. 94-95. Know what symptoms identify your upsetness.

☮ Take a time out when your Anger Cues present themselves.

☮ Own the need for the time out, telling your partner, "I'm too upset to talk about this right now. I need to take a time out."

☮ Leave for 20-30 minutes or an hour.

☮ Do something physical (run, walk, bike, chop wood, etc.) or relaxing (deep breathing, prayer or meditation).

☮ Pay attention to your self-talk. Make sure it's positive.

☮ Don't drink alcohol or drive fast.

☮ Return in 20-60 minutes.

☮ Check in — Ask your partner (and yourself) either, "Are you able to talk about this now?" or "Can we talk about this tonight after dinner (or some other time)?" Decide together on a good time for discussion of the issue.

☮ Post this process in a convenient place.

☮ These are the **Anger Cues** (see pages 94-95) I first identify when upset:_____

_____

☮ These are the **Activities** I find most helpful during a time out:_____

_____

_____

☮ The positive **Self-talk** I use during my Time Outs is:_____

_____

_____

☮ I have found I typically need ____ minutes for an effective time out.

Time Limits

☮ My partner and I have discussed whether or not to set a **Time Limit** for our discussions: ____ Yes ____ Not Necessary.

☮ The **Length** of our Time Limit is: _____

☮ We have used this Time Limit **successfully.**

Chapter 7

Calming the Beast Within

The Task of Emotional Regulation

S*hane, tell us your story. How did you get here?"*

Grinning sheepishly, he begins, *"Well, it was pretty stupid, actually. My wife and I ran this bar together and it wasn't doing very well. Actually it was losing money. So we got into this argument about money as we were standing in the bar and it got a little loud. Her ma was there, as usual, and she called the cops and took Betty into the house with her. I just stayed in the bar and started drinking. I had just started watching the Packer Game when the cops arrived and when they called me on the phone and told me to come out, I said I would after the game was over."*

"Well, they weren't too happy with that response, so they cut the cable for TV reception. So I went and got the radio and turned on the game. They tried to call me again, but I pulled the phone out of the wall so they couldn't.

"Apparently they called the SWAT team, because the next thing I knew, I heard someone on a bullhorn, telling me to come out. I still wasn't ready, so I pulled out a shotgun I kept behind the bar and

waved it in front of the window. At that point, they cut the electricity so I couldn't even listen to the game and called out that I should come out or they were coming in.

"At that point I decided I was being pretty stupid. It was half time anyway, so I called out for them to come in, that I wasn't coming out, but I had put the gun down. I knew I would end up being face down on the ground and decided I would rather assume that position on the carpeting of the bar than in the gravel driveway.

"The next thing I knew, the SWAT team storms through the door and down I go. What an idiot I was—having trouble with money, I make the situation worse with fines, counseling and legal fees, and almost get myself killed in the process!"

While each of the chapters in this book is important in its own right and in the position it plays with respect to controlling or managing your anger, this chapter is, by far, the most crucial to master. If you have not been exposed to the issues presented here before we recommend reading this chapter several times and giving some thought to the concepts discussed. This is a technique anyone can learn, but it does require practice and repetition.

When they are exposed to something new, most people benefit from reading or hearing the information several times. When I present this information to a client in a session, and I use this technique with almost every client I work with, I typically explain and review it a number of times so that it becomes almost second nature to the person I am working with. Only then will it be accessible during times of intense emotion.

One important point about feelings—they aren't right or wrong, good or bad. They just are. All people, children and adults, have them. They are simply part of our human experience. In the example above, Shane no doubt had feelings of frustration and fear about money in the argument he had with his wife, then about the police interrupting his game. The feelings are not the issue; we can all probably understand how he must have been feeling in those circumstances.

Where Shane got into trouble was in his actions. You see, while the feelings are acceptable, what may not be is how they are expressed. The behavior that accompanies our feelings, such as expressing anger by yelling at parents, hitting a sibling or waving a shotgun in front of the SWAT team is definitely not appropriate. Also, while we cannot eliminate feelings from our existence, we can have some effect on the extent of negative emotion we are willing to endure.

Events, Thoughts and Feelings

What is emotional regulation? What we are referring to when we talk about emotional regulation is a cognitive behavioral technique we frequently use in therapy to help people change their thinking process to cope with, and reduce, all types of negative emotions—anger, fear, grief, jealousy, sadness, frustration and the like. While there are minor differences in application, techniques similar to this are taught by many therapists and have a number of different names, but most are based on work pioneered by Aaron Beck and Albert Ellis. For the sake of simplicity, and for reasons that will become obvious, we call it the Event, Thought, Feeling Process. It is easy to learn but, as we have said, it does require practice.

The basic premise is that any event, anything that happens in our lives, is neither good nor bad, but neutral. We give it meaning by the thoughts we have about it. These thoughts give rise to our feelings and these feelings, in many ways, direct the actions we choose to take in response to the event.

The process can be diagrammed as follows:

By way of illustration, we will walk through the process with the simple example of a rainstorm. A rainstorm is neither good nor bad, but neutral; it just is. Any meaning it has for us comes from the thoughts we allow ourselves to have about it.

Assume, for example, that you are a farmer. You planted your crops a month ago, but nothing is sprouting because there has been no rain. The ground is so dry it has developed large, deep cracks. You need a good crop this year because last year there was a drought. If this crop doesn't save you, the bank will foreclose and take the farm, which has been in your family for five generations. It is important to you to be able to pass it on to your children as well. You are pondering these heavy thoughts, and your very existence, as you stare out the window of your farmhouse one day when suddenly the skies open up and it begins to rain.

You will have some pretty predictable thoughts about this neutral event, the rainstorm. You may think:

☮ Thank God — now I will have a good crop.
☮ The bank won't take the farm.
☮ I will be able to pass the farm on to my children,
☮ I won't have to look for another job."

Your feelings will flow directly from these thoughts. Given the probable thoughts listed above, you will most likely feel very relieved, excited, hopeful, happy and at peace.

If you are like most of us, you will also act in accordance with your feelings. Others will probably be able to guess some of the feelings you are experiencing just from observing you. You may be grinning from ear to ear as you watch the rain fall. You might be on the phone with your banker, saying, "Looks like you're not going to get it this year!" You may be on the phone with a friend asking, "Do you want to do something today? It's raining so I can't plow." Or, you may express your pleasure and relief by dancing out in the cornfield in the rain! But we will be able to tell, just by looking at you, that you are experiencing some pretty positive emotions.

If, however, instead of being our farmer, you are the single parent of four children under the age five, who had been planning a picnic at the beach for this very day, you may have quite a different reaction to this turn of events. You know that the kids have been looking forward to this picnic for more than a month and are so excited that they jumped out of bed this morning and right into their swimming suits. Then they chased each other around the house, collecting and blowing up all the beach toys they could find. They are now loaded in the mini-van and you are headed out the back door with the picnic basket over your arm, when the same neutral event occurs — the skies open up and rain begins to fall.

Your thoughts about this event will most likely be very different from those of our farmer. You might have thoughts such as the following:

- ⊕ "Oh no — the kids are going to be so disappointed!
- ⊕ They'll be climbing the walls!
- ⊕ What am I going to do with them all day?
- ⊕ This will be a nightmare!"

The feelings arising from these thoughts will most likely be some variation of frustration, disappointment, irritation, panic, aggravation, anger and, perhaps, depression. Your actions in the expression of these feelings may include snapping at the kids, slamming things around the house, giving up and slumping down in a chair or venting on the phone to a friend. And, watching you, any observer would detect the negative emotions and know you are anything but happy, excited and relieved.

Using Emotional Regulation to Manage Emotions

It is when you become aware that you are experiencing negative emotions, such as anger, frustration, hurt, fear, jealousy and the like, that you must learn to remember that you are creating this situation for yourself. Your thoughts are your captors, your prison and the creator of your misery. I don't mean to imply that bad things don't happen to people sometimes. Or, that you should or can be expected to enjoy them. But, when you are feeling negative emotions, know that your thoughts are creating your emotional reaction to the event you've experienced. That fact alone empowers you to change it.

How do you do that? Take the example of our parent and the disappointed children. Rather than going with the negative set of thoughts that first popped into your head, imagine the difference if you entertained these thoughts: "Well, I need to come up with plan B. Let's see, we'll put a video in the VCR and have a picnic on the living room floor. We'll save the beach for next weekend and, after lunch, we'll all go out and splash around in the puddles!"

This change in your thinking process and the addition of those "Replacement Thoughts" leading to "More Positive Feelings" can be diagrammed as follows:

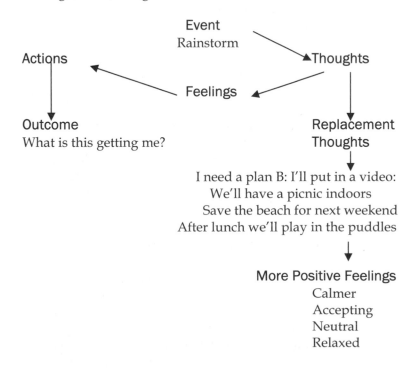

Event
Rainstorm

Actions

Thoughts

Feelings

Outcome
What is this getting me?

Replacement
Thoughts

I need a plan B: I'll put in a video:
We'll have a picnic indoors
Save the beach for next weekend
After lunch we'll play in the puddles

More Positive Feelings
Calmer
Accepting
Neutral
Relaxed

Granted, it probably won't make you happy, excited and relieved like our farmer, but you will most likely be a whole lot calmer, more relaxed and more neutral about the event than with the former set of thoughts. That's the effect the thinking process can have: enabling you to **choose** your reaction to events over which you, in most cases, have no control. For most of us, in this society, there are only too many such situations in our lives. What do you have to lose by managing your emotions more successfully?

While utilizing this process typically takes some work, it does get easier with practice. You are likely, at first, to notice that you remember to pay attention to your thoughts only after you have **again** reacted emotionally to a situation. But, in many cases, there is emotional baggage remaining that you can work on at that point with this process. The more you work with this, the earlier you will notice the effect you have. Pretty soon, you will stop yourself in mid-sentence as you react to an event and, before long, you will be thinking through the entire reaction before even opening your mouth.

As you get more accustomed to thinking this way, you will notice, also, that your mind takes over and completes the process for you. After a while, you might start down the path of a negative reaction, and your thoughts will stop suddenly, seemingly of their own accord. You may think, "Wait a minute, I don't have to go there. I can think about it this way instead!" It will seem as involuntary as the negative thinking does to you now — only you won't be nearly as miserable! But, as with any change worth making, it does take practice to make it work.

The Concepts of Repetition and Outcome

Two more points about the Event, Thought, Feeling Process bear mention here: repetition and outcome. First, if an event has happened to you a number of times in a similar manner, you are likely, in that instance, to move so quickly from Event to Feelings and Actions that you are not consciously aware of the Thoughts at all. They are, indeed, there. You will just have to work harder, and slow things down even more, to get to them.

Because this is a repeated experience for you, your thoughts have taken the same route many times in the past. Thoughts that we have create a neural pathway in our brain. Each time we have a similar experience and the thoughts repeat themselves, they follow the same pathway. Once an experience has repeated itself a number of times, your thoughts have dug a deep trench in your brain, as it were. Each time the same experience and thoughts happen, it takes less time to get through them and on to the feelings and actions. And each time the trench gets a little deeper and a little wider. Let me give you another example.

Let's say you've had a previous relationship in which your partner took to going out with friends and, when this would happen, frequently he would hook up with another woman and become involved in an affair. Whether this happened to you once or a thousand times (hopefully you did not choose to stay in the same relationship that long), you have a pattern of thoughts that will tend to happen pretty much automatically when your new partner announces he will be going out with friends Friday night. It goes something like this:

Event
Your partner announces he's going out with friends.

Actions
You ask him 20 questions:
- Where are you going?
-Who will you be with?
You forbid him to go
You get upset and start an
  argument
You give him the silent treatment
You attack him when he gets home

Thoughts
He'll meet someone else;
He'll find someone he prefers to me
He really doesn't care about me
There's something wrong w/me
I'm unlovable!

Feelings
Hurt, Afraid, Jealous
Insecure, Lonely, Angry

Because of your life experiences, you are uniquely set up to react negatively to this situation. How you react is often largely dictated by what has happened in your past as well. But, just knowing this, you have the power and ability to change it!

It is also important, in the context of relationships, to think about outcome. You want to get in the habit of asking yourself, "What's my outcome here?" and "Are my actions getting me the result I want?"

In the example presented above, if you act on the first set of thoughts, your actions are likely to be snapping at your partner, giving him the silent treatment, or starting an argument. We are upset because we are afraid our partner will leave or not be faithful to us and we are feeling emotionally distant from him. Choosing those actions, however, we end up with exactly the opposite of what we want; we get greater emotional distance, rather than the closeness we prefer.

The bottom line in this exercise is, we want to feel closer to our partner, but all our actions are achieving is greater distance. In reacting to an event in the context of a relationship, always ask yourself, "Is this getting me greater emotional closeness? Or greater emotional distance?" Then act according to what you would prefer.

If worrying about what our partner might get into is not going to make us happier or make us more content, what might replacement thoughts be in a case such as this?
How about these:
☮ This is a new relationship
☮ This is a different partner
☮ He and I have a good relationship
☮ I know I can trust him
☮ I know he cares about me

Again, this is how the replacement thought process might be diagrammed:

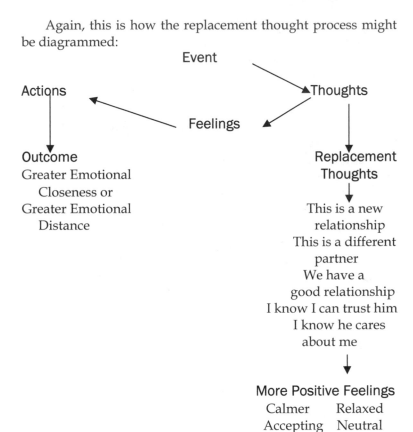

You may not find yourself happy and excited about your partner going out with his friends, but you will most likely be much calmer and more neutral about the experience than if you went with your first set of thoughts. You will be less likely to push your partner away with distancing behaviors and more likely to act in ways that increase emotional closeness with him.

In creating replacement thoughts, is it important to be genuine. Don't attempt to create positive thoughts that you can't believe, such as telling yourself you have no reason not to trust your partner if she has cheated repeatedly in the past. In that case, you may first want to ask yourself why you stay in the relationship in the first place. What are you getting out of the deal that keeps you there? Are you with her only because you feel you cannot find another partner? Do you have a need to "save" her from herself? Or, is it that you truly enjoy each other's company when you are together and her affairs take little away from the relationship? If that is the case, your positive thoughts may need to be about this conscious choice on your part: "I know she sometimes sees other men, but our relationship is a good one and I can live with that."

Know, too, that the first time you travel this new path with your thinking, you will have to work at it to come up with the replacement thoughts. Remember, all of those old familiar destructive thoughts have dug a pretty deep trench by now. Creating a new path can take some work. But the more you force yourself to go through the exercise of creating positive thoughts, the easier and more automatic it becomes.

Emotional Regulation and STOP!

Before continuing on with the next concept I will present, it would be good to read over the first part of this chapter to get it secure in your mind. Take a few minutes now to skim over the previous eleven pages, then, after you have taken an opportunity to do so, read on.

Brain Development

We humans have three parts to our brain:
- ⊕ the **reptilian brain**, which is located at the brain stem and controls instinctual behaviors, such as breathing, heartbeat and swallowing,
- ⊕ the **limbric brain**, which was the second stage to develop and acts as the center of emotion and
- ⊕ the **neocortical brain**, which is capable of thought, logic, will and choice.

We tend to assume that the neocortical brain is the most valuable and powerful brain because it controls our logic and reasoning. Human beings like to think of themselves as primarily rational beings that can control our lives and world by using reason and skill. We like to downplay the importance of emotion in our lives.

However, our survival in the face of danger or threat depends on instinct and emotion, not reason. In a life and death situation, stopping to think can result in injury or death. When seconds count, thinking is too slow. As emotion and instinct are instantaneous, it is these reactions that help us to survive. As we discussed in Chapter Three, the fight, flight or freeze reaction is triggered by a real or perceived threat to our safety. At most times, if we stop to think about what our response will be it is too late. Logically, it makes no sense to run back into a burning building. However, if our child is trapped inside, emotionally that may be exactly the reaction we have. Logic has nothing to do with it.

Scientists are doing some interesting research in the area of brain development. We used to think that children's brains were fully developed in infancy. But remember, we now know that our brains are not fully developed until 18-25 years of age. This means that a child or an adolescent will think differently about an event than an adult.

The Logical Brain vs. the Emotional Brain

The emotional brain reacts quickly, but is inaccurate. When emotion is in control, memory is limited. For this reason, we may not remember what we do or say when we are extremely upset. The more intense the emotion, the less accurate you may be.

Further, to access memories, positive feelings about your partner for example, you would need to be in a different emotional state. And you cannot be in two emotional states at the same time. Therefore, when we are angry at our partner, it is natural to only be able to get in touch with things she does that lead to a negative reaction on our part.

When we are able to access our logical thinking brain, we can quickly reason our way out of emotional and illogical upsets. It is very easy at those times to choose an outcome that gets us the payoff or goal we are looking for. However, it can be very difficult to access logic when we are very upset. As our emotional and illogical brain is stronger and more powerful than our logical, rational brain, it can quickly overpower logic and we can choose behaviors that are not in our best interest and, thus, get us exactly the opposite outcome from what we are hoping and looking for.

Some of the research that is being done involves infrared photographs of the brain in action. Scientists have taken pictures of the brain of an individual who is extremely emotionally upset; then of the same individual after they have calmed down and are in a problem-solving mode. In the first photo, only the emotional regions of the brain are showing as active. No logic or reasoning is being used. In the latter, only the area governing our rational thinking, the neocortex, is activated. This is truly fascinating stuff!

I have a wonderful example of this principle in action. I worked for while with a woman I will call Karla. Karla came into counseling to deal with some things that had happened in her childhood. She was happily married when we met and had nothing about her current life that she wanted to change. In fact, she told me that her husband was a kind and caring man and that they had a very good relationship. But Karla had had several experiences in childhood that she wanted to work through.

Karla and I began working on her childhood issues and about the fourth time we met, she came into my office, sat down hard on the chair and stated, "I'm afraid my husband doesn't respect met, doesn't love me and we'll probably end up getting a divorce!" I was rather surprised, given how she had spoken of their relationship previously, and asked why she would say such a thing.

Her response floored me. She promptly replied, "He won't pick up his dirty socks and throw them into the hamper!" Still not understanding how this could completely devastate a healthy relationship, I probed for more.

Karla responded, "I spend all day and every night taking care of our home and our child. I make sure the house is clean, our daughter is cared for, that we have good food to eat and I am exhausted! The only thing I ask of him is to pick up his dirty, stinky socks from next to the recliner where he drops them every day when he comes home from work. But every night when I drag my exhausted body to bed at 11:00 p.m., there they lay. So I have to pick them up and put them in the hamper myself! I think that means he doesn't respect all that I do for us and for our family, so he probably doesn't love me and we'll probably end up getting a divorce!" You can see and hear the emotion here.

I should add that Karla was not working outside the home at the time as she was about eight months pregnant with their second child and spent her days at home caring for their nine month old daughter. Hormones undoubtedly played a part in her reaction, but I would agree that being a homemaker is about the most thankless job imaginable. I did this for two years myself and, not only do you not get the paycheck at the end of each week to reward you, you typically do not hear a "thank you" and most of your hard work goes unnoticed as a clean house is quickly dirtied. Then you can start all over again!

Now, if you can get into the mindset of the Event, Thought, Feeling Process, you will be able to identify the negative and destructive **Thoughts** that Karla was using to get herself into trouble here. Then, moving on to feelings, we can tell she was **Feeling** hurt, unappreciated, unimportant, afraid and frustrated. So, acting on those thoughts and feelings, how do you suppose she welcomed her husband home each day when he returned from work?

Right! She was on him as soon as he walked in the door. So, what **Outcome** was she getting? Well, she was feeling all of those negative feelings because she was emotionally more distant from her husband than she wanted to be. But her actions were buying her more of the same. Rather than drawing him close to her, she, herself, was pushing him away and getting exactly the opposite of the Outcome she desired. Reacting with her strong emotions, Karla was not thinking logically about her situation or the effect of her behavior on her husband or their relationship.

I suggested to Karla that her husband was probably exhausted when he came home from work as he had been working overtime for the past month. In fact, I was quite sure that the one thing he looked forward to at the end of the day, was seeing and spending time with her and their daughter, and that the socks were probably the last thing on his mind. In fact, I supposed that in some ways it was a compliment to her that he wasn't racing the socks to the hamper, as he was focused on spending his time with her.

Karla looked at me suspiciously, raised one eyebrow and said, "I'll have to think about that." She came back two weeks later a different woman. She stated, "This Thinking Process changed my life! I still don't like the socks on the floor. But I don't take it personally anymore. I know it just happens, but that it doesn't mean my husband doesn't love me!"

Two weeks after that appointment, I met Karla's husband for the first time. As I was explaining the Event, Thought, Feeling Process to him, he began laughing as he recognized himself in the "socks on the floor" example. But, he added, "Now that I understand how important it is to Karla, I really do make more of an effort to get my socks in the hamper!" And they lived happily ever after! Or, at least I haven't heard from them in the past two years, which is typically a good sign!

Each of us has events in our lives that prompt strong emotional responses. If we can train ourselves to calm down, take a time out and shift into our logical thinking brain when we are feeling very reactive, we have a great deal more control over the outcomes we receive. But there are other variables at work here as well.

When we are being triggered by a provocative issue, something to which we react strongly, it can be difficult to switch into our logical brain and think constructively about what we can do to bring about the outcome we desire. When we are very upset, it is incredibly difficult to access our logical brain; difficult to even access the Event, Thought, Feeling Process at times like those. Yet, that is the time it is most essential to do so. There are several things you can do to make your rational thinking more accessible to you, which we will discuss in the next several pages.

But just understand that our emotional brain, which pre-dates our logical brain both individually and historically, is far stronger and more powerful than our logical brain and in direct competition, will win out every time. It does not mean you are weak or that you have no determination to get a handle on this anger thing. It simply means you are human and your brain is operating as it was designed to, to protect you and invoke your survival instincts and behaviors.

Innate Worth

To begin our discussion of how to access our neocortical, or logical, brain during times of strong emotion, I want to spend some time talking about innate worth and negative beliefs. We are all born with a sense of innate worth. It is the birthright of every human being. If you look at any baby, you will see and appreciate his value as a human being. It is the truth that each of us is as valuable, lovable, worthwhile and acceptable as any other person.

As we travel our path through life, we begin to lose some of our sense of innate worth. We question ourselves, our abilities, our value as a human being. When this happens we take an emotional "hit." When we are angry, it is a sign that we, perhaps subconsciously, are questioning our innate worth. Something has been triggered in us that does not feel good; we are feeling lacking or inadequate in some way. Our reaction to that feeling, our secondary emotion, is anger.

Taking a look at the flip side of this issue, when I believe in my innate worth, no one can threaten it, no matter what they think, do or say. When I believe in my innate worth, I can handle any issue, problem or situation in my life simply as events that must be dealt with. They are not a measure of my worth. They just are.

It is only when we begin to doubt ourselves and question our innate worth that we begin to get into trouble with anger in our life and relationships. For this reason, only we can be the solution to this problem. No one else can fix this for us. The solution lies with the individual.

We must each take responsibility for our innate worth. We must work to appreciate, value, respect and protect it. When we have a strong sense of ourselves as worthy human beings, we can be OK even if we make mistakes or do things that are harmful to ourselves or others. We are not swayed or overwhelmed by the behavior of others, nor are we at the mercy of external events that are out of our control.

Emotional Wounds and Negative Beliefs

The losses we suffer when our innate worth, our sense of value in ourselves, takes a hit, can be called emotional wounds. Each of us incurs a substantial amount of these wounds as we wend our way through life and they accumulate, causing us to be more or less reactive to life events than persons with a greater or lesser amount of these wounds. Obviously the more wounds we have, the more times we have been kicked in the teeth, so to speak, the more reactive we tend to be.

It is not hard to accumulate emotional wounds for several reasons. First of all, even in the best of families, our parents contribute to this process. They are, after all, only human, and at times will do and say things that are harmful to us emotionally.

Secondly, as we discussed previously, a human brain is not fully developed until we are between 18 and 25 years of age and younger persons tend to process life events differently than adults. This can cause emotional wounds as well, depending on what we tell ourselves about a given situation.

Take the example of a five year old child looking to play a game. He asks his mother who responds, "Not now, honey, I'm busy. I have to make dinner." He moves on to his father who tells him, "I'm sorry son; I have to mow the lawn." As adults we can only imagine the number of tasks these parents have on their plates and can empathize with their choice to decline their son's request this time. To a child, with an immature emotional brain, this kind of an event can send the message, "I am not important. Even my Mom and Dad don't want to play with me."

The child files this experience and belief away, only to be triggered in his adulthood when he asks his wife to do something with him and she, also being busy and overwhelmed, responds with, "Not today I have to make dinner," or walk the dog, do the laundry or whatever. Feeling unimportant to this most important person in his life, he then behaves in ways that get him exactly the opposite outcome from that which he desires: he complains, whines, yells or simply withdraws in silence, leading to greater emotional distance from his partner. He no longer consciously remembers the incident at age five, but his emotional brain does and triggers that emotional response. He may be aware of feeling unimportant and, unless he is able to do something to flip himself into his logical brain, he will be acting on the basis of those feelings and probably doing more damage to the relationship.

There are a number of negative beliefs about ourselves that we may collect over the years, but if we let ourselves think about it, one or two of the following usually sound and "feel" more familiar to us than the rest. These are most likely the ones which we collected as children. It is a useful experience to become aware of these beliefs so we can correct them. We will be able to watch for them to be triggered and counteract them before they get us into trouble.

Notice, also, that the example above is something that probably happens everyday in very healthy, positive, nurturing homes. Imagine the experiences built up when a child is raised in an abusive or neglectful home environment. The more of these experiences we have, the more reactive we are likely to be.

Some of the more common Negative Beliefs that get us into trouble tend to be the following:

☮ *I am unimportant.*
☮ *I am worthless.*
☮ *I am powerless.*
☮ *I am helpless.*
☮ *I am inadequate.*

There are no doubt others that trigger people as well, but these tend to be some of the more common ones. If you are aware of a different belief that you find yourself reacting to, please add it to the list on the summary page at the end of this chapter. This will help you to keep it in your awareness so you will be less reactive to it.

STOP!

So, now that we understand why we react to certain triggering situations, what are we going to do about it? We are going to STOP! It is a simple technique, but it's not easy and it takes practice.

Remember the Event, Thought, Feeling process we discussed earlier in this chapter? It is an extremely effective technique all on its own. However, there are times when we are feeling something very intensely and are unable to access our thoughts, positive or negative. At those times, our best option is to incorporate STOP! in combination with the Event, Thought, Feeling Process.

The method is this: Whenever you are aware that you are reacting emotionally to a situation, you are going to imagine a "Stop Sign" flashing three times. Say to yourself, "STOP! STOP! STOP!" This is important because there is something magical about the way our brains react to three repetitions that is more effective than repeating "STOP!" either two or four times.

If you are not driving in a car or operating heavy equipment, you may find it easier to close your eyes and imagine the Stop Sign. It will be helpful to get a clear visual image of the sign flashing "STOP!" at you. If you are not out in public, it can also be helpful to actually say your three

"STOP!"s out loud. This invokes another sense, hearing, into the experience. But even if you are driving or standing in line at the grocery store, as long as you can imagine the Stop Sign and say "STOP!" three times in your head, you can make this work for you.

Saying "STOP!" as described above will enable you to switch your thinking from your emotional brain to your logical, rational brain. You will then be able to identify what is triggering you and choose to replace those destructive and negative thoughts with more positive replacement thoughts that will take you to a different place and a more positive outcome.

The Effect of STOP!

When you use STOP!, it will not make you thrilled that your partner doesn't have time for you, but it will make these experiences less painful. It won't feel like fireworks going off; it will be more like someone opened up a window and let in a breath of fresh air. It may feel like a heavy sigh or a little bit of weight being lifted off your shoulders. The situation will feel manageable; like something you can handle or tolerate and deal with. And the technique will enable you to flip into your logical brain to decide how you do want to deal with the event.

At that point, after you've repeated STOP! to yourself three times and feeling slight relief, I want you to ask yourself the following very important questions:

"What am I reacting to?"
"Why am I reacting to this situation?"
"What negative belief is being triggered?"

If you sit quietly for several minutes after asking yourself these questions, the answers will come. Think about it; let the negative belief sink in for just a minute. That will enable you to let it go. You have to "Feel it to heal it." Then you will be able to figure out what belief and experience are being triggered and what you need to do about them.

All of this can take place when you are taking a time out. You can deal with the situation and be ready to deal more positively with your partner, child, co-worker or whomever, upon your return. This would be a wonderful way to spend your time as you take your walk, go for a leisurely drive or chop some wood.

Once you are able to identify the negative belief that is getting you into trouble, try to look a little deeper to determine the first event in your life that led to the belief. This will be easier for some than for others. If you are able to discover this event, please keep this in mind as we continue with the thinking process. Even if you cannot bring to mind the original event, stay with me here.

The next step is to respond to the negative belief and choose replacement thoughts that will lead you to a different result and outcome. Respond immediately with a statement contrary to your negative belief, because these statements are not only untrue, they are harmful and damaging to you emotionally. Our goal is to get rid of them. The following are the response statements I am talking about:

If your Negative Belief is:	Use:
I am unimportant	*I am important.*
I am worthless.	*I am worthwhile.*
I am powerless.	*I am powerful.*
I am helpless.	*I am capable.*
I am inadequate.	*I am valuable.*

If your negative belief is not one of the above, come up with a feeling statement that is the opposite of your belief and repeat it to yourself.

After responding to your key negative belief, flip into the replacement thinking that we discussed in the section on the Event, Thought, Feeling Process. Turn around the destructive statements about the event in your mind. Several statements that tend to be pretty universal and work in most situations include:

☮   *This is not about me.*
☮   *I don't have to take this personally.*
☮   *This is not the end of the world.*
☮   *S/he does love me.*
☮   *I don't have to react to this.*
☮   *I can let this go.*

For most people, three or four statements are plenty to get them to the replacement feelings. You should notice that you become calmer, more relaxed, more accepting and more neutral about whatever the triggering event is than if you go with your first, destructive thinking. You should then be able to think about your Outcome and choose actions that will have a greater likelihood of achieving the outcome you desire.

You may want to refer back to the previous diagram of an upsetting situation. When we incorporate STOP!, our diagram looks like this:

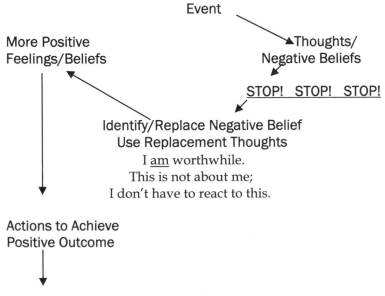

Event

More Positive
Feelings/Beliefs

Thoughts/
Negative Beliefs

STOP!   STOP!   STOP!

Identify/Replace Negative Belief
Use Replacement Thoughts
I am worthwhile.
This is not about me;
I don't have to react to this.

Actions to Achieve
Positive Outcome

Outcome: Greater Emotional Closeness!

We can follow the same model quite easily, but by using the image of the stop sign and identifying the underlying negative belief, which we then replace with a statement of our innate worth, we can more easily access, not only our thinking brain, but the replacement thoughts necessary to move us to a point of acting in accordance with our own best interests. Give it a try, but do not expect perfection. Don't expect yourself to remember to use it in every potential situation.

As an example, let's walk through this new process with the example of our partner going out with friends that we used earlier in this chapter. Let's assume that, finding yourself too upset, you are unable to access the Thinking Process. You use the STOP! Technique and watch what happens:

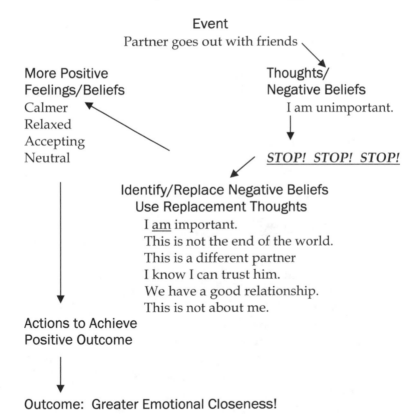

Event
Partner goes out with friends

More Positive Feelings/Beliefs
Calmer
Relaxed
Accepting
Neutral

Thoughts/ Negative Beliefs
I am unimportant.

STOP! STOP! STOP!

Identify/Replace Negative Beliefs Use Replacement Thoughts
I am important.
This is not the end of the world.
This is a different partner
I know I can trust him.
We have a good relationship.
This is not about me.

Actions to Achieve Positive Outcome

Outcome: Greater Emotional Closeness!

The Path of Progress

The development of the ability to use this process is not smooth. Most people start out with the best of intentions, but end up forgetting about thinking when they are upset. They will remember two hours later and get upset with themselves for having done "it" again! Don't worry—it should get easier to remember and closer to the time of the upset. You may initially remember two hours after the fact, then one hour, finally as you are in the middle of an outburst, then in mid-sentence and, finally, before you open your mouth. This is a typical progression. It will get easier!

Also remember to practice this technique in a wide variety of situations. Start with things that bother you only a little and work up to the more upsetting situations. If the first time you use this is when you come home find your partner in bed with another man, it won't do a bit of good. You must work up to the most upsetting situations by using it regularly to deal with those minor irritations each of us experience three or four times each and every day: traffic, waiting in lines, interruptions, co-workers and minor events involving partners and children.

As we said when introducing this technique, it is simple, but it is not easy. You must practice using it in order for it to be accessible to you in times of great upset. The more you do practice it, the more accessible and powerful it will be. Like the Event, Thought, Feeling Process, it will become quite automatic for you as well. If you practice and use it regularly, you may find yourself using it without even realizing you are doing so. That is true success!

Also, the more you identify these Negative Beliefs for yourself, the less of a hold they have on you. If you work with them regularly, you should find yourself becoming less and less reactive to situations in your life. You may be surprised by the thought, "Gee I would really have been upset about that situation a year ago. It really doesn't bother me now." This is our hope for you. Practice regularly and you, too, can easily have this result!

Blind Rage

Another unique aspect of invoking our strong emotional brain is the concept of blind rage. We have all heard people talk about situations in which they were very upset and have no memory of what they did or said, similar to the example of "Travis" at the beginning of Chapter Three. You may even have had this experience yourself.

When our emotional brain is engaged in a highly agitated state, it is not uncommon to have no recall of our behavior. This is similar to the "blackout" periods experienced by someone with an alcohol problem. The adrenaline is flowing and your rational brain has no recollection of what you may have done in this highly aroused state.

The Thinking/STOP! technique is helpful for even this type of a situation. As long as you practice using the technique when less aroused, it can be available to you even when you are extremely upset. It is truly an amazing process!

Further, now that you are aware that this tool can be helpful in a blind rage situation, you have no excuses. Sometimes angry partners deny responsibility for their actions using the excuse that they are not aware of their behavior when angry. We would suggest that, rather than looking to excuse or deny responsibility, you now have a responsibility to practice the technique that can help you change this behavior. And improve all of your relationships in the process!

Other Difficult Emotions

As helpful as this technique is for situations involving anger, it is also extremely useful and just as effective for dealing with any negative emotion: depression, anxiety, frustration, jealousy, fear, hurt, guilt and so on. Use it as often as you can identify a difficult emotion to reduce the amount of time you are troubled by these feelings.

We often tell our group that if they take nothing else that we have taught with them when they leave, we want them to take this technique. It's simply that important. It is the most effective technique we know for getting a handle on upsetting emotions. Practice it and use it regularly. It really does get easier and you won't be disappointed!

As in previous chapters, read through the summary on the next page to review the material presented here. We have also included blank STOP! and Thinking Process diagrams in Appendices F and G. Many people find it helpful to hang one or both on their refrigerator to help them regularly remember the process. We even had a group member that was the leader of a roofing crew and he tacked it up on the roof they were working on each day to keep these ideas in mind, both for himself and his workers. Others have found it a useful exercise to make a number of copies of these forms to write out their Negative Beliefs and Thoughts, as well as their Replacement Thinking whenever they have an upsetting event. However you choose to use them, the forms are there in Appendices F and G.

Good Luck!

"Calming the Beast Within" Summary*

☮ Spend some time thinking about **Events** that trigger strong negative emotions for you. List the most common:

a. _____

b. _____

c. _____

☮ Identify the **Negative Thoughts** that cause trouble for you in these events (i.e. *"She's going to leave me!"*):

a. _____

b. _____

c. _____

☮ List the **Feelings** typically arising from these Negative Thoughts:

_____

_____

_____

☮ Identify the **Behaviors** (yours) that often result from these Negative Feelings:

a. _____

b. _____

c. _____

☮ The **Outcome** typically associated with these Behaviors is:

___Emotional Closeness   ___ Emotional Distance
(With Partner)   *(From Partner)*

☮ List **Replacement Thoughts** you have developed to use in the above situations:

a. _____

b. _____

c. _____

d. _____

☮ The **Negative Belief** most familiar to me is:

_____

(Example: I am unimportant.)

☮ I can turn that belief around with the **Positive Statement:**

_____

(Example:: I am important.)

* Please also refer to Appendices F and G for diagrams of the Thinking Processes.

"I am an old man
and have known a great many troubles —
but most of them never happened."

~Mark Twain

Chapter 8

Too Much Of a Good Thing

The Concept of Control

Afer introducing the concept of control in relationships and making the point that it is only an imbalance of power that causes problems with the law and the relationship, Jason raises his hand.

"Well, my situation doesn't bear that out. I didn't exercise an imbalance of power or control."

"How so, Jason?" guessing where he was going with his question and wanting him to commit himself a little further.

"Well, I needed to hit Shelly. We were driving home from a picnic, where we'd both been drinking. She was questioning the steering on the car, so I swerved it back and forth to show her it worked fine. She lost it and started screaming and trying to get the keys out of the ignition, so I reached over and punched her in the face just to calm her down.

*"I was going to pull over and just get out, but didn't want to leave our 4 year old son in the car with her. We had a ways to drive and she kept trying to get the keys, so I **had** to hit her whenever she would*

try to get the keys. Finally I pulled into the driveway and she jumped out and ran off. I looked all over for her but couldn't find her. After the police came, they found her hiding in the neighbor's garage. She got blood all over their new car."

"Did she need medical treatment?"

"Yeah, uhh, they said she had two black eyes, um, a broken jaw and I guess a couple of cracked ribs. She was in the hospital about a week but I couldn't go see her."

"Jason, I'm guessing you knew she was frightened when you were swerving the car, right?"

"Yeah, I guess."

"Do you think some part of you enjoyed scaring her?"

"Yeah, it shut her up and kept her in her place."

"And she must have been pretty frightened to stay hiding in the neighbor's garage, as injured as she was."

"I guess." Jason is suddenly sounding less certain of his methods.

"Perhaps this was an imbalance of power and control after all."

In order for a relationship to be healthy, each party needs a measure of control. The amount needed by, and acceptable to each, is largely determined by the type of relationship and by agreement between the parties.

A relationship between parent and child will necessitate the parent having a larger portion of control, at least until the child is in her teen-age years. At that point, the parent may feel like he has no control at all, so vast is the change. But this is an important step in the child eventually achieving independence from her family of origin.

In the context of an employer/employee relationship, again control must be shared. However, while the employer often maintains a larger portion of control while the relationship continues, it is still within the employee's prerogative to terminate the relationship entirely. Therefore, there must be a balance of control with which each party is comfortable in order for the relationship to continue.

When we get to the intimate relationship, the balance can be ever more difficult to achieve and assess. Both parties need to feel in control within the context of the relationship for them to want the union to continue. Put more simply, who wants to be in a relationship in which they are forever feeling bossed around?

Sometimes both partners accept a relationship in which one partner initially has a greater amount of control as it meets his need to be in charge and her need to be taken care of or instructed or guided as to how to behave. One reason for this might be a difference in age between the parties. What often happens, however, is that the controlled partner eventually becomes dissatisfied with her role and seeks to change it. This is a crisis point for the relationship as it must now adapt to her new needs or it will probably end.

In this day and age it is simple enough to end a relationship and seek another that is comfortable and fulfilling. It thus requires negotiation and the achievement of an agreement between the parties in order for control in an intimate relationship to be balanced and acceptable to both partners. But when and how does this happen?

The Natural Process of Relationships

There is a predictable process that occurs in the development of an intimate relationship. Initially, connection and commonalities are the focus, but this soon gives way to conflict and/or identification of the ways in which we are different from our partner. This does not mean the relationship is flawed. All of this is normal within the natural flow of relationships.

Merging

Early in any relationship there is a focus on togetherness. Couples marvel at the depth of their connection and the many things they have in common. Differences are not acknowledged. If they are noticed, they are minimized or brushed beneath the surface as unimportant.

The emphasis is on closeness and togetherness. There is very low anxiety at this stage of the relationship and a high level of satisfaction. They attempt to please and accommodate each other as long as possible, giving up the "me" for the "we". This state does not last forever, however.

Conflict

Eventually, this leads to unresolved and unacknowledged issues resulting from personal differences that have actually existed all along, but have been ignored. At this point, these issues can no longer be denied. The individual feels a strong need to express his own individual needs and preferences, in spite of the fact that this will cause conflict in the relationship.

This stage is normal in every relationship. We must remember that when we are choosing a life partner, we come to that place as two individuals who have been raised in two entirely different families of origin. The concept that opposites attract is not merely a myth.

Many a time I have had a couple in my office in which the wife is content to stay at home and have few friends and the husband is an ambitious mover and shaker in the business community. Or, perhaps, she is the social butterfly, enjoying all forms of social discourse, while he is uncomfortable in groups larger than two. While these partners are initially attracted by their differences, it is these differences which generally will raise conflict when this new stage of the relationship is reached.

Now, instead of being thrilled that she is being taken care of by her ambitious and well-providing husband, she is lonely and wants him to sit with her on the sofa to keep her company. Instead of enjoying her sociability with others, he is jealous that she is talking and flirting with other men. The conflict has begun.

While this is a normal phase in the development of any relationship, there is an adjustment that must occur at this point if the relationship is to survive. How this couple deals with this conflict must change in order to accommodate and resolve this conflict.

Power Struggles

Some couples deal with the developing conflict by engaging in repeated power struggles, often over the same mundane or ridiculous issues, about which neither truly cares. What is happening here is that each partner is trying to establish some power in the relationship in order to feel some semblance of control.

What is truly occurring, however, is that each party is attempting to force the other to give up or give in. When this pressure is exerted, the only choice is to detach or leave, either physically or emotionally. Parties may choose to stay in the relationship but be completely emotionally uninvolved with the other partner. Or they may choose at this point to simply leave the relationship as the repeated conflicts and power struggles for control grow tiresome; they simply give up.

If the relationship does continue, continuing conflict is the result. It is often accompanied by resentment, bitterness, disinterest and feelings of dissatisfaction and oppression. In sum, it is neither a happy nor fulfilling relationship for either partner.

Differentiation

There is another choice in relationship development, however: that of differentiation. Differentiation is simply a long word that means maintaining one's individuality in the context of a relationship.

Just as a child will grow and separate from parents to establish a separate identity as part of normal healthy development, so too must individuals in a long term intimate relationship develop and define their own identities. When the conflict begins to appear, couples who are able to differentiate work to define themselves while in the relationship, understanding that this an important task if the union is to continue. At this point, the focus is on the self, not the other.

This represents a shift from the other-focus during the merging period of relationship development. It requires each individual to be honest with himself and his partner and that each takes action he believes to be the best for him, regardless of what may happen to the relationship.

While this sounds incredibly self-centered, an example may help to illustrate why this is actually a healthy response. Take the example of Joe and Mary. Joe is an athlete and spends time while he is alone by running, biking and working out. He eventually meets Mary and, early in the relationship, he gives up his workout routine in order to devote time to his new partner.

Eventually, he will begin to feel frustrated, however, at having no time to himself to work out. His resentment may show and he may blame his partner for expecting or demanding so much of his time, though he was the one who initially validated those expectations.

His task at that point is to talk with his partner about his need for time for himself to meet his own needs. We will discuss in Chapter Ten more about how to have these difficult conversations, but know that they are crucial to the survival of the relationship.

If he makes his needs known, this crisis can lead to personal integrity, growth and change, or bitterness and resentment. The relationship could still end, but the only way he will be able to happily and contentedly continue in the relationship will be to attempt to make his individual needs known. Refer to Chapter Four on the Basic Needs of all individuals for a discussion of why this is important.

Two Do Not Become One

One of the most dangerous beliefs we are trained to expect regarding relationships is that "two shall become one." We get this from many religious marriage ceremonies and the notion of romantic love. This can, however, be extremely destructive to the individuals involved in the relationship.

In many wedding ceremonies, partners light a unity candle with two individual candles, and then extinguish them. This powerful symbol creates the expectation that we will give ourselves up to this new union. If and when that proves difficult, we may feel we have failed or are somehow inadequate at being unable to fulfill this very basic expectation.

Terry and I thought long and hard about the symbolism of this tradition when we married. This was the second marriage for both of us and we wanted to be realistic about our expectations upon entering into our marriage commitment. We ultimately decided to use the two individual candles to light a unity candle, but to leave the separate candles lit, rather than to extinguish them. This was meant to reinforce the idea that although we were creating a new entity, our marriage and family by this ceremony, we were not extinguishing the two individuals that were participating in and creating this union.

Couples that enter into such a union expecting not to have separate needs or preferences are setting themselves up for failure or unrealistic expectations. We believe that in order for couples to succeed, they need to know that it is normal and acceptable to have individual needs within the context of a relationship. Only then will they be able to make informed decisions and take responsibility for getting their needs met.

Dangerous and Unrealistic Expectations

There are a number of expectations that many of us received from our parents, our church, or former partners that may be contrary to an evolved and informed view of relationships. For example, in past generations, male/female relationships were often patriarchal and male dominated.

While this may have been most efficient in earlier times, as we have evolved from authoritarian dictatorships to more democratic societies, so, too, have marriages and families changed. These old, outmoded expectations cause harm to the development of a healthy union and tend to create much conflict between otherwise amiable partners. We will take some time now to dispel some of these myths.

1) That My Partner Will Be Supportive at All Times
This is simply unrealistic and it cannot happen. No partner can or should be available at all times; it is unrealistic to expect or

demand this type of support. Needing or expecting this from a partner makes you needy and dependent. Also, any partner who makes herself this available is not meeting her own needs.

In times of conflict, it is normal for your partner to become angry at you and may think you are being selfish or ridiculous. What is important here is that we develop the ability to give ourselves what we need emotionally and not expect or require that it come from others. We need to be able to soothe, comfort, calm and support ourselves. This helps us not overreact to another's behavior and to handle the pain and discomfort of growth and change. See Chapter Seven for a more extensive discussion of dealing with these feelings.

2) That a Partner Will Not Do Anything To Upset or Hurt Me

It is very possible that two people can love and respect each other and still do things the other will not like and will find upsetting and hurtful. This is simply the natural result of any relationship being comprised of two separate individuals with different life experiences, beliefs, needs and desires.

As David Schnarch explains in *Passionate Marriage* (W. W. Norton & Co., 1997), your relationship will push you to make some difficult choices. These choices are not easy to make and, while they can often be delayed, they cannot be put off forever. When faced with one of these issues, we can choose to: 1) give myself up for the relationship; 2) force my partner to give up herself for the relationship; 3) withdraw emotionally or physically from the relationship or 4) grow up and take the risk of defining who I am within the relationship.

This is the process of differentiation that we have been discussing. Only the fourth choice will bring about positive growth and change for both the individual and the relationship. The first three may keep things together for awhile, but eventually more resentment and conflict will result.

3) That My Partner Will Stop Any Behavior That Makes Me Uncomfortable

Again, your feelings and insecurities are your own to handle. Refer back to Chapter Seven if you need to for some ideas on how to do this. Any sign of change in a relationship is likely to trigger anxiety and insecurity, even if it is for the better.

For example, your partner gets a big raise and promotion at work. You are excited and celebrate her success, but then start to feel insecure. You question her commitment and what you have to offer her. You begin to feel inadequate.

At this point you have two choices: respond as a responsible adult or as an immature child. A responsible adult is aware of his fears and insecurities. He takes responsibility for them and soothes and calms himself. He supports his wife and is proud of her achievement.

An immature child, on the other hand, will attempt to get his partner to care for his insecure feelings. He will need her to constantly reassure him of his importance and downplay her achievement so he doesn't feel bad. He may complain about the time she spends at work, refuse to do more than "his share" around the house and make demands that will force her to choose between her new job and him.

His partner thinks about going back to her old position to relieve the stress. He supports that idea. Which relationship is likely to last?

4) That My Partner Should Try to Calm and Soothe Me When I Am Upset

This, also, represents an emotional dependency. We are each responsible for our own feelings and need to learn how to soothe and comfort ourselves. In the face of conflict, comfort and support must come from within. An angry partner is involved in dealing with his own hurt and will be unable and unavailable to soothe yours.

5) That I Will Always Feel Close to My Partner and He to Me

This is another unrealistic expectation. It is normal to be out of synch with your partner at times because you are each separate and unique individuals with different needs. Every person has both a need for closeness and a need for autonomy. Both are essential. Allow this ebb and flow of closeness and distance in your relationship and learn to soothe yourself while in the process.

6) That If I Am Upset About Something, My Partner Should Be Upset About It Too

Again, you are not clones of each other and will not feel the same way at many times. This is a symptom of enmeshment and a lack of differentiation. Enmeshment occurs when two people fail to acknowledge that they are separate persons with different needs and desires. It often stems from an anxiety or fear of separateness. Part of being an adult is caring for others without being overwhelmed by their emotions or reactions.

7) That Couples Should be Able to Negotiate and Compromise on Any Issue if They Love Each Other

While it is easy to negotiate and compromise on issues that are not important to us, there will inevitably be issues on which it is neither possible nor desirable. These are issues of integrity, about who you are as a person, apart from your relationship.

Most couples have several issues about which they have the same argument over and over again and about which they are in emotional gridlock. You may have the same frustrating argument over and over and both are sure your partner is wrong.

The way out of this gridlock is by differentiation. You must give up trying to control or change your partner and focus instead on yourself. Think long and hard about why the position you are taking is important to you and whether you are willing to make any compromises or changes that will benefit the relationship. Again, the focus here is on defining yourself.

Once you have been honest with yourself, the next step is to communicate this to your partner. Disclose your thoughts and feelings about this troublesome issue to your partner along with your self-discovery process. Sharing with your partner the questions you are asking yourself may help her to understand why you feel as you do. She may not agree, but may be able to be more understanding or accepting after you share your thinking with her. The relationship could still end, but whatever decision you make comes from a place of integrity within yourself, rather than being about her and her reaction.

8) That If a Couple Knows How to Communicate Effectively, They Should not Have Conflict or Unresolved Issues

Couples have few communication problems during the merging process of the relationship. Any difficulty seems easily resolvable. During the conflict stage, however, these skills seem to disappear. While they are still present, the desire to use them is often missing.

Again, during the initial courtship, differences are not obvious or identified. Each person is committed to doing anything to make his partner happy. Once this stage has passed, however, personal differences are starting to be felt.

Further, while communicating agreement is easy, communicating differences is not. This produces anxiety and conflict. Often couples stop talking in order to avoid their differences. They decide it is safer to keep their thoughts to themselves rather than share them and risk further conflict.

9) That How My Partner Looks and Acts Reflects on Me and She Should Be Careful Not To Make Me Look Bad

If we are expecting each relationship to contain two separate and unique individuals as we have discussed, we cannot assume they will choose their actions based solely on how they reflect on their partner. This can lead to situations in which my partner may appropriately behave in a manner that meets her needs, which are different from mine, but which I may not like or appreciate as her actions may reflect less than favorably on me.

If this belief is operating in a relationship, the partner who is feeling offended at his partner's actions may put himself in the position of trying to "stop" her from behaving in a way he views as inappropriate. He may attempt to control, punish or change her behaviors, seeing her as an extension of himself rather than as a separate person in her own right. He is thus depending on her to calm his insecurities and anxieties and protect his fragile ego from harm, all expectations inappropriately foist on another person. He needs to be able to deal with these issues himself.

The healthy way to view this issue is that each of us is a separate person, with different likes and needs. In a relationship it is important to know we are loved and valued for who we are; for our own uniqueness. This does not happen if you are only a reflection of your partner and your acceptance depends on how well you make her look.

Conflict Is Normal In Relationships

Conflict is a normal part of any relationship between two or more persons. Especially when we are talking about an intimate relationship, with another person who will touch us more deeply and know us more personally than perhaps any other living being, we must expect to encounter some conflict.
If it does not appear, one person, or perhaps both parties, are not truly investing themselves in the relationship.

In thinking about why this is so, imagine how a couple comes together. We have two separate individuals, raised in entirely unique families of origin, getting to know each other. Eventually they decide to marry or live together and expect to do so harmoniously all the time.

However, each has been raised in a different home with its own set of beliefs and expectations and ways of doing things. Even something as simple as decorating the Christmas tree or hanging the toilet tissue can lead to some significant conflict. The real miracle is that couples don't experience more conflict, not that they experience any at all!

Further, some issues take on an added emotional significance that fuels the fires and our expectations. For example, Christmas is a very emotional issue for many persons due, in part, to the significant memories and attachments each party has associated with it through the years. Thus, interfering or disagreeing with any of our partner's expectations regarding this most significant issue can lead to an all out war.

Therefore, it is not whether a couple experiences conflict that determines the health of the relationship, but how they handle it. We will discuss negotiation and conflict resolution techniques in Chapter Ten. For now, just know that conflict in any relationship is normal and to be expected. It does not mean there is something wrong with the relationship but rather that both parties are engaged and involved in it.

Difficult Relationships Do Not Mean You Have Chosen the Wrong Partner

Partners are most often our best teachers. They come into our lives to teach us things we need to learn and present us with situations in which we can choose to grow. But it is often the very thing that most attracted you to this person that you find most upsetting or annoying later in the relationship.

For example, perhaps you are a quieter person and, when you met your partner, you were attracted by how easily she seemed to interact with others in a social setting. Now, when the two of you go out for an evening, you find it nothing short of infuriating that she can so easily make conversation with everyone at the party; flip sides of the same coin.

In coping with a situation like this, you can either struggle to change or control her and end up simply frustrating yourself, or you can work on your own feelings of insecurity ("Maybe she'll find someone she likes better than me") and inadequacy ("I'm not outgoing enough for her"). We will discuss in Chapter Ten some more positive ways to resolve conflicts such as these, but a review of the Thinking Process outlined in Chapter Seven will be helpful as well.

Leaving Is Not Your Only Option!

Another assumption many people make is that when a relationship is experiencing difficulties, regardless of whether it is a significant amount of conflict or a great deal of emotional distance, the best solution is to leave. While this is an option, it may not be the best one to choose.

Many of us find ourselves in relationships that are quite similar to past relationships we have had. When we are seeking an intimate partner, we are really looking for someone who reminds us on some level, often a very subconscious level, of one of our primary caregivers as a child. As an adult, we seek to replicate this relationship and have it come out with a happier ending. All of our relationships with primary caregivers are imperfect in some ways: perhaps our father was emotionally distant or our mother was emotionally abusive. In addition, as a child, we do not have the same power in the relationship as the adults we are relating to. As adults, we seek to replicate the relationship by choosing a partner that may be emotionally distant or abusive as well and take the power we now have as an adult to "fix" or improve on that relationship, i.e. to find the happy ending.

Most people are not aware that this is what they are doing. In fact many of my clients are surprised in our first counseling session when upon hearing their family and relationship history, I can say to them, "I see you married your mother." But upon thinking about it, most can identify a number of occasions in which their spouse has reminded them of that parent.

It is therefore a useful exercise, in most cases, to put some effort and energy into trying to resolve the issues in your relationship. You may see a counselor or therapist, either alone or with your partner; you might speak with a pastor or priest; you might read books that you find helpful on conflict resolution, such as this one; you might just make a plan to sit down and talk with each other on a regular basis to keep trying to work out the issues coming to the surface. But in most cases, unless you have tried any or all of these endeavors, leaving is the least beneficial option.

If you do simply leave, what is likely to happen is that you will end up in a relationship in which you are struggling with the same or similar issues. You have not worked them out yet so they will follow you from one relationship to the next. In the meantime, you have the financial and emotional expense of starting over. Invest the time and energy necessary to try to resolve the issues you are dealing with in the first relationship. You will save yourself much grief and expense!

The Goal of Relationships

It would be beneficial to spend some time discussing the purpose or goal of relationships at this point. What are we looking for when we become involved in an intimate relationship with another person? What are we attempting to achieve or accomplish in doing this?

Relationships tend to be about meeting needs. Take a look back at Chapter Four where we talk about the basic needs we all have as human beings and the different ways we can meet them. Being in a relationship can help to meet many of those needs rather easily and conveniently.

For example, living with a partner can certainly meet our emotional and social needs. That goes without saying. It's an easy fix. But if we look a little more closely, a variety of other needs can be met in this relationship as well. We can feel a spiritual connection with our partner in a good relationship, thereby occasionally satisfying that need.

Further, a healthy sexual relationship can satisfy some of our physical needs. In addition, if our partner helps out with cooking and cleaning, this can help to satisfy our physical need for good food or fuel for our body and free up time so that we can invest in doing things to meet our creative and intellectual needs. Interesting conversations with our partner can challenge us intellectually as well. Therefore, an intimate relationship can do much to help us, as individuals, to meet our needs.

A caveat to this, however, is that you will want to avoid expecting that all of your needs will be met by this one relationship. Truthfully, demanding that this union meet all needs puts too much responsibility on the relationship to keep you happy. The relationship is then weighted down by that demand; these expectations are too heavy for one contact or partner to meet. This tends to lead to disappointment and conflict, rather that closeness and harmony. Therefore, be sure to balance your needs between and among relationships in your life. It is fine to expect that your partner will meet many of them, but guard against expecting her or this relationship to be the "be all and end all" for you.

The other factor that it is important to remember is that there are two people in this relationship. Therefore, there are two sets of needs to be met. Your partner has her own set of needs and desires as she is an independent entity as well.

For a harmonious fulfilling relationship, most persons will want to spend some time thinking about and focusing on the needs of their partner and how they can help to meet them. Remember, just as she cannot meet all of your needs, you cannot meet all of hers, either. Do not expect that of yourself. She will still need to spend time with friends and family that may not include you. This is not a detriment; it can only enhance the relationship.

If two persons are in a relationship and spend all of their time together in an attempt to meet all of each other's needs, one of them soon becomes redundant. It does not take long for one of them to disappear, either physically or emotionally. This is what is meant by enmeshment. So you will want to support the ways in which your partner goes about trying to meet her individual needs. Remember, your goal is to support her being happy and fulfilled in the relationship as well.

For many couples today is it simply too easy to walk away from a relationship. Partners don't need to stay together for the same reasons they did in the past. Both genders have greater freedoms in how they may support themselves and get what they need so that clinging to a bad relationship is not as necessary as it may have been in the past.

We don't mean to imply that there is not an emotional and financial cost involved in leaving a relationship; just that anyone who really wants out of a relationship can usually find a way to get there. If it isn't by filing for divorce, it may be just living separately until it is financially feasible to file papers. For this reason, you will want to be sure your partner is as happy and fulfilled in your relationship as you are so that she continues to want to be there.

Intimacy~Passion~Commitment

While we are on the issue of relationships, there is one other group of concepts we would like to explore. A healthy intimate relationship is composed of three key components all dependent on the issue of trust. Ideally, these should all be met or exist at approximately the same level.

Intimacy is the first component and comprises the sharing of thoughts, feelings, hopes, dreams, expectations, needs, values and beliefs. It is the feeling that your partner is also your best friend and that you can and want to share most things in your life with her.

Passion is the dating, romantic, sexual part of your relationship. It is the feeling that you are attracted to your partner and want to be sexual with her. It can also be described as the chemistry between you.

Commitment is the promise you make; the contract you keep. It can be made to a God or higher power in front of a pastor or priest, to a judge or justice of the peace or simply to yourself or your partner. But this is the contract you make to stay with the relationship both when things are easy and when they are not.

For a healthy, balanced relationship, you want relatively high and consistent levels of each component between you and your partner. If you have a relationship with intimacy and passion, you may have great sex and stay up talking and planning all night, but that's as far as it gets due to the lack of commitment. Eventually the relationship will fail because of a lack of follow through.

If you have intimacy and commitment, the component of passion or chemistry may be lacking and could cause you or a partner to seek attention elsewhere. Finally, if you have passion and commitment, your relationship may consist of great long term sex, but a true connection or meeting of the minds will be lacking. Any of these deficits can usually be endured in the short run, but most lead to either an ending of the relationship or chronic dissatisfaction if left unchecked for longer periods of time.

Underlying each of these components is the concept of trust. If you do not trust your partner, you will not feel comfortable being intimate or sexual with her for the long term, nor will you believe the commitment she offers you. A lack of trust eventually leads to either a major change or progress in a relationship or the ending of the relationship.

The "Good" Partner

When we get to talking about what we want in a partner, be aware that we all have expectations of what a good husband, wife, mother and father will be like that we have developed in childhood based on what we observed from the adults and families we were exposed to. These expectations can remain quite subconscious and cause trouble for us only as we become aware that our partner is not meeting them.

If you find that you are getting into conflict about roles in your relationship, focus on what you think are the characteristics of a "good partner" (i.e. faithful, loyal, good cook, sex partner, housekeeper, provider, nurturer, teacher, etc.). Once you have done so, use the communication and negotiation skills discussed in Chapters Nine and Ten to discuss these with your partner and explore the possibilities of negotiating a more fulfilling relationship for both of you.

Examples of an Imbalance of Power and Control

To further illustrate what an imbalance of power and control can look like, we would like to share a few other examples with you that we have experienced in our group work. Because our group is made up of men, all of these examples except the last involve men exercising inappropriate control over their partner. But, as you will see from the final example, men by no means have a lock on these types of expectations or actions.

The goal of most controlling behaviors is "to get what I want when I want it." Most often this is done through the process of intimidation, or threatening the safety or security a partner feels in the relationship. These behaviors often stem from feelings of powerlessness, anxiety, inadequacy and helplessness and the resulting attempt to control a partner is but a feeble attempt to resolve an uncomfortable situation. If you see yourself in any of these examples, please read over this chapter again so you can begin to take a look at the thinking that enables you to justify these types of actions. They can be very subtle, but are undoubtedly damaging your relationship more than you are aware.

⊕ Dan was first discussed in Chapter Two regarding a particularly disturbing situation in our community in which an 82 year old man, during an argument with his wife of 60 years, calmly took out his gun and shot her twice in the head. In response to police questioning, he quickly admitted, "Sure I did it…I just couldn't take it anymore." Dan cut the clipping out of the newspaper and hung it on the refrigerator in his home, telling his wife, "See, that's what happens…" Dan and his wife have since divorced.

⊕ In the beginning of Chapter Ten we will meet Marco, who in trying to prevent his estranged wife from taking off with his truck, picks up a railroad tie and proceeds to shatter the driver's side window as she is attempting to drive away.

⊕ And then we have Tiara, who wants to have her way in the relationship so badly, she prevents her partner from having access to keys to the car or apartment, so that if they get into an argument, he is unable to leave. However, if she wants him to get away, she has figured out she has only to call police and tell them she is afraid of him and she will get her wish. He stays in the relationship for the son they share.

These examples exhibit an attempt to exert an inappropriate level of control over a partner. Read through the summary on the next page to identify any lingering controlling beliefs you may be struggling with and the sections pertaining to those issues, then move on to Chapters Nine and Ten where we will discuss how to actually resolve conflict with a partner.

Remember:

"We cannot control the wind;
but we can adjust our sails."

~Anonymous

"Too Much of a Good Thing" Summary

☮About Relationships:
~Each partner in a healthy relationship must retain a measure
    of control.
~Early in a relationship the focus is on merging.
~Later, areas of conflict develop which lead to power struggles
    which must be resolved for the relationship to
    continue.

☮The following are unrealistic expectations in a relationship:
--A partner will/should be supportive at all times
--A partner will not do anything to upset or hurt me
--A partner will stop any behavior that makes me
    uncomfortable
--My partner should try to soothe me when I am upset
--I will always feel close to my partner and he to me.
--If I am upset about something, my partner should be
    upset about it too
--Couples should be able to negotiate and compromise on
    any issue if they love each other.
--If a couple knows how to communicate effectively, they
    should not have conflict or unresolved issues
--How my partner looks and acts reflects on me and she
    should be careful not to make me look bad.
--A good relationship is one without conflict
--Difficult relationships mean you chose the wrong partner
--If you are having relationship problems, leaving is your only
    option.

☮The following statements are true about relationships:
--The goal of a relationship is to meet some of our needs
--Good relationships require an equal measure of Intimacy,
    Passion and Commitment
--Roles in a healthy relationship should be negotiated.

Chapter 9

Everything and Nothing

Communication Styles in Relationships

Jeremiah *is sent to us after an arrest for threatening his wife with a firearm. "I didn't threaten her," are his first words, "I never said I was gonna shoot her."*

"What happened?" we ask, already knowing the answer.

"We were arguing again. Something about her always wanting to go out with her friends. I was just asking her a few simple questions, you know, like who was gonna be there, where they were going, what time she was going to get home, if she was attracted to any of the guys…All of a sudden she went off on me. Well, I just sat down and started cleaning my gun."

"Your gun?" we ask.

"Yeah, I like to keep it clean and in good shape. I learned that in the military."

"Can you see how that might send a threatening message to her – do what I want or I'll use this on you?" we suggest, trying to help him

to see what might have led to his arrest, if he is interested and open to it.

"I guess. She said she was scared," is the noncommittal reply.

Very often couples will come in for marital or relationship counseling and, when I ask them what they view as the most important difficulty in their relationship, they respond by saying, "Communication problems." This is a pet peeve of mine because we hear this phrase so often and the word "communication" is used so frequently and in so many settings, it has become virtually meaningless.

Most often, the couples I work with are communicating very effectively. What most of them mean by "communication problems" is "My partner doesn't agree with me!" or "She isn't doing what I want her to." For this reason, I always inquire about the details of these supposed "communication problems."

In one recent session, the young husband explained their communication problems as, "I want to have sex three times a week, while she would be content with once a month." There is no communication problem here. Each party has clearly conveyed his position and fully understands that of his partner. Their problem is conflict resolution, not communication.

If this is true for you as well, read over this chapter on communication, but then move on to the next, which focuses on healthy and positive negotiation techniques so that you and your partner can work out the issues upon which you disagree. Most likely if you have been together any length of time, you have a pretty clear understanding of your partner's position on many issues. Achieving a mutually satisfying compromise or solution, however, requires different skills, which are addressed in Chapter Ten.

What is Communication?

The ultimate authority on meaning, Webster's Dictionary, defines "communication" in many ways, but the definition most specifically appropriate for our discussion here is, "a giving or exchanging of information, signals, or messages by talk, gestures, writing, etc."

In truth, we are communicating all the time, whether it is with our partner, friends or strangers. We do this both intentionally and unintentionally. And, we communicate with words and silence, gestures and withdrawal, tone of voice and choice of words, facial expression and eye contact.

For example, you walk into a grocery store where you know no one. You do not make eye contact and change direction to walk away from anyone who begins to approach you. You are clearly communicating that you do not wish to have any interaction with these people you don't know. And you have not uttered a word. You may not be aware of the message you are sending—or, perhaps, you understand it perfectly.

Or, you walk in the door from work and your partner greets you with a cheery "Hi Honey!" and a smile. She is communicating that she is happy to see you. If you respond with a "Hmph!" and refuse to look up or make eye contact, then move on to the bedroom to change clothes, the message you are sending her is that you are not interested in chatting with her at the moment and, probably, that you are not in a very good mood altogether. Again, few words have been spoken, but both her message and yours are clear.

In reality, communication encompasses all of the messages we send out to the world at large, both verbal and nonverbal. These messages tend to dictate the responses we receive and, most often, the outcome we get from any situation we are involved in, those involving people and those that do not.

If you come home from work and your puppy greets you excitedly at the door, but you kick it away, you will train your puppy that you do not want its affection and it will begin to avoid you. This is the outcome you have chosen and set up for yourself. On the other had if you pet it affectionately and rub its tummy, it will most likely greet you every day. Again, you have created your own reality by your communication style.

The Importance of Our Awareness

It is important for each of us to be aware of how we are communicating so that we can make informed choices about how we are coming across and the outcomes we are seeking for ourselves. Just as the Event, Thought, Feeling Process helps us to make choices to achieve a desired outcome, being aware of the messages we are sending, both verbally and nonverbally, allows us to choose the response we are most likely to or want to receive from others.

In most cases, and this is no exception, awareness is power. It is only when we are aware of how we are being received that we are able to make changes if it is not getting us what we want. If we are pushing people away with our communication style, we want to know about this and look at the various components of our communication, so that, when we choose to, we can change some things and achieve a different outcome. If we are being walked on as we are not asking for what we want or are inviting others to refuse our requests, we are being too passive and knowing this, gives us the opportunity to change it.

For example, imagine you own a business. A new customer enters your establishment and requests a price quote on a product. You respond by saying loudly and intensely, "Well, ours is the best in the business so the price is high and you can't get it for a month but that's just the way it is. If you don't like it you can look somewhere else!" while getting very close and staring directly at them, daring them to question you further. Your new customer is likely to walk out the door. Most people don't like to be bullied, especially where money is involved.

On the other hand, if you respond with slouched shoulders, making no eye contact, by saying, "Well, our price is kind of high at $_____; do you think maybe you can pay that much or should I see if I can do better?" you are inviting the customer to respond with, "No, can you do any better?" You are being too passive.

If you can have someone watch you interact with people, or have a friend or partner that you trust give you feedback about your predominant communication style, you can learn to make changes that will get you more of what you want. It is important to get some impartial feedback, either from a partner or friend. If no one is willing or available to provide this, you can get this information by recording yourself on either a tape or video recorder so you can observe yourself directly. However, if no one is willing to give you feedback this is probably an indication that you are typically communicating pretty aggressively and those who know you don't consider it safe, emotionally or physically, to be honest with you. Set up your recorder as soon as you can!

We all use each of the following communication styles at one time or another, with the possible exception of the passive aggressive style as that tends to be a special and deceptive variation of the aggressive style. However, most of us have one style we use predominantly. Most people find that it benefits them to use an assertive style more often than not, as others tend to respond most positively to that type of communication. Therefore, you are likely to get consistently better outcomes if you can err on the side of using assertive communication techniques most consistently.

Communication Styles

Below are descriptions of the most common communication styles, along with real life examples of what each style can look like in everyday conversation. Read them over with an eye toward identifying which style you believe you use most commonly. Once you have determined which that is, ask your partner, if you are in a relationship, or someone else you trust, such as a friend or family member, if you are not currently involved with a partner, to read them and give you that feedback as well.

Again, if you find others unwilling to do this, you may be erring on the side of communicating aggressively more often than not and will want to explore some type of electronic recording means to enable you to observe yourself in communication with others. If others will be recorded as well, be sure to inform them of the fact and secure their approval.

As we explore each style, I will describe what they look and sound like in terms of choice of language, tone of voice, body language, gestures, etc. in order to give you a true feel for the communication that occurs. Each description will then be followed by an example to illustrate an actual situation in which it was used. It is my hope that in this manner you will develop the ability to easily identify these communication styles, whether you are using them or witnessing someone else use them. Only when you can easily identify these styles in practice will you be able to make choices about how you want to be perceived by people you are communicating with.

Aggressive

The message given or implied in an aggressive communication is "I'm OK—you are not OK." Another form of this is the idea that "any differences between us are bad and when you don't agree with me, you are wrong." The aggressive communicator sees the world in terms of win-lose situations and always positions himself to win, even at the expense of others. The world view of this person is that the outside world "dumps all over me" and I lash back at the world.

The aggressive communicator tends to be threatening, punishing and blaming, in that he often refuses to take responsibility for his own actions or decisions. He uses power to his advantage and attempts to get his way by making threats and being forceful and demanding. He also tends to minimize his role in any negative behavior and to be controlling and defensive. The aggressive person is often feared and resorts to humiliating and sarcastic responses to get his way.

The tone of voice used is typically some combination of loud, threatening, demanding or forceful. There is often a "tone" or attitude associated with these communications. The aggressive person often uses profanity and his gestures tend to be threatening, such as a fist in the air or a finger pointed in the face. Body language tends to be closed and very tense. He may also resort to a dirty look or the evil eye to get others to fall into line. Any physical contact tends to be abusive and threatening as well.

The aggressive person's focus is to beat out others and get what he wants at all costs. He chooses **FOR** others and they know it; he does not hesitate to step on their rights in order to enforce his. He gets what he is entitled to and then some. He puts himself up by putting others down and his defensive pattern is outright attack. In terms of responding to a situation, the aggressive communicator tends to over-react.

My favorite example of an aggressive communicator is Jesse, a former member of our Anger Management Group:

> *Jesse is an extremely intimidating person, but is only partially aware of this fact. He bullies to get his way, but is not completely cognizant of why people go along or agree with him. On some level, he seems to feel he is just entitled to get things his way. Jesse is a very large man, standing about 6'5" and easily weighing over 350 pounds. In addition, he has a deep, booming voice that tends to get both louder and deeper when he is excited. One evening, our office manager had left me a note to let Jesse know that he owed $30 on his bill. As he came in the door, I smiled and greeted him and he responded positively. However, as I introduced the subject of the payment with him, he became immediately defensive and responded loudly with, "What do you mean I owe an extra $30? That's not fair! This is all I can pay!" I explained where the bill had come from and he merely walked away and into the group room with a growl of "Hrrmph!" If he reacts to this extent to a polite business contact, I can only imagine how intimidating and aggressive he can be with an intimate partner in a conflict at home.*

Jesse is classic in his aggressive communication style, however. His defensive response and verbal attack in reaction to some unwelcome news, even on a business level, was designed to get his way, i.e., to get me to back down. When that didn't happen, he was aggressive again and cut off the contact. I will tell you he did make the payment eventually, but never ceased to complain about it, making his case until the end.

Someone less experienced with the aggressive personality, might have been tempted to let it go. I suspect that many persons often acquiesce in response to an aggressive person. It is often easier and less painful than asking for what is legitimately due from him.

Passive

Passive communication takes a one-down position and typically contains the message "You're OK — I'm not OK." The focus in disagreements is that any difference between us is bad and I am either wrong or at fault in some way. The passive persons sees life in terms of win-lose situations as does the aggressive communicator; the difference is that the passive person is always in the "lose" position and expects this. The world view of this person is that the outside world "dumps all over me" and I expect this and allow it to happen as external forces, such as others, life and stress, control my life.

Quite the opposite of the aggressive person, the passive communicator tends to feel threatened, punished and blamed for negative events. He also tends to see himself as responsible for negative outcomes and to be dependent, controlled and fearful, typically harboring many guilt feelings for his lack of assertiveness. He tends to be acquiescing and manipulative. He procrastinates and lives his life by "shoulds:" "I should do this, I should do that." Due to his passivity, however, he puts off taking any action. He tends to be insecure, has few opinions and tends to be self-effacing and resentful of others who get more of what they want.

The passive communicator's tone of voice is typically meek, soft and submissive. He may have a tendency to slouch or cower and usually makes little eye contact. He qualifies his communications with submissive terms, such as "Perhaps we should do such and such" or "Maybe this would be a solution." Body language is withdrawn, slouched or cowering and he tends to shy away from physical contact and keep to himself.

When responding to a challenge, rather than attack or assert, the passive person either flees or gives in. Socially, he puts others up by putting himself down; again, the opposite of his aggressive counterpart. He tends to be a wonderful martyr and, in decision-making, his reality is that others choose for him and he lets them. As a result, he under-reacts to challenges he is facing. When he does succeed, it is because he has lucked out rather than taken action to allow himself to succeed. He does not get what he is entitled to and does not enforce his rights, but allows others to infringe upon them.

The example I offer involves an individual client I have known for many years who I will call Amy:

> *After many years without a partner, Amy was being courted by a man who lives in her apartment complex. An extremely passive person, Amy would never have approached Sam, even though she had found him attractive. When she told me about the relationship, Sam had invited Amy to dinner on two occasions at his apartment, once inviting her up for shrimp and the other, ordering out pizza. "Well, how was it?" I asked her, curious about this new development in her life. "It was OK," she started, hesitantly, "I like him and enjoy his company. But I don't really like shrimp and the pizza was sausage and I don't really care for that either." "Did you tell him that you didn't like shrimp when he invited you? Or that you would prefer some other type of pizza when he was ordering?" "No, I just ate it; I didn't want to make a fuss."*

I suspect that Sam, like most of us in a similar situation, would just prefer for Amy to be honest about her preferences. After all, if the relationship is to continue, he will eventually learn these things about her anyway. The difference between Amy and Emma, who is discussed under the passive aggressive heading, is that Amy ate the food without stating her preferences, but also without complaint. Emma would probably have eaten food also, but then criticized the food and choices after the fact.

Assertive

The message in assertive communication is one of acceptance: "I'm OK and you're OK." Another way this can be expressed is by the attitude that any differences between us are just differences, not good or bad, right or wrong and nothing more or less. Difference is OK. The assertive communicator seeks win-win situations in most every case and looks to find a way that everyone can succeed. The world view of this person is that life goes on as it must, but ups and downs are handled from an internal sense of self-control. In other words, some days you get the elevator; some days you get the shaft.

Assertive communications and communicators tend to be engaged in negotiation and compromise when conflict is presented and are powerful by using their own internal controls. Rather than threatening, punishing or blaming, he knows how to say no and set limits for himself. He lives life on his own terms and by choice and chooses to look for mutually agreeable solutions to problems. He is opinionated but respectful of others. He is careful to accept responsibility for his own actions and lives life by the Serenity Prayer:

"God grant me the courage to change what I can
The serenity to accept what I cannot change and
The wisdom to know the difference."

The assertive person's tone of voice is typically confident yet respectful. He maintains appropriate eye contact and comfortable facial expressions. Gestures tend to be open, relaxed and comfortable; body language is open and accepting. If there is physical contact, it is appropriately warm and reassuring, such as a hand on the arm or shoulder that expresses support. Words used are courteous, accepting and respectful and in responding to any situation, the assertive person evaluates the circumstances, makes a choice for himself, but not for anyone else, then takes action. He is not about forcing or imposing his will on others but is accepting of differences between them.

Socially, he puts himself up, expressing healthy self-confidence, but does not do so at the expense of others as the aggressive communicator does. When he wins, he does so honestly, not because he beat others down, and, rather than over-reacting as the aggressive person does, he acts directly and appropriately for the situation at hand. He enforces his rights but does so with respect for the rights of others and takes only what he is entitled to.

The example we offer here is of our youngest daughter, Meghan, with regard to an incident that occurred when she was about ten years old:

> *Meghan has always had an uncanny sense about dealing with people. One day she was asking me to buy her an inexpensive item that she wanted from a local store. We were saving money for our upcoming family vacation, so my response was, "No, not today." Without missing a beat, Meghan looked up at me and responded, in a very pleasant tone of voice, devoid of attitude, "Mom, I know we're saving money for our trip, but it would really mean a lot to me if we could get this for me today. I will do extra chores to help out around the house. Please can we get it?" How could I refuse? She was practicing a life skill that I wanted to encourage her to use. I also advised my oldest daughter, Kate, who was 17 at the time and had witnessed the entire interchange that she could learn a thing or two from her baby sister, as she tended to use a more aggressive communication style at this time in her life.*

Passive Aggressive

The passive aggressive communication style is actually a variation of the aggressive style, but borrows behaviors from the passive approach to manipulate a given situation. An individual using this style may have learned to communicate aggressively, but received messages that this was unacceptable or learned that it did not have the desired effect in certain situations.

The passive aggressive person pretends to be very compliant, appearing for all intents and purposes as a passive communicator, refusing to stand up for himself or assert his rights or privileges. This goes on until either the individual can no longer maintain this approach or something happens to force him to lash out. Other times, this is planned all along, playing at passive and then attacking others when they feel you are an easy mark or just a nice easy-going person.

The example I offer here is of a woman I met when she was elderly who I will call Emma:

> *Emma had grown up during the depression with all of the destructive messages about what nice girls should and shouldn't do. On the surface Emma appeared sweet and accepting. Underneath however, she had the claws of a tiger. As an example, when being invited out to dinner and asked where she wanted to eat, she would sweetly reply, "Oh I don't care, dear. You choose. I would be happy to go anywhere." The restaurant is chosen by her companion, but shortly after arrival, Emma pronounces the service as lousy and,"Oh, it's so smoky in here. And the wait! Will we **ever** get a table?" When ordering her meal, Emma is asked what type of dressing she would like on her salad. She responds sweetly to the waitress, "Oh it doesn't matter, dear, what ever you choose will be fine." Once the salad arrives, however, the dressing is too salty or she doesn't like the taste of it. And on and on and on.*

On the surface and to outsiders, passive aggressive people seem very sweet and unassuming. Once you spend time with them, however, you may find yourself wanting to head for the hills as it can be extremely frustrating on many levels. Even addressing the passive aggressive behavior directly does not work; the communicator always has an excuse or a reason for his behavior. And they are far better at playing the martyr than even the passive communicator. Just remember, there is a price to pay.

This person should be viewed as similar to the aggressive communicator, only sneakier and more underhanded. They are much harder to pin down as they will most often deny their anger and unhappiness. The aggressive person will often admit he is power hungry and self-centered. The passive aggressive communicator will be all sweetness and kindness, even when confronted, denying any negative feelings. They can be incredibly difficult and frustrating to deal with.

If you are in a position of communicating with someone like this, understand that most passive aggressive people harbor strong and longstanding feelings of anger, hurt and frustration. Your only hope of helping them to understand how they are coming across is to get them in touch with those long buried feelings. But for someone in her later years, like Emma, who has relied on these tactics for most of her life, the hope of making any true lasting change, unless she is strongly motivated to do so, is slim. Good Luck!

Use of Communication Styles

As previously stated, we each use all of these various communication styles, with the possible exception of the passive aggressive style, as that is a unique and specialized variation of the aggressive approach. It takes a certain amount of cunning and manipulation to pull that off successfully; one must be quite motivated to use it and most persons will not sufficiently value such deceptive communication to put the time and effort into staying three steps ahead of persons they are dealing with.

For the rest of us, however, we need not swear off all communication styles other than the assertive. There are times when it makes sense to respond passively. For example, in a large group of people, it may be wise to sit back and accept information that is being given and wait to have questions answered in a more private manner. Or to go along for awhile to see what happens in a given situation before asserting your preferences.

With regard to the aggressive choice, I would maintain that, with the possible exception of an immediate physical attack or threat, it is always better to use an assertive approach, rather than aggressive. I believe you are more likely to get what you are looking for and can feel better about your methods, with an assertive response.

Give some thought and do some research into your typical communication style. If it is not assertive, think carefully about what you could modify (tone of voice, choice of words, body language, gestures, etc.) to change it to more of an assertive approach. Then try it out and watch what happens. But above all, develop the awareness of the style you are using to communicate so that you can make more conscious choices about how you want to be perceived.

Silence As Communication

Often when couples come to me for marital counseling and we get into that all-important "communication problems" discussion, I will hear the complaint that one partner doesn't talk. Most often, the complaint sounds something like the following: "He comes home from work and doesn't say anything. I ask him what's wrong and he says, 'Nothing.' Then when we sit down to talk about our relationship, he doesn't talk to me! I don't know what to do." Her partner will often respond, "I just don't have anything to say."

Make no mistake about it: silence **is** a form of communication. What it means, however, can be difficult to determine and may depend on the individual using it and/or the incident in which it is being used. When silence is an issue in a relationship, couples need to have a conversation, either on their own or with a neutral third party, such as a therapist or counselor, to discuss what it means. In this way it can be accepted and appreciated and need not present a threat to the relationship.

Silence can have several or multiple meanings, however, and I want to discuss those briefly here. In this way, when you get to the point of having this conversation, you will have a bit of direction to guide your conversation. The following are the most common meanings of silences:

☮ Timing is a Problem

Timing may be causing the silence if, for example the children are playing in the next room or either partner is about to leave for work or to go out for the evening. The silent partner may then just be choosing to put off the discussion for a more convenient time.

A simple solution may be to say something such as, "I would like to talk to you because our relationship is important to me, but why don't we set a time to do it that's more convenient for all of us." Notice I have not said anything unduly negative or threatening. Comments that threaten either the partner or the relationship are provocative and abusive and should never be used as grounds to change the timing of a conversation.

☮ It's Not Safe to Talk—Either Physically or Emotionally

Women tend to fear for their physical safety while men tend to be more afraid of an emotional outburst. If there has been a history of violence in the relationship and the female partner is asked, "What's wrong?" she may be reluctant to say anything for fear of being physically hurt. On the other hand, women are more likely to react emotionally during a discussion about the relationship. Many men have an aversion to tears and will bend over backwards to avoid saying anything that might lead their female partner to cry. This could be causing his silence. Or, perhaps his partner has a history of becoming verbally aggressive when she hears something she doesn't like. This, also, may prevent her partner from opening up to her.

If you are the partner who is trying to avoid the outburst, choose a "no-problem" moment to be honest with your spouse. Tell her you want to be able to talk with her about your relationship, but you want it to be safe to do so. You can also look ahead to the next chapter and use some of the ideas in the Negotiation and Partnership section to have this conversation. If you are a female partner who is afraid of a physical reaction, please have this conversation only in the presence of a neutral third party who can help to enhance your safety, such as a counselor or therapist.

☮ I Don't Have the Words or Skill to Tell You What I'm Thinking or Feeling

This response is more likely to come from a male, than a female partner. Women are socialized to be focused on relationships and to be able to talk at length about them, as well as our thoughts and feelings about how it is going. Most men don't have this experience and many reach adulthood without any clue about how to identify, much less talk to a partner about their feelings or relationship.

If you are a male and this is how you are feeling, be honest with your partner. She can help you learn how to have these conversations and model for you how to do this. This can make the difference between having a healthy, lasting partnership or a marriage that ends in divorce. It's really that important.

☮ Really, Nothing is Wrong

If you are silent, but everything is fine, please tell this to your partner in a reassuring manner. If you say this, however, your actions should support it. Don't tell your partner that everything is fine, then in the next breath ask if she's ever thought about seeing other people. Use this only if you are fine with how the relationship is going.

A simple variation is, "I'm fine about the relationship; I just had a rough day at work, lousy night's sleep, stomach virus, etc." But be honest. Don't use this as a tactic to avoid a meaningful and necessary conversation with your partner.

☮ I'm Angry and I'm Punishing You With Silence

Using silence to punish a partner when you are angry is inappropriate and abusive. If you use this tactic, please review Chapter Two on abuse and violence in relationships before continuing and make a pact not to use this technique again. There are many appropriate times to use silence; this is not one of them.

☮ I'm Not Sure What I'm Thinking, Feeling

Sometimes it takes us some time to sort out what we are thinking or feeling. If we try to rush into talking with our partner before we have it all figured out, we can end up doing more harm and causing more pain, than necessary. Give yourself the time to think through your feelings before discussing them with your partner so that you can articulate what you are needing and why.

⊕ I'm Just Not Ready to Talk

A variation of the above is that I may think I know what I am feeling, but am just not ready to share it yet. This is an appropriate reason to delay the conversation wit your partner. However, you will want to say something like, "I'm still working on sorting out what is going on with me and I'm not ready to talk about it yet. When I've got it sorted out, I will let you know and we can set up a time to talk."

If you can, say something reassuring to your partner, such as, "Don't worry; I'm not thinking of leaving. I just have some things I'd like us to discuss." If you can't reassure your partner, please work on getting yourself ready to talk as quickly as possible to avoid causing her any undue worry or misery.

Misunderstandings

A couple who experiences regular misunderstandings truly does have a communication problem. The problem may be one of needing to listen better to each other. Or, it may be repeatedly interpreting events and statements in the most negative manner possible. Consider the following example:

> *A man is driving down the road. A woman is driving down the same road from the opposite direction. As they pass each other, the woman leans out the window and yells, "PIG!!" The man immediately leans out his window and yells, "BITCH!!" They each continue on their way and, as the man rounds the next curve, he crashes into a huge pig standing in the middle of the road.*

This is one of those email "forwards" that seem to circulate regularly. I received this one from my sister several years ago. However, because it does a rather exceptional job making the point it does, we have incorporated it into the unit on communication unit that we do in our group.

Misunderstandings can cause a great deal of relationship stress at home and at work. To avoid this, when communication is important, practice repeating back to the speaker what you heard them say. For example: *"Let me see if I understand you clearly. You said......"* or *"You feel* _____ *because* _____."

If the example above seems to summarize your experience with your partner, either one or both of you may want to seek counseling or therapy to see what you can do to change this experience. Or, perhaps, just reading the example above and trying out the repetition technique can teach you to interpret conversations you have with each other in the most generous light possible in an effort to reduce your frustration and improve your relationship.

Obstacles to Support and Open Communication in Relationships

Open, assertive communication enhances support and trust in relationships. Most often that is our goal. There are persons and occasions, however, when we may be seeking to muddy the waters or be less than open because we are afraid that support and closeness will require further changes on our part. Maybe we fear that we will have to give up time with our friends or hobbies that we enjoy. We may be frightened of making the anticipated change or actually quite comfortable in spite of the conflict and the possibility of having to change keeps us stuck.

If you are in that type of a situation, and apprehensive of change for that reason, know that taking the risk and attempting to make the changes most often results in a closer, more fulfilling relationship even if the initial change is difficult or uncomfortable. Further, using the negotiation skills outlined in Chapter Nine you should be able to achieve a balance between your needs and those of your partner. If your goal is a close, healthy relationship, take the risk and make the changes.

Communication Summary

☮I find that I am communicating primarily in the following communication style:

___Aggressive   ___Assertive

___Passive   ___Passive Aggressive

☮My evidence for this is:_____

_____

☮I want to make a change so that I communicate more often in the _____ communication style. The behaviors I am looking at changing include: _____

_____

_____

☮I find myself using silence at the following times:

___Timing is a Problem   ___I Don't Have the Words

___It's Not Safe to Talk: ___Nothing is Wrong

    ___Emotionally   ___I'm Angry & Punishing

    ___Physically   ___I'm Not Ready to Talk

___I'm Not Sure What I'm Thinking or Feeling

☮My Partner and I have Misunderstandings Regularly. This is what we are planning to do to minimize them:

___Listen More Closely   ___Check Out Assumptions

___Repeat Statements   ___See a Therapist

☮My Partner and I will do the following to increase the level of Support and Open Communication:_____

_____

_____

_____

"Ninety percent of the friction of daily life is caused by the wrong tone of voice."

~Anonymous

Chapter 10

My Way or No Way

The Concepts of Negotiation and Partnership

Following up the concept of power and control with those of negotiation and partnership, Marco comes to mind. Marco was arrested as his marriage was ending. His wife had sold several of their vehicles without his agreement and he came out of his home one day only to find her about to drive off in his truck.

"So, how did you get arrested?" we ask Marco as he explains the story to us.

"Well, I tried to get into the truck to stop her, but she locked the doors, so I picked up a piece of wood and popped the window out so I would open the door."

"Where did you get the wood?" we ask, patiently, knowing the story from the police report, but wanting the rest of the group to hear it from Marco.

"Well, it was a railroad tie that we were going to use for landscaping. It was laying nearby."

"When you say you 'popped' the window out, do you mean it all came out in one piece," we probe again.

"No, it broke," is the reply.

"Do you mean it cracked in two or how did it break?" we ask again.

"Well, actually, it shattered all over the place," is the now meeker response, *"But I **had** to stop her from taking it."*

"Do you think that could have been frightening, to be in a truck and see a railroad tie coming at you and the window shattering?" we ask again.

"Yeah, I guess it could have been," Marco finally admits.

"Can you think of any other way you could have worked that out between yourselves?" we inquire.

"Yeah, we probably could have worked it out through the divorce process, I guess," is the reply.

If we accept, as we discussed in Chapter Eight, that conflict in a relationship is inevitable and even healthy, we have to decide what to do when it happens to us. You could respond as Marco did and very aggressively insist on getting your way. But be aware there are legal and emotional consequences to acting as he did. True, his relationship was all but over, but he had extensive legal expenses, was required to attend our group and had an extremely limited placement schedule with his children as a result of his actions. There is a better way.

Negotiating the Negotiable

But before we get to the techniques of negotiation, we must be sure that this issue we are trying to negotiate is, in fact, negotiable. So before we get to the practice of negotiation, we want to explore different types of issues that couples face and how we will know if it is an appropriate subject for a negotiation.

What is Negotiable?

An issue is open to negotiation between partners if it is not entirely one person's right to make the decision. If only one of the partners has the right to decide a particular issue, it may be open to discussion with the other partner, but not negotiation.

Many couples get themselves into a bind by attempting to negotiate what are actually individual issues. Individual issues are those that it is the responsibility and right of one or the other to decide. A controlling partner, however, often has little trouble making a case that as these issues have an indirect impact on him or the relationship, they should be negotiated and often the reasoning behind this is that "I should get my way."

While many individual issues do have an indirect impact on a relationship, any actual decision making should rest with the individual as the outcome will have a direct impact on her level of happiness and satisfaction within the relationship. In addition, it will also affect the number of her needs being met. Let me give you some examples.

If my partner hates his job and is miserable there, it should be solely within his control whether or not he leaves it and searches for a different occupation or employer. If he truly desires to make such a change, it is for him to decide. His needs and happiness are at stake.

If a partner wants to go back to school to pursue additional education or training, it should be solely up to that individual whether or not that happens. Again, her happiness and fulfillment is dependent on her needs being met. If she is wanting to pursue an education or different line of work, that should be her decision.

But what about the family who depends on her income, I am asked? Read on. There is a difference between offering feedback and actually making a final decision.

Decision-Making vs. Feedback

When we are in a relationship, it is acceptable and necessary for open communication and a healthy relationship to discuss issues that concern the relationship and even offer feedback to our partner with regard to issues that are solely within her realm to decide. This is simply a part of a healthy relationship.

That does not mean, however, that if you offer negative feedback regarding an issue, your partner must direct her decision in accordance with your wishes. Feedback is simply that: an opportunity to share your opinion with your partner. The ultimate decision must lie with her.

For example, if you dislike your partner's friends, it is acceptable and appropriate to share that with her. Her choice to spend time with them, however, remains with her. And remember, it would be a controlling behavior to hit her with 20 questions about the time she spends with them upon her return. That would eventually have the effect of causing her to choose to isolate herself, rather than enduring another round of interrogation when she gets home.

You would most likely eventually get your wish; at some point if this behavior continues she would probably choose not to spend time with her friends, but at the price of her isolation, resentment and most likely emotional distance. Do you begin to understand how all of these behaviors and issues are inextricably linked?

If she thus finds herself unfulfilled and unable to meet her needs in this relationship, her logical choice is to begin to think about leaving it—again, the opposite outcome of what you are looking for. Therefore, once you have discussed the situation and offered your feedback, you must back off and accept her decision.

We have included our checklist entitled "Whose Decision Is It, Anyway?" in Appendix H. Please look it over and complete it to the best of your ability. If you are currently in a relationship, have your partner complete one as well, but both of you do it separately. Then share your responses and discuss the results.

Mutual Agreement

The principles listed above are guidelines that work best in a healthy growing relationship in which both partners are committed to each other. If, after an honest discussion with your partner, you both agree that a different rule or expectation works best for your relationship, you are free to set another guideline. Just be certain that if you do choose to vary from these recommendations, you are both in true agreement that the new rule is best. Take care to ascertain that neither of you is pressuring the other to go along with a more controlling arrangement in order to maintain peace in the relationship.

For true compromise to exist, both parties should feel free to bargain in good faith and safety. Using the negotiation guidelines outlined below can help to ascertain a true "meeting of the minds" if you are looking to develop guidelines that work best for your relationship.

Guidelines for Fair Negotiation

The following represent the guidelines we have developed to share with our group to teach them how to work through an issue that arises in an intimate relationship and reach a mutually satisfying solution. These guidelines will also work in other negotiations as well, probably with even more success, because the greatest difficulty most of us have in negotiating is reaching agreements with an intimate partner. This is because, again, that person touches us more deeply than anyone else in our lives. We are also most often quite emotionally invested in the outcome of these conversations, where with our friends and employers, we may not be as emotionally connected to the issue being discussed.

Negotiate by Mutual Consent—the Timing Issue

When you are seeking to negotiate an issue with a partner, both of you must be willing and able to participate fully in the process. Do not start a discussion at a time when one or both of you are not truly available to invest yourselves in the task. Couples who do this are just creating an invitation to disaster.

A bad time would be when either of you is already angry, rushed, tired, hungry, distracted or otherwise already dealing with a negative or difficult emotion. Additionally, if one of you is headed out the door to get to work on time or headed up to bed, it is the wrong time for such a discussion.

Instead, agree to discuss the issue at a mutually agreeable time when you are both likely to be in a good frame of mind, you are alone together and will both have the time for a meaningful discussion. A good discussion demands two ready and willing participants.

Another component of the timing issue may be that some preparation needs to take place before the discussion should happen. If you are discussing how much of your annual income each of you wishes to put into a savings account, you may need to postpone the discussion until you can collect the necessary documentation needed to make a reasoned decision, such as pay stubs, savings account statements, documentation of other financial obligations, etc. Forcing this discussion to occur prematurely could simply waste time and lead to hard feelings.

Set the Rules

Once you have determined that it is a good time for the discussion you want to have, the next step would be to sit down with your partner and set some ground rules for your negotiation. After you have done this one time, you can always refer back to the same set of guidelines each time you have a talk, but this first time, put some effort into laying out the expectations each of you has with regard to how this conversation will proceed.

When you have set a series of guidelines or ground rules, should one of them happen to be violated or broken during the course of the negotiation, the best choice would be to stop the discussion immediately and set another time to conclude it. Violating rules that have been mutually set indicates that one or both of you is operating primarily in your emotional brain and from a reactive standpoint. Little good is likely to be accomplished at that point. It's best to err on the safe side and pick it up another time. Remember, you have the rest of your lives together. Don't make the mistake of rushing to resolve an issue only to further damage the relationship.

The following are some guidelines that work for most couples. Feel free to adapt or modify them as you wish, as long as the changes are mutually agreeable to both of you.

1) Discuss, Don't Yell

As indicated in Chapter Seven on Emotional Regulation, the best discussions between couples happen when both are speaking and interacting calmly and respectfully. Accordingly, your goal should be that each of you gets to say what you think and that you will both speak in a calm tone of voice. You are trying to have a discussion to resolve a problem. When a couple is yelling at each other, both are talking and nobody is listening.

As we discussed previously, listening is the most important communication skill that we can use. Accordingly, we will want to be doing more listening and thinking than talking in this discussion. If you can take the time to truly hear what your partner is saying, you have a much better chance of happening upon a solution that meets both of your needs.

To that end, you will also want to make sure that each of you gets a chance to speak. Often in couples, one partner is more verbally skilled than the other. Many times this is the female partner, but this is not always true.

If the more skilled partner goes on at length and the other person feels he never gets a chance to talk he will stop listening and the negotiation will end. He may go along with what the talker is pushing for, but it will not be the type of result or solution that both will be able to live with long term. It may also result in bitterness, resentment or passive aggressive noncompliance on the part of the less talkative partner.

2) Stick to the Present

When you are negotiating an issue, do not bring up events that have happened in the past to add fuel to the fire. If there is a previous incident that still remains unresolved, set a separate time to discuss and resolve it to the extent that both of you will be able to put it to rest. If your partner is still raising an issue from the past, that is a sign that it remains unresolved for her, even if you had felt it was behind you as a couple.

Many of our group members complain that their partners keep bringing things up from the past. When questioned further, they admit that they had not really discussed or resolved the issue, just hoped it would go away. This usually does not work because if an issue is unresolved for one person in a relationship it is unresolved for the entire relationship.

Put some effort into finding an acceptable solution that both of you can live with, then agree that it is over. At that point, neither of you should again raise the issue unless it arises in a new situation.

3) One Issue at a Time

This is another common problem with which many couples struggle. They start with an issue that has been raised, and during the discussion, one partner, usually the one who is feeling defensive about his role in this situation, will raise a completely unrelated issue on which the couple is conflicted. It may sound like this:

Her: I feel hurt when you tell me you'll be home for dinner but show up two hours late.

Him: (feeling defensive): Well, what about the time you stayed out until two in the morning with that trampy girlfriend of yours. (he raises a completely different issue — her staying out late in the evening and spending time with a friend he doesn't care for — her individual decisions, remember?)

Her: (She now decides to get into the fray with:) Well, what about the time you stayed out until 5 am then drove home drunk?

We now have a third issue in the mix and are no closer to resolving the first issue than when we started. In addition, we now have some hurt feelings to be soothed and it would be best to postpone any attempt at constructive discussion to another time. If this process continues, this couple will never get anywhere; all problems and issues of concern will remain unresolved creating further emotional distance and one will probably choose to leave, either emotionally or physically.

Couples who deal with conflict this way are doing a dance. They are waltzing around one issue, then another, but not spending enough time with any of them to truly resolve anything. Eventually they just get tired of getting nowhere and end the discussion.

To truly resolve a conflictual issue, you must limit each discussion to just one issue. If a new issue arises during the course of a discussion already in progress, acknowledge it and consciously save it for a later time. If you need to, make a list of other issues for later discussions. In this way you will be able to devote your entire attention and focus to finding the best solution for the issue at hand, thereby increasing your likelihood of success and relationship satisfaction.

4) Stay Above the Belt

When we live with or are intimately involved with a partner, we learn how best to hurt them. We come to know where they are vulnerable and how best to put them in their place. If we use this information to get our way in a negotiation, we may win the battle, by getting them to go along with us, but we will probably lose the war.

Unkind, hurtful statements about your partner's character, appearance, personality, or family only lead to anger and retaliation. This technique does not engender the closeness and trust we are seeking, but breeds resentment and emotional distance, the very things that lead to a dissatisfying or terminated relationship. Remember, our goal is peace, gentleness and a mutually satisfying solution.

5) No Violence

Physical and emotional attacks violate all of the above rules and completely eliminate the mutual consent necessary for an honest discussion. They void any positive resolutions that can result from such a discussion and lead to further damage in the relationship.

The Process of Negotiation

Now that we have set some ground rules for our discussion and talked some about what not to do, let's focus on how you want to proceed. The following ideas are well-known components of the negotiation process, whether it is occurring in a business or employment setting or in an intimate relationship. Read them over and, in your next discussion with your partner, see how many of them you can follow.

1) Look 'Em in the Eye

Go into a negotiation session with the expectation that you will both give and receive respect. Expect to be treated respectfully by the person you are speaking with and that you will treat her with respect as well. In the event your partner is not being respectful to you, do not use that as an excuse to treat her disrespectfully. Do not let her actions dictate yours. You are free to choose to take the high road even if she chooses to grovel in the dirt. In the event of abusive behavior, however, I would end the discussion and set it for another time.

As part of treating each other with respect you will want to both be comfortable, preferably sitting side by side or at right angles to each other, if possible. Seating yourselves directly opposite each other is a more aggressive, confrontational stance and often leads to conflictual discussion.

Work to listen as your partner speaks and strive to make eye contact when you are talking. Take care to set up your environment so that you are alone in the room and any distractions, such as the television and telephone are eliminated. Men tend to be more visually stimulated than women, so will usually have a greater difficulty maintaining eye contact with a partner when a television is within view. Men, do not feel defensive or blamed by this; it's how you are programmed. Just take care to eliminate these distractions in conversations that are important to you.

To this day, even after being married 18 years, Terry and I have to make sure he is facing away from a television if we happen to be eating in a restaurant that has one in order for us to be able to have a conversation—even if the program is one he has no interest in. Once you understand these things about your partner, you can choose not to take them personally. After all, it is not about me; he would be doing the same thing with any one!

So, set the stage for your discussion to increase the likelihood of success. Seat yourselves appropriately and eliminate all the distractions you can. Then expect to be treated with respect and to return the favor.

2) Own Your Own Stuff

While we will discuss this more fully in Chapter Eleven which deals with honesty and accountability in relationships, in general, it bears mention here that in order to negotiate an issue and reach a solution, you must each take responsibility for what you bring to the table. Own up to your own idiosyncrasies and work on your own issues. If you have had a former partner who was unfaithful to you, recognize and admit that you may be more sensitive to that possibility occurring in this relationship than the next person. By the same token, recognize that it is your issue to deal with; your problem to solve. Don't expect your partner to make it go away.

By the same token, accept your stuff but not that of your partner. Understand that some of the issues are hers as well. We can come into a relationship as a co-dependent person, comfortable with taking responsibility for all the issues in our relationships. Thus we can prevent our partner from taking responsibility for her own issues. Take care not to make that mistake either. Both can prevent the relationship from being all it can be.

3) Come Back to It If You Must

If you can, bring your discussion to a mutual conclusion. Take the time to resolve it to everyone's satisfaction. If you do not, it will just resurface again and again.

However, if the situation seems irresolvable on the first, or even the second or third attempt, do no hesitate to take a time out and plan to come back to it another time. These issues aren't created for either of you overnight. It is unrealistic to expect them to be resolved in a half hour. Some of the larger issues may require many attempts before they are reasonably settled. But don't despair; the end result is worth the effort.

4) Use "I Statements" to Define the Problem

One important concept in beginning the discussion is to state the problem. The person who most strongly views the situation as a problem should take responsibility for putting into words why it bothers him. This should be done in a calm, non-blaming fashion.

A helpful technique in stating a problem is the use of what are called "I Statements." This is nothing more than a feeling statement with a reason attached. For example, "I'm hurt that you came home late for dinner. " The sentence starts with the word "I" followed immediately by a feeling word. To refresh our memories, feeling words are those that state actual feelings, such as hurt, scared, frustrated, anxious, confused, irritated, upset, jealous, angry and the like.

If "angry" is the feeling that jumps into your sentence, try to dig a little deeper to understand the primary emotion. Remember, anger is a feeling that comes second. Typically arriving before the anger are feelings such as hurt, fear and frustration. You will gain more out of the experience if you are able to identify the true underlying emotion.

Also, if you are tempted to add the words "that" or "like" after your feeling word, be aware that you are stating a thought, not a feeling. An example of this would be, "I feel like you are a jerk!" Go back to the drawing board and try again. A likely candidate in this case might be "I'm frustrated that..."

5) If Appropriate, Identify Long and Short Term Goals

If the problem you are discussing is one in which short and long terms goals are appropriate, set them. Common examples may be when discussing how to get out from under credit card debt, establishing a savings plan or planning additional leisure activities.

Short term goals related to credit card debt might be to use them only when an emergency arises and to pay four times the minimum payment each month. Long term goals may be to have all balances paid up and carry only one card for emergency situations.

6) Brainstorm Solutions

This is the fun part of negotiation and compromise. This is where, with the problem clearly stated, you get to sit down and list all possible solutions to it. It matters not that some might seem quite outlandish or impossible to achieve. Your goal here is not to evaluate the solutions for reasonableness but simply to come up with every idea either of you can think of. This is called brainstorming.

Persons who use this process regularly will tell me that it is often some part of the most ridiculous idea that is suggested that becomes the best, most satisfying solution. Engage your entire brain. Use its silliness to access your most creative problem-solving abilities. And have fun with it.

7) Look for a Win/Win Solution

This is the part where you go down your list of solutions and evaluate them. Eliminate the completely unworkable ones. But take a long hard look at the silliest ones. Some part of it might end up being the most creative solutions. Take turns with your partner suggesting solutions to eliminate from your list. Those left comprise your best ideas for handling the problem—at least for now. A better solution may present itself at a later time.

Keep in mind as you look through your list that you are seeking a solution both of you can live with. You do not want a result that only you will be happy with or one that only pleases your partner. This will not lead to long term happiness. Remember, in order for the relationship to continue, both of you must be getting your needs met. If it is only working for you, you may soon be in it alone.

8) The Compromise Issue

When you are dealing with an issue for which compromise is possible, that can be the best solution for all. Each of you giving up something for the good of the whole can build closeness and connection between you. Both of you may also be more able to live with the solution also if is partially your way.

Be aware, however, that there are issues for which compromise is not going to be helpful. Say, for example, you and your partner are trying to decide what kind of new car to buy. You would like a sports car and your partner wants a new pickup truck. You agree to compromise. If you look for something halfway between those examples, you may end up with a four door Pontiac that neither of you wants to drive!

A better solution in that case may be for one of you to be charitable and say, "I know your desire for the truck is stronger than mine for the sports car. Let's get the truck. Maybe next time we can get the sports car."

Guard against the temptation to **require** that next time we must get the sports car, as circumstances may change in the mean time or you may receive other considerations, such as getting to decide where you will go on vacation next year that make up for the vehicle decision. Try to take each new issue or dilemma as its own unique situation to be handled independently.

9) Respect Emotion: Feelings are OK; Behavior May Not Be

Often while a couple is discussing a problem one or both parties may shed some tears. Crying is a valid response to how we feel and need not get in the way of reaching a solution.

As women tend to cry in the midst of emotionally upsetting situations more readily than men, largely because of their socialization as discussed previously, some men assume tears are a manipulation, designed to get their way. Understanding why their partner may be experiencing this reaction may help a male partner understand and accept that crying can just be an honest expression of emotion.

Whatever the reason for it, the appearance of tears may signal a good time to take a break from your negotiation.

Remember, when negotiating you want your logical brain to be engaged as much as possible to achieve the best, most workable solutions. If you are in tears, it may be difficult to have a calm, rational solution-focused discussion. Nothing will be harmed by taking a break for a few hours or for a day or two.

We also want to emphasize the importance of accepting feelings. Feelings are expressions of emotion and need to be accepted. They are neither right, nor wrong; they just are. What may be right or wrong, however, are the actions associated with our feelings.

For example, punching a wall is a very clear expression of emotion, both anger and the underlying emotion of frustration. However, this choice of behavior is problematic in that it will typically frighten and intimidate a family member. Additionally, you then must either fix the wall or hire someone to repair it.

Take a look at your actions associated with certain feelings and determine if they are acceptable. As discussed previously, our actions and behavior are learned and represent choices on our part. We may choose to learn different actions if the ones we are using are not leading to the outcome we would prefer.

10) Use Words That Help

In choosing the words you want to use in discussing an issue with your partner, understand that your words are powerful. Aside from what we are saying, the manner in which we say something may have a profound effect on how it is received and the outcome we experience.

When you have a point to make, think carefully about what you want to say and how you want to say it to get the most positive result. Focus on "I Statements" and words that will be gentle and positive. Statements that are powerful in discussions between couples include:

I'm sorry
I was wrong
I appreciate…or Thank you for…
I love you.

You will get much further and have a much more pleasing outcome and relationship if you can focus on what your partner is doing right, rather than on what she is doing wrong. Remember, according to the law of attraction, you will draw to yourself more of what you focus on. Choose wisely!

11) Avoid Words That Hurt

Some words are just programmed to invite conflict. Any sentence starting with the word, "You" is pretty much guaranteed to be fighting words. People faced with a "You statement" tend to feel backed into the corner as if they have to defend themselves against something. This is not the attitude you want to engender in a partner when you are looking for compromise or cooperation.

If the word "You" is followed by an "always" or a "never" the argument is all but guaranteed. Most people confronted by a "You always come home late" or "You never buy me flowers" will inevitably find themselves looking for the one occasion on which they arrived home on time or actually did buy flowers in order to prove the accuser wrong. The discussion then focuses on the one exception to the generalization that has been made and away from any type of workable solution. Avoid these accusatory statements at all costs.

Another approach that will usually guarantee an argument is the question "Why?" When faced with a "Why did you do that?" question, most persons again feel put on the defensive or backed into a corner. The message is that they must justify their actions and choices to their interrogator. The focus becomes making excuses for past behavior and, again, veers away from any prospective solution. This does nothing but sidetrack true progress in a discussion and cause hard feelings. Avoid asking why.

12) Keep Your Cool

When discussing issues with your partner, you will accomplish more if you can stay calm and in control. Look back to the chapter on Emotional Regulation. That is when we find the most positive solutions. If feelings and emotions become too overwhelming, take a break and come back to the discussion at an agreed-upon time. If your partner needs such a break, graciously provide one. You will be rewarded by achieving a happier, closer, more fulfilling relationship.

13) Be Clear About Solutions Reached

When a decision has been made or a matter settled, clearly restate what has been agreed to and what actions will be taken, by whom and when. For example: "When I will be late for dinner, I will call and let you know by 5:00 p.m." In this manner, everyone will have an understanding of the solution. If the solution is complex or involves financial arrangements or commitments, you may want to write it down so each of you can keep a copy to refer back to. Clarity breeds trust.

Remember, a discussion or disagreement between partners has the purpose of clearing the air and expressing deep feelings in order to build greater unity and emotional closeness. Keep in mind your goal of sharing your lives with each other. Further, remember the discussion of basic needs. Individuals are programmed to seek to get their own needs met. In order to keep your partner happy and invested in the relationship, her needs must be met as well. For that reason, her happiness should become an important goal for you, as should yours for her.

We have summarized the main points of this chapter on the following page. Read it over to assess your progress in the areas of negotiation and compromise.

We also suggest to our group when we go through this unit that those in a committed relationship select an issue that is not too serious and work through the process of negotiating a solution with their partner. Practicing these techniques before the need arises or an urgency is present can help to make them more accessible to you when you truly need them.

Good luck. Remember, do not hesitate to take a break if emotions run high or get in the way of your progress.

"My Way or No Way" Summary

☮ **Decide What Is Negotiable***
~If it is a matter for individual decision, provide
feedback (i.e. friends, telephone, computer use)
~If it is a relationship issue, joint decision making is
appropriate (i.e. parenting, housekeeping)

☮ **Negotiate By Mutual Consent—Is This a Good Time?**

☮ **Set Some Ground Rules**
1) Discuss, don't yell
2) Stick to the Present
3) Discuss Only One Issue at a Time
4) Don't Hit Below the Belt
5) No Violence of Any Kind

☮ **Follow the Negotiation Process**
1) Make Eye Contact
2) Take Responsibility for Your Own Issues/Actions
3) Take a Break if You Need to; Come Back to it Later
4) Use I Statements to Define the Problem
5) Identify Long and Short Term Goals
6) Brainstorm Solutions
7) Look for a Win/Win Solution
8) Reach a Compromise if the Issue Permits
9) Respect Emotion; Take a Break
10) Use Words That Help: I'm Sorry, I Was Wrong
11) Avoid Words That Hurt: You, Always, Never
12) Stay Calm
13) Be Clear About Solutions Reached

* See also Appendix H: Who Decides?

Chapter 11

The Path of Obfuscation

Honesty and Accountability in Relationships

W*e had just introduced the idea of defenses in group and defined the three main ways of not taking responsibility for our actions: minimization, denial and blame.*

Troy piped up excitedly, "Oh, I did all three! A couple of years ago, my wife and I were doing a home repair project and she was holding something I was drilling. Well, the drill slipped and I drilled right into her hand. And she's crying and bleeding there, and I felt just terrible, but the first thing out of my mouth was a denial. I said, 'I didn't do that!' Then I went on to say, 'Well, it's not that big-a hole,' and then, 'It wouldn't have happened if you would let me buy decent tools.' Those would be minimizing and blame, right?

He had hit the nail right on the head. This remains our classic example of attempting not to take responsibility for behavior we are not proud of.

Taking responsibility for our actions is an important element in developing a good relationship. But it is helpful to understand why that is important and why is the impulse to defend ourselves so tempting? Just as physical defenses were necessary to our earlier ancestors for survival, psychological defenses are necessary for our emotional well-being. However, inappropriately used, they can get in the way of a truly intimate relationship. However, this is one more behavior you can change and make more adaptive by taking a closer look at it and making some different choices. The end result: a stronger, closer, more loving relationship with your partner.

Owning Our Own Stuff

In all relationships, there comes a time when we do something we do not feel good about so we attempt to make ourselves feel better by denying our responsibility for the action. I love the example of Troy above, because anyone can understand how awful he felt drilling into his wife's hand as well as the fact that it was unintentional. It easy to see why he would want to avoid responsibility for injuring his partner in that way.

Owning our own stuff is simply the act of taking responsibility for our own actions and behavior, both the good and the bad; the actions we are proud of as well as those we don't feel so good about. It may be something as simple as saying, "I'm sorry," or something as large as writing out a full confession. But it is an important relationship skill to know how to be accountable and to have the emotional strength to do so.

Further, the better we feel about ourselves, the less we need to hide behind defenses and the more we are able to accept responsibility for our actions. If our self-esteem is not what it could be, we have a responsibility to take care of ourselves and make some changes so that we can truly invest ourselves in this relationship.

In every relationship there are two people. Both partners have some responsibility for what happens between them. Responsibility may not be 50/50 in every conflict or occurrence, but over the course of the relationship, each is 50 percent responsible for the outcome of the union.

Seeing our "stuff" with clear eyes helps us to take responsibility for it more easily. After all, it is easy to deny what we refuse to see. It also helps us to make better choices in the future if there is something about our contribution to the relationship that we want to change.

Why Do It?

Why is it important to accept responsibility for our role in what is happening in our relationship? First of all, we cannot change what we do not see and chose not to be aware of. Thus, we can remain stuck in unhappy, unfulfilling patterns for years with little hope of change. Therefore, one way to find our own happiness is to attempt to change what we can to improve our relationship.

The second and most important reason to take responsibility for our own mistakes or bad behavior is that it enhances trust in the relationship. If our partner knows that we will accept responsibility for our role in relationship problems and take care of changing what we can to make things better, she is likely to be more accepting of our efforts.

Additionally, she is likely to be more committed to the relationship as she sees the effort we are making and can be confident that things will eventually improve. Finally, it connects and bonds the two of you as a couple, both taking responsibility for your part in the relationship and remaining committed to working on it together.

Obstacles to Accountability

Alright, so if this is such a good thing to do for ourselves and our relationship, why don't we just do it? The answer, in a word is "defenses." Defenses are little tricks we play on ourselves; mind games we use to make ourselves feel better about what we have done.

Imagine yourself in Troy's position, just having drilled a hole in your wife's hand. How are you likely to be feeling? Probably pretty lousy--and also perhaps incompetent, frustrated, scared and worried about how badly she is hurt. Wouldn't you want to find a way out from under that emotional pain and responsibility if you could?

It is only human nature to want to feel good about ourselves and our actions. We have a need to feel capable, competent and confident. Defenses are simply one attempt to help ourselves do this.

The Deadly Trio: Minimizing, Denial and Blaming

There are many defenses available to us when we are attempting to deny responsibility for our behavior. We like to focus on the three Troy used, minimizing, denial and blame, as they are the most common and the easiest to understand. But let's look at them in greater detail.

Minimization
We define minimizing in our group as "making something seem less than it should be." Examples we give include a comment after a physical altercation with a partner, such as, "Well, I just pushed you a little," and "Well, I didn't really hit you," or "I just punched the door." All of these are designed to lessen the responsibility one feels for behavior which, no doubt, caused emotional or physical harm to a partner or intimidated her, causing fear.

Look back to Troy's minimizing comment, "It's not that bigga hole," again attempting to minimize the damage he had done to his partner's hand. While it would not feel good to accept that you have caused this damage and pain to your partner, think about the effect of minimizing the responsibility for the damage. It is easy to see that would do nothing to endear or bring you closer to her!

Denial
Denial is simply refusing to acknowledge that something happened. Troy's first statement was a denial. Upon realizing what has happened, he responds, "I didn't do that!" Again, most likely as reality sets in, even he cannot believe he has done such a thing. But it is difficult to deny when only the two of you are there, the drill is in your hand and she is the one bleeding.

A report we sometimes hear from women in abusive relationships is that their partner will physically abuse them one evening, then upon waking the next morning, will observe their bruises and black eyes and ask, quite innocently, "What happened to you? Did you walk into a door?" Again, imagine the effect of that behavior on a relationship over time. Over and over her reality of the experience is invalidated. Eventually it is normal for her to begin to question her own sanity and recollection of the event.

Blame

Blame is simply laying the responsibility for the event at someone else's feet. Troy does this quite handily by his comment that, "This wouldn't have happened if you'd let me buy decent tools!"

Other reports of the use of blame include, "I was drunk and didn't know what was happening," and "I wouldn't have _____ (hit you, left, punched the wall, etc.) if you'd shut up." Again, all responsibility for the action taken is laid at the feet of another party.

How to Do It Better: the Five A's

So what do we do instead? We know this is human nature. How do I deny this normal human tendency and start making a change? By using the five A's:

1) Awareness

The first step is to simply become aware of when you are using these defenses. In our discussion of communication styles, we identified that just becoming knowing which style we are using gives us the ability to pay attention to what we are doing, the outcome we are getting and decide to make some changes. The same is true for defenses.

For the next few weeks, pay attention to how you respond when you know your partner is not happy with you for some reason. Be honest with yourself. You are not sharing your observations with anyone else yet, so you have nothing to lose by taking a good hard look at your responses.

2) Admission

The second step, once you have developed an awareness of how you are responding to her, is to admit what you are doing. Choose just one occasion at first. Make it a safe one, i.e. that you forgot to feed the dog, not that you flushed her wedding ring down the toilet, so that even if she is upset, you have little to lose.

Pay attention to your feelings and her reactions. What you are likely to notice is that she is a lot easier on you than you have been and would be on yourself. This knowledge is likely to make it easier to accept responsibility in the future.

3) Acknowledgement (Validation)

The next step is acknowledgment. You are validating her feelings here and admitting that you have, at times, not taken responsibility for your actions. This is setting the tone for the future of your relationship
.

4) Apology

When appropriate, apologize. You can simply say, "I'm sorry," or you can be more specific if the situation warrants.

Men often have a harder time apologizing than women do because they tend to get many messages while growing up that it is not manly or masculine to apologize. Further, men are often trained that to apologize is to admit weakness and they are typically socialized to deny or at least not openly admit any sign of weakness or vulnerability. Take a risk, men, apologize. It can make a world of difference in your relationships!

Also, know that saying "I'm sorry" does not mean you are the only one at fault and that you are responsible for all bad things that have happened. If you like, you can make your apology more specific. You can say, "I'm sorry you are upset about this weekend. It was not my intent to hurt your feelings." Notice you have not said, "I was wrong," yet it still comes across as a genuine expression of emotion and responsibility. Work to find language that you are comfortable with so that you can, in good conscience, be true to yourself and to your partner in the apologies you make and the responsibility you accept.

5) Action: Alteration of Future Behavior

The final step in taking responsibility for our actions lies in the action stage. It involves an alteration of future behavior to avoid hurting our partner again. Simply learning to take responsibility for your actions is not enough. If you engage in behavior that you are aware hurts or upsets your partner, you can apologize until you are blue in the face but if your behavior does not change, your relationship will not improve. If you are doing the same thing that hurts her over and over, your apology becomes meaningless and further diminishes her trust in you.

For example, you went out one night and ended up kissing another woman. You decide to take responsibility for your actions, so you come home, tell your wife and apologize for your indiscretion. How many times do you think that would work before she looks at you and says, "I don't want to hear it"?

In most cases, if you are apologizing for an action, you will want and need to look at changing the behavior that is causing the problem. If you do not, the apology eventually becomes meaningless.

Take a look at the chapter review on the following page and think carefully about how much responsibility you are accepting for your own actions in your relationship. Remember, developing more awareness and accepting responsibility for your own "stuff" can only enhance your relationship by developing trust and emotional closeness.

The Path to Obfuscation Summary

☮ Take Responsibility for Your Own Actions to:
1) Find Greater Happiness
2) Enhance Trust in Your Relationship
3) Connect Emotionally With Your Partner

☮ Be On the Lookout for Obstacles to Accountability:
1) Minimizing
2) Denying
3) Blaming

☮ Rather Than Defenses, Use the 5 A's:
1) Be **Aware** of Your Use of Defenses
2) **Admit** Using Defenses and Bad Behavior
3) **Acknowledge** and Validate Your Partner's Feelings
4) **Apologize** for Bad Behavior
5) Take **Action: Alter** Future Behavior

"Happiness is not having what you want —
it's wanting what you have."

~Spencer Johnson

Chapter 12

The Green-Eyed Monster

Dealing With the Jealousy Issue

Robert comes into group a broken man. His beautiful, professional wife has filed for divorce due to his arrest incident.

"I was just jealous," he nearly whimpers as he is telling his story for the first time. "We were out at a local club and I thought she was flirting with some guy so we got into an argument. She said she was going home, but I didn't believe her. I'd had a lot to drink so I wasn't real 'with-it' but eventually I looked around and she was gone, so I drove around looking for her, sure she went with another guy. I finally ended up at home. She was there after all and the argument continued. I was so angry I just started hitting her and darned near killed her. If her mother hadn't come into the room, she would probably be dead. And there was no other guy at all! It was all a mistake and now I've lost the most important thing in my life."

A common dilemma among couples is the issue of jealousy. At least half of all of our group members report that their own jealousy has caused problems in their relationships in the past. It bears a look then, at what this mysterious emotion is and where it comes from. As with any difficult emotion or reaction, the better we understand it and the more awareness we have of how it affects us, the greater our power to handle it is a positive manner.

The Seeds of Jealousy

We come to the point of jealousy from many different avenues. There are some commonalities, however. But before we look at those, because jealousy is such a troublesome issue, it makes sense to take a look where it comes from. In dealing with any problem or issue, understanding why and how it is causing a problem for us is half the battle of making a change in the pattern.

☮ Childhood

Often-times jealousy is rooted in childhood experiences. Perhaps our parents brought home a new brother or sister and, all of a sudden, our lives changed dramatically. Maybe they had no more time for us. Perhaps we were no longer the "apple of their eye." The attention we experienced diminished to the minimal amount necessary to keep us alive. And, worse yet, we had to share our bedroom, our toys, everything that was precious to us with this new little intruder. He was no picnic either. He cried all night, smelled badly and destroyed our toys.

Remember from our discussion of brain development that our brains are not fully developed until we are 18-25 years of age. Therefore, our hopelessly undeveloped brain is not going to begin to understand that this is a natural event and will not last forever. Our reaction is to feel cheated and displaced. We may carry this experience throughout our lifetime, superimposing the lack of time and attention on anyone with whom we develop an intimate partnership.

Remember we are seeking to replicate a relationship with one of our primary caregivers and have it come out with a happier ending. Perhaps the issue we are struggling with is feeling displaced and jealous. We then set the stage in our relationships to never have enough of our partner's time or attention and to be jealous of her contacts with any others, especially other males who may be taking our place.

Do you see how once we are aware of the problem and the source of these feelings, they become easier to deal with? We can talk to our partner about our childhood to help her understand where they come from. Then we can take responsibility for changing them ourself.

☮ Past Experience

Previous relationships are also a typical source of jealousy. Perhaps we had a high school sweetheart and had dated for our junior and senior years. We attended Homecoming and Prom and had discussed marriage and children. Then, all of a sudden as senior year was drawing to a close, she was discovered in a late night tryst with the captain of the football team. The relationship ended and we have never been the same.

We will then tend to superimpose her actions on every other partner we date. With each new relationship we find ourselves being hyper vigilant, waiting for the betrayal that we know is to come. So certain are we that the infidelity will occur that we accept it is only a matter of time.

The greatest difficulty here is that we often create a self-fulfilling prophecy in this situation. We are so certain our partner will leave us for someone else that we question her every move and interrogate her at every opportunity that you are not together. Eventually, she decides that if she is going to be guilty either way, she might as well succumb to the attentions of the attractive co-worker you have been accusing her of sleeping with all along. What does she have to lose?

We fail to see how our actions have led to this behavior, or how we have perpetuated our own problem. All we can see is that our suspicions have been confirmed. They are then likely to be repeated again in our next relationship.

☮ Control

Very often persons who are jealous feel an overwhelming and disproportionate need to control their partner. Often this can come from childhood or past relationships as well, but if you find yourself in this situation, take another look at Chapters Eight and Ten discussing appropriate and healthy control in relationships.

☮ Fear

The most basic reason underlying any jealousy we feel is fear. Regardless of what has happened in our childhood or what our past relationship experience has been, when we are feeling jealous we are experiencing a fear that our partner will leave and find someone better. If we are able to deal with this fear, we can alleviate the jealousy and move on to a happier, healthier relationship.

☮ Inadequacy

Underlying the fear that supercedes jealousy is often a deep sense of inadequacy. Look at it this way, if we felt confident in ourselves and in what we have to offer a partner, why would we question whether she wants to be with us. If we believe in ourselves, we are confident that she is the lucky one and we have nothing to worry about.

The Common Denominator: Fear

No matter where our jealousy comes from, the common denominator is fear. Fear that we are inadequate, fear she will cheat, fear that we are not good enough, fear that we will be replaced by another as happened in previous relationships or our childhood.

Understand that everyone feels fear. I have recently become aware of a quote by one of my favorite and most admired artists, the great Georgia O'Keefe. She said:

*"I have been terrified every day of my life,
but that has never stopped me
from doing everything I wanted to do."*

Fear is a painful and difficult emotion to deal with, but deal with it you can. It is entirely within your control to let fear rule your life or to stare it in the face and make a change. We challenge you to choose the latter!

How Jealous Are You?

We have a quiz that we have written for use with our group when dealing with the jealousy issue. It is attached as Appendix I. Take some time and work your way through this quiz to assess the depth of your difficulties caused by jealousy. When you have gone through it, ask your partner if she would take a look at it as well. Then, when she has done so, sit down and discuss your responses.

Make sure she feels safe having this discussion with you. If emotions start to get out of control, stop and come back to this conversation another time. There is no time limit for this. You do not need to resolve it today. Better to be safe and positive than to do damage to the relationship. You have the rest of your lives together.

What to Do Instead

If you do identify jealousy as a significant issue for you, what does that mean? What can you do about it? Why should it matter that you are now aware of this problem?

Remember that awareness is half the battle toward resolution. Being able to say, "I am a jealous person," or "I have a problem with jealousy," puts you very close to actually changing that behavior. That is a valuable place to be and can make a world of difference with your partner and in your relationship. Then move on to the techniques below:

☮ Think Outcome

Ask yourself how your jealousy is affecting your relationship. Is it bringing you closer to your partner or driving you further apart? If it is not having the outcome you desire, what risk do you take in changing your reactions? What do you have to lose?

Take a look back at the example of Robert at the beginning of this chapter. His lovely wife was so special to him, he became very jealous and abusive when she left the club without him. As a result of his abuse he lost the relationship. We recently learned that she has now obtained a Restraining Order against him. Not only are they divorced, but he can no longer have any form of contact with her. Is this the outcome he wanted? We think not.

☮ Revisiting Emotional Regulation

If you find yourself in this dilemma, know that this is a very appropriate use of the Thinking Process explained in Chapter Seven. An example illustrating jealousy is also included in that chapter. If you are still struggling with this issue, put more effort into practicing this thinking process and working on your replacement thoughts. You have nothing to lose and everything to gain, especially a richer, closer, more satisfying relationship!

Take a look at the summary we have prepared on the following page to assess your progress in dealing with this very troubling and problematic issue.

The "Green-Eyed Monster" Summary

☮ Jealousy is a common issue for couples, especially when anger is an issue for one or both of them.

☮ The Seeds of Jealousy are rooted in:
~Childhood Experiences
~Past Relationships
~A Need to Control and Belief That This is Justified
~Fear that Our Partner Will Leave
~An Underlying Sense of Inadequacy

☮ The Common Denominator is Fear:
~Of Abandonment
~Of Inadequacy
~Of Being Left

☮ If we get a handle on our Fear, the Jealousy goes away

☮ Take the Jealousy Quiz in Appendix I to understand what situations trigger your fear and jealousy

☮ Instead of giving in to the Jealousy, do the following:
~Be **Aware** that this is an issue for you — this alone can prepare you to deal with jealousy when it arises
~Think about the **Outcome** you want for this relationship
~Revisit Chapter Seven to review **Emotional Regulation** and Replacement Thinking

*"If you always do what you've always done,
you'll always get
what you've always gotten."*

~Anonymous

"Only the brave know how to forgive...
A coward never forgave; it is not in his nature."

Laurence Sterne

He Doesn't Deserve to Be Forgiven!

The How and Why of Forgiveness

Devin clenched both his jaw and his fist as he spoke. "I'm just not ready to forgive him yet; he doesn't deserve it! He had no right to do what he did to me."

Devin was describing an incident in which his brother had emotionally, then physically attacked him. A leader in our group, Devin was one week shy of graduation when this incident happened and had handled the provocation by his brother quite appropriately until it finally became too much for him and he had responded physically.

Now, a week later, his brother was remorseful and seeking forgiveness, which Devin was withholding. Feeling out of control in the incident, and ashamed at reacting violently after 19 weeks in group, the only thing Devin could hold onto was his absolution. But this was keeping him stuck in the same destructive and violent pattern he and his brother had shared for the past 30 years. The only way for Devin to let go was to forgive and move on.

Why is forgiveness so difficult for us? We hang onto every vestige of the harm another has caused us trying to squeeze every last smidgeon of life out of it. We seem to want to hang onto the most difficult and painful moments life has thrown our way as if they are something to be savored or enjoyed. What is it about being wronged that makes it so hard to let go and forgive?

There are many aspects of human nature that play a part in our hanging onto resentment and bitterness. We may feel that if we let go and forgive our wrongdoers, it will condone or make their hurtful behavior acceptable to us or to the world at large. It may feel as if what they did was OK if we let them off the hook and refuse to hold a grudge.

Or, we may be afraid forgiveness will open us up to further hurt or injury. If they get away with hurting us this time, they may try it again. Or do something worse.

We also may be afraid of appearing weak or helpless if we forgive someone who has hurt us in the past. We may be afraid others will think less of us if we are the bigger person and choose to let go rather than harbor a grievance. Or that these others may, perhaps, try to hurt us as well.

Finally, we may want to exact more mileage out of the incident. Perhaps we want to punish our wrongdoer a bit— make them a little sorrier for what they have done to us or exact a larger price for having "done me wrong."

Because of their beliefs and characteristics unique to this personality style, persons with an anger problem tend to have a more difficult time forgiving and letting go of grievances than the general population. Many of the persons I have worked with on anger issues really have to struggle to be able to forgive even the most minor transgressions; even something as insignificant and impersonal as a car cutting into their traffic lane a bit too quickly.

Upon experiencing an incident like this one, one former client followed the offending car to a "Stop" sign, pulled over in front of it to prevent the driver from moving on and proceeded to jump out to scream threats at him for 15 minutes! Forgiveness? Not much. I would hate to be the person who truly hurts this man!

What Forgiveness Does NOT Mean

One of the most important reasons we struggle with forgiveness is what we tell ourselves about what it will mean to forgive. To dispel some of these myths about forgiveness, we will spend a few minutes on looking at what forgiveness does NOT do.

☮ Forgiveness Does Not Condone Their Actions

One of the most difficult wrongs to forgive can be unfaithfulness or betrayal on the part of an intimate partner. Many persons, whether they choose to stay in the relationship or end it at that point, are afraid to let go and forgive the unfaithful partner assuming that will mean that what she did was OK or acceptable. Forgiveness does not mean this to anyone observing it!

This is an extremely well-entrenched and destructive idea as it keeps many innocent partners stuck in an angry and bitter spot for a very long time. You are doing nothing but harming yourself if you subscribe to this idea. To help dispel this notion, talk about your fears and your pain with persons you can trust. You will most likely be surprised at the support you receive and at how inaccurate this notion is.

☮ Forgiveness Does Not Erase History or Minimize the Positive Parts of Your Relationship

Other persons assume that if I forgive my wife for leaving me, it will erase our history of being happy together. It will be as if our life together had never existed. This, also, is an extremely common sticking point for persons experiencing intimate betrayal. Hopefully, reading it in black and white type will help believers realize how ridiculous it is. Nothing can erase your life or history together.

Every couple that gets divorced did have some happy, emotionally connected moments. If they did not, they never would have gotten together. Nothing can erase those moments, either in reality or in your own mind. You know what you had. Forgiveness allows you to move on with your life and to invest emotionally in your future. It does not destroy or eliminate your past.

☮ Forgiveness Does Not Invalidate You or Your Pain

Another erroneous belief, closely related to the first two, is that if I forgive my partner or transgressor, it will invalidate me as a person. The pain that she caused me will not matter or will be insignificant as I will no longer be holding onto it.

Nothing could be further from the truth. This is an experience you can learn and grow from. You can use this pain to make changes you believe are necessary in your life and relationships. You can choose to see this pain as a gift that can give you the ability to learn some things about your way of being that you had no reason to learn before. But forgiveness cannot invalidate you or your pain. It is real. Forgiveness just prevents it from controlling your life.

☮ Forgiveness Does Not Mean It Was Your Fault!

Some people feel that if they forgive someone who has wronged them, it absolves the other of any guilt or responsibility for the wrongdoing and lays the fault at their own doorstep. For example, a husband whose wife has been unfaithful may fear that if he forgives her actions, others will see her affair as his fault; as if he was not a good husband.

Looking at this from the outside, it is easy to see how invalid this assumption is, but his reasoning can seem pretty infallible to one in the throes of this difficult situation. If you have been guilty of making this assumption in the past, look at its invalidity with clear eyes now so you will be able to see that whoever has done something to cause you pain is completely and totally responsible for her actions.

How Failing to Forgive Keeps Us Stuck

When we choose to hold onto an injury or hurt, seeking some revenge or justice, we may think that we are punishing the evil doers or those who have "done us wrong," but, in reality, we are punishing ourselves. You see, in holding onto those negative experiences, we choose to commit our energy and our precious resources to that end as well. Just as it takes over 50 muscles to frown and only four to smile, it costs us much more to be mad at someone, and to maintain that anger and hurt, than to choose to let it go and move on.

When we choose to mire our lives in our hurts and transgressions, we have less time and energy to focus on the good things in our lives, our partner, family, friends and the like. We can become driven by that negativity, so that our family and friends want to spend less time with us and we have a hard time acknowledging and appreciating what is good in our lives.

In the extreme, the hurt, anger and quest for revenge can take over our lives, becoming an all-encompassing goal or mission we take it upon ourselves to exact or accomplish. In these situations, little energy or focus is directed at loved ones; virtually all of our energy is focused on our enemies.

Even in a less extreme situation, refusing to forgive is keeping you stuck. It is tying up additional resources and you are choosing to sacrifice even more of yourself and your life to one who has hurt you in the past.

Don't make that choice. Choose to let it go. Choose this for yourself, for your life and for your loved ones.

On the way to our cabin in northern Wisconsin, we pass two small Baptist churches. Each has a message board out front and these often contain inspirational messages or thoughts to live by. One weekend as we passed a few years ago, the quotation on one of the boards read:

"Forgiveness is giving up my right to hurt you for hurting me."

I have since used that with every divorced client I have worked with and hope that it has made a difference. Both Terry and I think this quote speaks volumes and empowers us to forgive as a powerful and peaceful choice. We challenge you to choose peace as well.

Exercise on Forgiveness

To illustrate the burden resentment and bitterness can add to the load we carry, we want to share with you a meditation exercise, written by an anonymous author that was shared with our family by our children's middle school principal in a weekly newsletter one Friday several years ago. We were impressed with it and have been using it with clients ever since. It read as follows:

Take a potato and write on it the name of a person who has fallen from grace with you. Do this for everyone you have never forgiven. When you're done, gather all your potatoes and place them in a sack. Keep the sack next to you at all times and take it everywhere you go. How long would it take for you to grow tired of carrying it, or for your potatoes to sprout, fester and smell? Wouldn't it be nice to be free from the constant reminder of hurt, heartache and anger? By hanging onto things that are unpleasant, we create more anguish for ourselves.

When you forgive someone, you free yourself from an oppressive load of negativity. Forgiveness allows you to create peace in your life.

How true this is! Our potatoes or our resentments do act as constant reminders of the pain we have suffered. Why not choose to let them go and enjoy peace instead? What do you have to lose?

Preparing Yourself to Forgive

Once you have decided to forgive someone who has hurt you, there are several things you can do to prepare yourself to take that step. You will want to make sure that you are taking on the act of forgiveness in a thoughtful, contemplative manner, not just a cursory fashion. If you do the latter, your act of forgiveness will most likely not be effective and the resentful, bitter and angry feelings are likely to re-emerge for you the next time you have any kind of contact with the person who hurt you or when you find yourself in a situation that, on some level, reminds you of that hurtful event.

When you put energy into forgiveness and make an effort at letting go, you are freeing your energy to be focused on creating more positive things in your life. To that end, you will need to spend some time thinking about how the transgression affected you and how you have been holding onto it in your daily life. The following exercises will help you to do this.

☮ Letting Go of the Labels

When focused on a hurt or injury, it is easy to slip into "victim thinking." We feel sorry for ourselves because we were the "victim" of this person's bad behavior. The longer we hold onto this experience, the more the injury begins to define our life experience. Before long, it is difficult to look at the relationship or situation in a realistic manner.

As you prepare to forgive the person who hurt you, you must first work on eliminating these labels from your thinking and your conversation. The first step in this process is to make a list of any term you have used to define yourself in relation to the person who wronged you. Some examples might be "victim," "ex-husband," "dumpee," "co-dependent" and so on. Make the list as comprehensive as possible.

Then list the negative terms by which you refer to your offender. Again, list all of the less than flattering labels you have attributed to this person since the offense occurred. Some of these may include "jerk," "abuser," "bitch," "ex-wife," "dumper, and so on.

After making your lists, tune in to your conversations with others for the next few days. Listen for any other "victim"or "abuser" labels you find yourself using when talking with friends and support persons. Add these to your lists.

Then, make a pact with yourself not to use any of these terms in conversation for at least a week. During those seven days, really attempt to define yourself separate and apart from these old hurts. Refer to yourself only in the context of other aspects of your life, such as your interests, work, family or friends.

Friends can also make this change truly difficult by asking questions like, "So, have you heard from that witch lately?" If this happens, gently change the subject politely and move on. Most friends will eventually get the idea and remove their focus from this past injury.

For those who don't, you may need to say something gently about the change you are trying to make, such as, "I've learned it's not healthy for me to focus on past hurts so I'm making an effort at putting that situation behind me." For those who still don't "get it" cut them loose and move on.

☮ Letting Go of Old Debts—the "You Don't Owe Me" Exercise

Many of us keep ourselves stuck and focused on old injuries by convincing ourselves that our injurer still owes us something. If we feel entitled, we can convince ourselves that we don't need to forgive until that person has given us what we deserve. Some of these expectations may include money, a verbal apology, acknowledgement, an explanation of their behavior, and many others.

Make a list of debts you feel the offender still owes you. Be as comprehensive as possible, including everything to which you feel you are still entitled. Once you are sure you have included every presumed debt, use one of the following techniques to release them.

1) Collect as many small (or large) rocks as you have debts on your list. With a marker, write one debt on each rock. Take them to a lake or other body of water and release each rock into the water. Imagine these are your final connections to this person and that by returning these rocks to the earth, you are severing all ties to this person. If you will still have a relationship with this individual, as with Devin and his brother at the beginning of this chapter, imagine instead that you are severing only the hurtful aspects of your relationship and that your investment in the relationship will change.

2)   Buy a package of balloons and write one debt on each of the balloons with a marker. Blow them up and one by one, release each balloon-debt to the universe. Imagine that the balloons are the last remaining connections you have with this person. As you release your balloons, imagine you are releasing the last threads that bind you to your injurer.

3)   Write out an IOU. On it, list all of the debts you believe the offender owes you. When you are finished, look over the list. Ask yourself if your injurer can or will ever truthfully repay you. When you are ready, shred the IOU.

4)   Look over your list and practice simply saying out loud, with feeling, to a friend, therapist, an empty chair or a photograph of your injurer the words, "You owe me nothing. You are free!" Do not do this exercise until you can say these words and mean them, however.

☮ A Trip Down Memory Lane

This is a most appropriate technique when coping with the ending of an intimate relationship but may fit other wounds as well. To prepare yourself to let go of a hurt is to immerse yourself in the relationship you have had with your injurer. It is a way to chronicle your history with this person, both good and bad. This process could take some time.

Collect photographs, letters, mementos and any other things that remind you of this relationship. Spend some time looking them over and putting them in some kind of order. As you look over each photo and read over each letter, allow your feelings about this person, the relationship and the injury to come forth. After you have spent some time with these items and the scrapbook, put it away, out of sight. It is time to move forward.

☮ If I Forgave You.....

Often, we are hesitant to forgive as it may mean that we have to take on additional responsibilities in our lives. In a divorce or relationship-ending situation, forgiveness may mean having to take on additional responsibilities around the household or it may mean having to acknowledge and take responsibility for our role in some of the problems in our relationship.

As painful and uncomfortable as this might be, however, it is the only way to be in a position to truly participate in a new, healthier and more satisfying relationship in the future. If you can acknowledge your shortcomings or the things you did that made the relationship not work, you are in a terrific position to create a better relationship down the road.

If, however, you refuse to see or take steps to change your contributions to the difficulties in the relationship, you are setting yourself up to have the same problems in a future relationship. Remember, each partner has some responsibility for the problems in any relationship. Accept yours and you have the power to do and create something different!

In the case of Devin at the beginning of this chapter, letting go of his hurt and anger toward his brother may mean having to accept responsibility for letting himself be provoked to react violently at a point in time when he had nearly completed the group and felt he had made considerable changes in his beliefs, values and behavior.

Devin was quite a charming individual and he clearly enjoyed the fact that he had come quite a ways at getting control over his negative emotions. Accepting the need to forgive his brother, he would also have to accept the need to make further changes himself and these requirements would humble him a bit, in his own eyes and the eyes of group members who looked up to him as a leader and model of how to make these changes.

Another thing that can hold us back in the "If I Forgave You I Would Have to...." category is the possible need to justify or explain our forgiveness to persons who are emotionally supportive of us in our hurt. Many times, these helpful friends and family members can do a better job holding on to our hurt and pain than we, ourselves, do. They may remind us regularly of what was done "to" us and incite those bitter and vengeful feelings again just as they begin to subside.

Often these persons will have a difficult time accepting that you are ready or willing to forgive the one who hurt you and you may feel the need to either justify why you feel this need or to pretend you will never forgive. Many of these persons may have their own issues regarding hurt and forgiveness and it is more comfortable for them to focus on your hurt than their own.

Know this and make the best decision for yourself regarding forgiveness, which, for most of us, is to let go and move on even if your friend does not understand how you could even think of forgiving the one who caused you so much pain. You will also need to be careful not to take on their emotional issues in the process.

As you prepare yourself to forgive one who has hurt you, give some thought to what expectations you will have of yourself when you do forgive them. What additional responsibilities will you have of yourself; what will you have to take on in order to let this hurt go and move past it. Only by giving some thought to these things ahead of time will you truly be ready to accept them.

The Steps of Forgiveness

Once you have made the decision to forgive your transgressor, there are a number ways to carry out the task. I will explain three different methods in this chapter. There is no need to use all three. Simply choose the one that you feel fits you and your personality or, perhaps the particular transgression in question the best, and be done with it.

☮ Say "I Forgive You"

The first method we will discuss is also the simplest. When you are ready, simply sit down with a friend, a therapist or an empty chair and say words out loud to acknowledge your forgiveness. For the ending of an intimate relationship, this can sound something like:

"_____, *I forgive you. You have hurt me deeply but that does not mean we have not loved each other. Forgiving you simply means I no longer expect anything from you. You are free to go on your way as I am free to go on mine. You are forgiven and we are free."*

Notice that the offending party is not present and has no knowledge of this forgiveness. The injurer has no part in the forgiveness process. It is not about him; it only involves the person actually doing the forgiving. He may never know he has been forgiven.

For another type of transgression, such as Devin's at the beginning of this chapter, the forgiveness may take a form such as the following:

"_____, *I forgive you. You have hurt me but that doesn't mean we don't care about each other. Forgiving you this hurt simply means I expect nothing more from you to try to make it right. You are forgiven and·we are both free to continue our relationship as we so choose."*

Again, the offending party may never know he has been forgiven. It will be up to the "victim" to establish and set his own limits on the new relationship. This may mean limiting contact with the offender or controlling the circumstances of that contact, such as to not be around him in a setting in which he is likely to become angry or abusive.

☮ Name, Claim, Blame and Balance

The next method for forgiving involves four steps: name, claim, blame and balance. First of all, you want to fully explain and acknowledge the injury to yourself and one other person. Talk about it. Say whatever needs to be said before it is put to rest.

Next, claim this injury. Saying something like, "This happened to me." This statement indicates and acknowledges ownership of the wound. This is important to be able to let it go and move beyond it.

Third, identify who is responsible for the injury. Name the offender and hold him responsible for the wound. Acknowledge that he did something wrong, something hurtful to you. Be as specific as possible about the offender's hurtful actions.

Finally, balance the scales. Do something that will help you move beyond this injury and let it go. This may involve having a conversation with an empty chair, telling your offender how much you have been hurt. It may involve writing a letter directed at the offending person, but not giving or sending it to him. Remember, this act is for you. When you are ready to let go, the letter may be burned, shredded or flushed down the toilet. Imagine that the smoke, shredder or water is carrying away the hurt and pain you have felt; cleansing you to move on, free from the injury you have suffered.

☮ Six Steps to Forgiveness

This next method is similar to the second, but with a slightly different twist.

1) Identify the injury or grievance and review it fully in your mind.

2) Then, hold in your mind an image of whomever or whatever action is to be forgiven. Say aloud, "I release you from the hold of my pain, anger or vengefulness. " Spend a few minutes concentrating quietly on this statement; repeating it out loud several times.

3) Next, imagine what your life will be like without the injury or grievance that has been disturbing you and tying up your energy for some time.

4) Reach out to someone you have hurt and attempt to make amends yourself in your other relationships. This will prepare you to let go of your own hurt.

5) Next, ask for the help of your Higher Power, whether it be God, spirit or some other force of nature, to forgive this transgression and let it go. Know that whenever you ask, help will be given. It can also be helpful to pray for the person you want to forgive and to think of two or three good things about them.

6) Finally, be patient. Forgiveness, and the healing that follows, often occurs in its own time frame which may not be our own. If you attempt to follow these steps, but falter, keep trying and be patient. Stay alert to any shifts in your thinking, feeling or relationships as they may be indications that change has happened. If you

allow yourself to think about the injury at those times, you may find it no longer bothers or disturbs you as much and that true change has, in fact, occurred.

Repeat these steps whenever you are aware of a hurt that is bothering or disturbing you. Remember to include yourself in your list of persons to be forgiven if there is something you need to forgive yourself for.

Summary

Forgiveness is a choice. No one can make you forgive someone who has hurt you. It is completely up to you. But for anyone with an anger problem, it is essential. The more you hold onto past hurts and grievances, the more you will be inclined to keep yourself angry, at your offender and at many others in your life. That anger will likely be visited upon those closest to you, your partner and other family members.

Remember, also, that forgiveness takes time. Be patient with yourself, but know that it is a goal worth pursuing. If at first attempt you don't succeed, keep coming back to it until you do. Forgiveness also takes great courage; it is an act of bravery to let go of a hurt or transgression. Appreciate the challenge and difficulties of this process.

Take a look at the summary on the following page that highlights some of the key concepts in this chapter. Read it over as often as you need to or whenever you are struggling to forgive someone.

And finally, understand that forgiving is for you, not for the person you forgive. He may never be aware that it has happened. Think of it as a gift to yourself so that you can move on with your life. Good Luck!

Forgiveness Summary

☮ I understand that forgiveness:

___Does not condone what was done to me.

___Does not minimize my history.

___Does not invalidate me or my pain.

___Does not mean the event was my fault or responsibility.

___Is beneficial for me, not for my transgressor, who may never know he has been forgiven.

☮ I understand that denying forgiveness hurts me and keeps me stuck in the past.

☮ I am ready to prepare myself to forgive _____ who has hurt me in the past I will do this by:

___Letting go of the Labels

___Letting go of Old Debts

___Making a Scrapbook of Memories of this Relationship

___Accepting the Responsibilities of _____ _____ that I will now have to take on if I forgive my offender.

☮ The method I will use to forgive my transgressor is: (Refer to chapter text for more information about these techniques)

___Saying "I Forgive You"

___Name, Claim, Blame & Balance

___Six Steps to Forgiveness.

☮ Repeat this process whenever you realize there is someone who has done something to hurt you and whom you need to forgive.

Do what you can,
with what you have,
where you are.

~ Theodore Roosevelt

Chapter 14

Why Can't I Do Anything Right?

Help for Partners of Angry People

Tell me about the most recent incident," I gently prompt the woman trembling on the sofa in my office. She is about 35, but looks 50. You can see she was once quite attractive; now she just looks tired.*

"Well," Misty begins hesitantly, "he came home from work in a bad mood and it escalated from there." She pauses to gingerly extract a tissue from the box at her side. I wait patiently, knowing she is preparing for the telling.

"He was upset that I had made meatloaf for dinner, so he threw it on the floor. I motioned for the kids to leave while he was going on about the food and the mess it made."

Knowing she had five children, ranging in ages from 4 to 17, I asked the obvious question, "Where did the children go?"

Her response was brilliant and heartbreaking at the same time, a true product of the nightmare she had lived for the past 18 years. "Well, they each have a job when dad gets upset. The oldest takes the cell phone, goes into the garage and calls 9-1-1. The middle two take care of the younger ones, to get them into their rooms and distract them. The little ones know to go along when they are told. I distract my husband so he takes his anger out on me instead of them."

There it was. The entire family had a plan for how to stay safe when dad's anger threatened them. The only problem was, Misty had finally had enough and was planning to leave. But she was worried about the safety of her children when they were with the father she no longer loved.

If you are reading this book because you have identified anger as a problem for yourself, good for you! It takes great courage to acknowledge and take responsibility for making personal changes. If you are in a relationship, however, I would ask that you read this chapter, so you will understand actions your partner may be taking and, after you have completed it, ask that your partner read it as well. Do not demand that he or she read it. Just make the request. Let it be up to your partner whether or not the chapter is read.

Both Men and Women Have Anger Problems

Men do not have the market cornered on anger. There are many angry women out there as well. But with women it often looks a bit different. Men tend to be socialized that it is acceptable and even expected of them to be angry and that is it acceptable to be violent when angry.

Women get the opposite message. As we discussed back in Chapter One, little girls are told "It's not ladylike to be angry," or "Good girls don't... (fill in the blank with: get angry, stamp their feet, yell, show their displeasure...etc.)". But when they burst into tears (often out of simple frustration, "Well then how am I supposed to act?") they get an arm around their shoulders and a "That's alright, honey." Therefore, when as adults they burst into tears during an argument, they are simply expressing anger through tears as they have been socialized or trained to do.

Some women **do** learn to express anger aggressively, however, and it often becomes quite explosive. Sometimes this reaction happens out of frustration or, perhaps, it is what has been modeled for them by parents or caregivers. These women have anger problems similar to the men who are angry. They are damaging their relationships, their children and their physical and emotional health, by allowing this intense emotion to get the best of them.

Anyone who has ever been involved with someone with an anger problem, has had the experience of feeling like no matter what they do, their partner is unhappy with them. It matters not if you are male or female; when you are dealing with someone who has a problem with anger, at some point you become the unsuspecting target of your partner's wrath.

As with the example of Misty at the beginning of this chapter, when I am working with partners of angry people, I hear many stories of making a favorite meal, only to be chastised because, "I'm not hungry for meatloaf," or "I wanted spaghetti tonight; can't you ever get it right?"

When the woman is the angry person, her partner may take care of her car, or the lawn or the children, only to be told that she really wanted him to do something else, like take her out to dinner, instead. But it doesn't matter, whatever he tries to do for her, it's the wrong thing.

Angry Partners Find Each Other

It may be that you picked up this book to help your partner deal with his anger, only to discover upon paging through it, that you have some work to do as well. Or, perhaps you chose this book knowing from the outset that both of you needed to learn to deal with anger more productively. That is really not surprising.

One thing we see regularly in our anger management group is that even though there are only men in the group, these men are often involved with partners who struggle with anger as much as they do. Perhaps these women do not become physical when angry, but are extremely emotionally abusive when upset, inflicting much emotional damage on their partners and their relationships. Or, although they tend to be smaller and less muscular than their male partners, some of these women are not above using a weapon to make a point.

I have heard many stories of the men in my group making amazing changes in their relationship, only to have their partners physically accost a man (or woman) who is harassing her, or maybe just in her way, when they are out for the evening together. The male partner is then made to feel like less of a man as he didn't "stand up for her" as she expected him to do. Clearly she has anger issues that need to be explored.

But even if that is not your situation, if you are seeing your partner as the only one with an anger problem, look carefully at yourself with regard to anger as well. You may even want to read over Chapter One with regard to issues with anger to determine if there may be other chapters that would be helpful for you to read.

Partners come together for a reason and often it is because they either have the same or complementary issues to learn about from each other. I often tell people that Terry was sent to me to teach me patience and I was sent to light a fire under him. He is patient and makes decisions cautiously while I tend to be more impetuous. We are dealing with opposite ends of the same issue and balance each other beautifully most of the time. The same is true for many couples.

If your issue is not anger, however, it may be assertiveness. You may be overly passive in your relationship and thereby not getting what you need. If that is the case, you may want to read over Chapter Ten on Communication Skills to learn how to become more assertive in your relationships. But try to take a step back and see the big picture. Note how your behavior complements your angry partner's actions, so that you make decisions that echo your needs or desires, rather than simply react to him.

Do Not Take Your Partner's Behavior Personally

We looked at several examples of unreasonable demands and expectations at the beginning of this chapter. These demands are not about you and it is important, if you are to continue in this relationship, that you learn not to take them personally. If you think back you can most likely recall a time when, nearly everything your partner has blamed for causing his unreasonable anger has been exactly the thing he desired. (i.e. "How could you make me meatloaf tonight!") While he may be more in the mood for meatloaf at one time than another, never should it be cause for anger or abusive behavior.

The fact that one time it is the perfect meal and the next it is viewed as an insult really establishes that the problem is neither you nor the meatloaf. It is your partner's anger problem and the underlying beliefs he has that allow him to insult and humiliate you for making him something to eat.

It is important if you are to survive this kind of a relationship with your personality and self-esteem intact, that you learn to not take these attacks personally. You may want to read over Chapter Seven on Emotional Regulation because you could use those skills to shrug off these attacks from your partner. Your replacement thinking could be:

- ☮ I know this is not about me.
- ☮ He is being unreasonable.
- ☮ I am not going to take this personally.

But read that Emotional Regulation chapter only if it is something **you** want to do, not because your partner thinks it would be good so you can help him or her master those concepts. You must take care of yourself in this relationship to minimize the emotional damage it can do to you.

The other question you want to spend some time thinking about is why you are in this relationship and subjecting yourself to this kind of treatment. Some persons find themselves in relationships with angry partners due to low self-esteem or an abusive childhood that set them up to expect to be treated badly. While I do not want to spend a lot of time exploring this here as it would take too much time and is more appropriately the subject of another book, please give some thought to this issue. Why do you accept the abusive treatment from your partner? Is it because you have some issues of your own to work on, in that on some level you believe you deserve to be treated badly? Or is it because you and your partner connect so well most of the time and have so many interests in common that you tolerate the angry outbursts to get what is good out of the relationship? Are you being honest with yourself with your answer to this question?

If you struggle with low self-esteem or believe you deserve the treatment your partner visits upon you, it would be good to find yourself some help as well. Locate a good book on these issues. There is a Reading List located in Appendix J. Or, better yet, find a therapist or counselor who is experienced in working with self esteem and abuse issues.

Whatever the reason you are staying in this relationship, I will tell you that angry, abusive behavior does not decrease, but increases and escalates without some type of intervention. It may start out as a bit of name-calling, move on to additional emotional abuse, then an out and out tirade and finally, a slap, push or something worse.

It is possible that this book can be the intervention that stops the escalation. If you have purchased this book for your partner, even if it is a last ditch effort to save the relationship before you leave, please be honest with her about the nature of your intentions and the toll her anger is taking on your relationship. If it is your partner who has chosen to read this book and merely presented you with this chapter written for partners, this is a good indicator of her level of motivation for change.

However, some persons for whom abusive anger patterns are long established and firmly entrenched may need more of an intervention than just a book. Persons in this position often need the imminent loss of a relationship or job, or perhaps police or other legal intervention to develop the motivation for change. Whether or not the book, alone, works, it can be a good first step and can be a supportive resource once the external intervention has occurred.

Do Not Take Responsibility for Your Partner's Anger

Some partners of angry people, in an attempt to make things better, try to take responsibility for making things right and for trying to prevent the angry partner from becoming angry. If you are attempting this, realize at once that you are fighting a losing battle. You should not and, indeed, cannot take responsibility for your partner's anger or for making it not happen. Remember, as we just said, it is not about you. Therefore, you are not causing it, nor can you change or fix it.

What You Need to Survive this Relationship

If you recognize the problems in your partner's expression and handling of anger and are committed to sticking it out and giving him the chance to make some changes, there are some things you need to do for yourself.

☮ Get Some Emotional Support

Find yourself someone to talk to. This person can be a friend, family member, co-worker or a therapist, but should be able to provide you with unconditional emotional support. The process of making any kind of long term lasting change in relationship and lifetime habits is a difficult one, fraught with many ups and downs. Any lasting change takes place in a three steps forward, two steps back fashion. Therefore, just when you think you and your partner have finally turned the corner on an issue or behavior, you are likely to be revisited by it.

Don't lose hope; you are truly not back at square one even if it feels like you are. If both of you remain committed to the relationship and the angry partner(s) continues to be committed to doing things differently, true lasting change is possible.

But this process will be easier if you have a neutral third party to talk to about it. Therefore, line up some support for yourself; someone to talk to and who will be there to help reassure you and boost you up when you are frustrated, disappointed, hopeless or disillusioned with how slowly change seems to be happening in your relationship.

This should be someone who is generally a positive person, who can see the glass as half full and who will not be pointing out all of the problems in your relationship. If you find yourself a negative person to talk with, you will generally find yourself feeling quite negative about any situation you discuss with her, so choose your support persons carefully.

☮ Understand You Deserve to be Treated with Respect

You must realize that you deserve to be treated with respect. No one deserves to receive the brunt of someone else's anger. As we said previously, your partner's anger is his responsibility. Expect him to deal with it and to learn to treat you with the respect you deserve. Don't fall into the trap of trying to make everything better for him. Remember, you are neither the cause nor the solution.

☮ Stress Management is Crucial

While there are many reasons to stay in a relationship in the hope that things will improve, especially if you have a great deal in common and a significant amount of no-problem time to make the investment worthwhile, please understand that this is and will continue to be an extremely stressful undertaking. It would be good for you to take a look at Chapter Three on Stress and stress management techniques to help yourself through this time.

There are many ideas in this chapter that will not only identify stressors but also suggest ways to take care of yourself to help manage your stress in positive, healthy ways. Most people can benefit from learning new coping skills. This chapter offers many suggestions for new ideas to try.

☮ Take Time For Yourself Away From Your Partner

Many persons with anger problems can be very intense in relationships. It is difficult to maintain this intensity for any length of time, especially for the partner without the anger problem. You will need to be cognizant of how his intensity is affecting you and be careful to take time away from the relationship when it becomes too overwhelming. Your angry partner will also need to accept that you will need to get away when his intensity becomes too much for you, and this acceptance could take some time to achieve.

In addition, in any relationship time away from your partner is a normal and healthy need. When each of you takes time away, you come back to the relationship refreshed and with more to share or give to the relationship than before. It is especially important in a relationship where anger is a problem to make sure this individual time is honored and respected. This can be one of the most important things you do to take care of yourself so that you can continue in the relationship.

☮ Re-Read this Chapter Regularly

This chapter contains many good ideas for coping with a relationship in which anger is a problem. Not only will re-reading it on a regular basis remind you to do these things to take care of yourself, it will also operate as a reality check when the temptation to believe you are always wrong and all relationship problems are your fault becomes overwhelming.

Angry partners are very good at playing the "blame game." It is easy to fall into the trap of accepting responsibility for all relationship problems absent this kind of a resource, especially for a responsible and accommodating partner, as many persons who find themselves in relationship with angry partners are. Read this over as double-check whenever you feel your self-esteem starting to slip or when you start to feel overwhelmed by the relationship.

Safety Planning

It is helpful in dealing with an angry partner to take steps to protect yourself when your partner chooses to lose control of his anger and direct it at you. Again, this can happen with both men and women. You, as the only rational person in the relationship at this time, will need to be prepared to take steps to care for yourself as your partner will not be thinking about how you are feeling or reacting to his anger.

☮ Get Yourself Out of the Situation

At times like this, even when it is just verbal and emotional battery, it is best to remove yourself from the situation for several reasons. First of all, leaving will prevent you from hearing or seeing what your partner is doing and will thereby prevent further damage to your self-esteem and your relationship. Secondly, there is some evidence that your presence as an audience serves to entice the angry behavior in order to provoke a reaction. If you leave, your angry partner is probably more likely to calm down and eventually let go of whatever she is choosing to upset herself with.

☮ Abusiveness Will Likely Escalate

There are times in a relationship with an angry person, when the relationship shifts from one of emotional and verbal attacks to one of physical abuse. Once that shift has happened once, it is likely to continue to escalate, with these attacks becoming more frequent and more severe, even if your partner seems ashamed and contrite afterwards and promises never to hurt you again.

Once this has happened, or if you have a strong feeling that it will happen in a particular conflict, you will need to be prepared to take steps to care for yourself and protect yourself physically from your partner. When the situation begins to escalate, if you can manage to leave the situation, do so at once.

☮ Holding, Chasing and Preventing You From Leaving

In many cases, your angry partner may try to further violate your person and your rights by preventing you from getting away from the situation. If you can get to the telephone, call 9-1-1 as soon as possible. Even someone who is loudly and irrationally swearing at you (or the police) can be arrested for Disorderly Conduct. This may lead to him being ordered to get the treatment he needs or getting his attention so he realizes how much of a problem he has. Either way, great change can result.

Many angry persons will try to prevent their partners from contacting police. They may try to convince you not to call, grab the telephone away from you or simply rip it out of the wall (this is an extremely common tactic; nearly half of our group members have done this at one time or anther).

This is the best argument for a cell or cordless phone I have heard. This way, once things begin to escalate, you can discreetly place the phone in an area where you will be able to get to it. Many people place the phone in the bathroom as most people will agree to let someone use the restroom even if they are extremely controlling and in the middle of an argument. Please consider this if your relationship has, or seems about to, escalate to physical violence.

Please also understand that chasing you down, holding you to prevent you from leaving and preventing you from calling police are abusive behaviors. These actions can qualify your partner for a Domestic Violence or at least a Disorderly Conduct arrest.

In a recent conversation with a representative of our local District Attorney's office, I was told that these behaviors could also elicit a charge separate from any Domestic Violence or Disorderly Conduct Arrest and could be called either False Imprisonment or Intimidating a Victim. Be sure to report them to police or, if police are not involved, know that these behaviors are a prelude to more invasive and extreme type of violence. Absent some type of intervention, this behavior will continue to escalate and lead to further trauma.

☮ Pack a Bag and Some Cash

Many partners find it helpful also to pack a bag of extra clothes and keep it in the trunk of a car they have access to. In addition, it is usually helpful to put aside a bit of cash, either in an account only you have access to, or better yet, hidden in a place where you can get to it any time of the day or night. Many of these altercations occur at the least convenient times, so you cannot always plan to have access to money kept in a bank or safe deposit box.

☮ Stay Calm

If your partner chooses to lose control of his anger and flight is impossible, keep yourself calm. Talk to him with a steady voice and move slowly. Keep your distance if you can. This may be the time to request a trip to the restroom to use that cell phone you have previously stashed there. Most abusive partners will let you use the restroom, even in the midst of a blind rage.

Even if that doesn't work, know that the calmer you can be, the calmer your partner is likely to stay. If you are emotionally intense, he is likely to escalate as well. Your life may depend on both of you remaining calm.

☮ Have an Escape Plan

One last item you will want to think about is where you might go if you can escape and do need to get away in a hurry. Learn whether there is a domestic violence shelter near you and memorize its address and telephone number.

Plan a friend you can stay the night with or a motel you know the way to where you can usually get a room. This way, you will be able to leave with a clearer head if matters escalate and seem to be spinning out of control. You may even want to write the friend's or the motel's telephone number and address and place it in your bag of clothing in your car.

These may seem like extreme steps, but if your relationship is moving in this direction a little planning can go a long way toward achieving your peace of mind. If you end up not needing the things you have prepared, all the better. But you will be feeling stronger and more empowered, knowing you have taken these steps.

If You Do Decide to Leave

Sometimes the only solution for the non-angry partner is to leave the relationship. Perhaps as much as she tries, your angry partner is making no progress on getting a handle on her anger. When you have discussed this with her, she has refused to seek further help in the form of group or individual counseling. You are feeling overwhelmed and resentful at the repeated attacks and find yourself become more bitter as time passes. At some point, your feelings for this person change from love and attraction to pity and an emotionally distant concern.

You are doing neither of you any good by being a martyr and staying in a relationship that leaves you cold. However, what I see as a therapist is that often people will stay in such a relationship until they happen upon a new partner they are attracted to. At that point, the solution becomes obvious.

However, it is better for you and for any subsequent relationship you find yourself in, to take time for yourself to adjust to the end of the first relationship before embarking upon a new one. I discuss this in my first book, *Child-Friendly Divorce*, at some length. Please review Chapter Ten of that book for more information about this issue.

I will tell you that an angry person will have a tendency to become more desperate if you talk about ending the relationship altogether. If you are male and in a relationship with an angry or abusive female, she is likely to pull out all stops to hurt you emotionally if you talk about leaving. Think *Fatal Attraction*. Remember the bunny in the soup came only after he left her and ended the relationship permanently. Take steps to protect your work and personal lives from this partner if you think, after knowing her, that there is a chance she could become vengeful and bitter in an attempt to get back at you.

If you are female and in a relationship with a male, know that your physical safety may be in great danger at this time. Of all the women killed by abusive partners, 85% have been killed when they were attempting to leave the relationship. This creates a desperation on the part of the angry partner that reduces inhibitions of getting caught and violating laws and personal values which may keep his behavior under control in most other situations.

Take extra precautions to protect yourself at this time. Keep your cell phone and money with you at all times and always let someone else know where you are going. Lock your doors and enjoy a bit of paranoia for awhile. Remember, it's

272 *A Peace of My Mind*

not being paranoid if he really is out to get you. Don't be a statistic!

Know also that domestic violence laws are being strengthened and revised on a regular basis. In Wisconsin, we no longer need the victim to press charges. This prevents the violent partner from leaning heavily on her to recant her story so he cannot be charged. The charging decision lies solely in the hands of the District Attorney's office.

Additionally, divorce laws are being revised provide protection for former partners and children during child placement arrangements. Wisconsin courts can require abusive partners to attend a batterer's treatment program or other counseling or to exchange placement in the presence of a neutral third party if there has been any history of domestic violence in the relationship, even if police and the courts were never previously involved. Many other states are revising laws to provide the same or similar arrangements. If you are leaving the relationship, and are or will be involved in child placement arrangements, be sure to check into the safeguards available in your locale.

In general, women are most likely to escalate their emotional attacks when desperation increases and men are most likely to react physically. Of course, there are exceptions to every rule, but if you can remember these two generalities, you will at least be on the lookout for danger or a threat of some kind. You may not ever see it, but you will more likely feel stronger, more empowered and less like a victim of your circumstances.

Take a look at the chapter summary on the next page and read it over for some assistance in considering which areas might bear further attention in your relationship. Know, however, that as the partner of a person with an anger problem, you will need to take steps to care for yourself and to keep yourself safe from harm. Good Luck!

"Why Can't I Do Anything Right?" Summary

☮ I will review Chapter One if I am concerned I may have anger issues of my own.

☮ I have reviewed Chapter Ten on Communication Skills to improve my communication with my partner.

☮I know not to take my partner's behavior personally. It is not about me, nor is it a reflection on me.

☮ I am not taking responsibility for my partner's anger. I know the problem is not mine to solve.

☮ I am taking steps to care for my self in this relationship:
~I am establishing my emotional support system and use it regularly.
~I understand I deserve to be treated with respect.
~I am practicing good stress management. These are some of the things I am doing to manage my stress:_____
_____
~I am taking time for myself away from my partner to spend alone and with my support system.
~I am re-reading this chapter as often as I need to to remember to care for myself.

☮ I have a Safety Plan in place for my own security. It is as follows:
___Cell Phone with me at all times ___Money available
___Clothing packed   ___Escape Plan
___Other Steps: _____

☮ If I decide to leave the relationship I will take these additional steps to be safe:_____

*"How wonderful it is
that nobody need wait a single moment
before starting to improve the world."*

~ Anne Frank

Chapter 15

Putting It All Together and Making It Work!

Summary and Conclusions

I can think of no better example of someone who is putting it all together and making it come out right than Tony. He initially came in for marriage counseling after his wife of five years confessed to a one night stand and told him she was no longer attracted to him. Tony was understandably hurt and angry and, in the course of an argument, hit and pushed his wife. Deciding that, whether or not the marriage survived, he needed to get a grip on his anger for his own sake and that of their four year old son, Tony asked to participate in the anger management group as a volunteer.

During his participation in the group Tony was able to look at his own controlling and abusive behaviors and make some changes in them. While he was in the group, Tony's father, with whom he was living at the time and his model for the abusive role he played in his relationship, became violent with Tony and his mother. Police were called and Tony was helpful in getting his father the help he needed as well, thus helping two generations directly and a third, Tony's son, indirectly.

We have covered an incredible amount of material in these few pages. It is almost overwhelming to think about all of the topics we have discussed. Know that it will and should take time to absorb all of this information and begin to put it into practice.

We would like to say a few words about that process as well. Most persons being exposed to new information need to hear it a number of times before they will begin to accept, understand and act on it as a part of their world view. We expect that most of the material covered in this book will be new to you, just as it is new to the members of our group. Therefore, do not expect yourself to be able to make changes without ever having to go over the chapter or the entire book again. It is human to need that repetition when exposed to a new idea.

However, just the fact that you have been exposed to new ideas is positive as well. We include here one of Diane's favorite quotations. Initially stated by Oliver Wendell Holmes, it reads:

"One's mind, once stretched by a new idea,
never regains its original dimensions."

What that means to us is that just by virtue of the fact that you have picked up and perused this volume, you will be forever changed by it. It doesn't matter that you may not practice every exercise or technique. You will be changed just for having read the book.

We also have some words of wisdom for those who have been challenged by these words and do want to try to make some lasting changes, however. Understand, first of all, that change is a process and we did not arrive where we are fully formed. It has taken us each a number of years to get here. Therefore, it will and should take some time to make true change in your life.

In our work, we call that "second order change." First order change is the kind of alteration we can all make that may last a week or a month. True second order change is something we only achieve by longer term effort. It is more permanent because it happens over time and results from a change in our underlying attitudes and beliefs that support our actions. That is the kind of change we wish for you; change that will happen to truly improve your life and relationships for the long term.

For you, this is our quotation, words from the patron saint of our children's elementary school:

"Have patience with all things,
but chiefly have patience with yourself."

~Saint Francis de Sales

Understand this will not happen overnight. As in the example of Tony at the beginning of this chapter, true change takes time. We have known him for in excess of three years and still occasionally have contact when he calls to check in and touch base with us about a family or relationship issue. He is doing very well and has made some remarkable changes, especially given the modeling that he received as a child, but he keeps working at it. That, more than anything else about him, makes him the role model to follow.

We have had others that have made faster and more miraculous progress, but Tony has the perseverance necessary to make truly remarkable changes. He keeps working at it and struggling with the ideas and concepts he first learned in our group. He is not perfect and has taken a few steps back from time to time. But he keeps picking himself up and getting back on the horse because his goal is to be a different kind of parent and partner than his father was and is.

That is what we hope our readers will work toward; not fast or remarkable progress, but the determination to keep coming back to it and looking at what is happening in your relationships with partners, children, co-workers and friends and questioning your role in what is taking place.

We have included our email address in Appendix J at the back of this volume. If you have any questions or comments about any of the material included in this volume, please contact us. With your permission, your information, whether it is a question, comment or a success story may be included in our second printing.

We wish you all the best of luck with this work. It is not easy but, if you practice it, it is simple. And it is so very rewarding!

Again, finally, we wish you Happy and Fulfilling Relationships!

☮ Appendix A
Peaceful Alternatives to Family Violence
Group Objectives

☮ Define violence and emotional and physical abuse.

☮ Explore the intent of abusive behavior and the impact of violent and abusive behavior on partners and children.

☮ Challenge beliefs and thinking that allow and promote the use of aggressive and violent means to achieve a desired outcome.

☮ Provide information about brain function relating to thinking and emotion, and the impact of strong emotional reactions on our ability to use rational thinking.

☮ Increase awareness and understanding of anger and explore how each group member experiences and expresses anger.

☮ Increase awareness of the use of defenses and tactics such as minimization, denial and blaming to avoid personal accountability for one's actions and challenge each member to accept complete responsibility for the same.

☮ Provide information and opportunities to learn and practice positive communication skills, conflict resolution, emotional regulation and relationship skills.

☮ Appendix B
Life Stress Survey

Directions: Determine which life events have occurred in your life over the past 12 months and circle the point value for these events. Fill in the number of times each event has occurred this year and calculate the appropriate point value in the blank in the last column. Add the points to obtain your stress score:

Life Event	Point Value	#		Points
Death of a Spouse/Partner	100	x	___ =	_____
Divorce/Breakup	73	x	___ =	_____
Marital/Relationship Separation	65	x	___ =	_____
Jail Sentence	63	x	___ =	_____
Death of Close Family Member	63	x	___ =	_____
Personal Injury or Illness	53	x	___ =	_____
Marriage	50	x	___ =	_____
Being Fired/Laid off at Work	47	x	___ =	_____
Marital Problems/Reconciliation	45	x	___ =	_____
Retirement	45	x	___ =	_____
Change/Health of Family Member	44	x	___ =	_____
Pregnancy	40	x	___ =	_____
Sexual Difficulties	39	x	___ =	_____
Addition of New Family Member	39	x	___ =	_____
Business Readjustment	39	x	___ =	_____
Change in Financial Situation	38	x	___ =	_____
Death of Close Friend	37	x	___ =	_____
Change to Different Field of Work	36	x	___ =	_____
Change/# of Arguments w/Spouse	35	x	___ =	_____
Mortgage/Loan for Major Purchase (i.e. home)	31	x	___ =	_____
Foreclosure of Mortgage/Loan	30	x	___ =	_____
Change in Responsibilities at Work	29	x	___ =	_____
Child Leaving Home	29	x	___ =	_____
Conflict with In-Laws	29	x	___ =	_____
Outstanding Accomplishment	28	x	___ =	_____
Spouse/Partner Begins/Stops Work	26	x	___ =	_____
Begin or End School	26	x	___ =	_____

Life Event	Point Value		#	Points
Change in Living Conditions	25	x	___ =	_____
Change in Personal Habits	24	x	___ =	_____
Conflict with Boss	23	x	___ =	_____
Change in Work Hours/Conditions	20	x	___ =	_____
Change in Residence	20	x	___ =	_____
Change in Schools	20	x	___ =	_____
Change in Recreation/Leisure	19	x	___ =	_____
Change in Church Activities	19	x	___ =	_____
Change in Social Activities	18	x	___ =	_____
Mortgage/Loan for Lesser Purchase (i.e. car or TV)	17	x	___ =	_____
Change in Sleeping Habits	16	x	___ =	_____
Change in # of Family Gatherings	15	x	___ =	_____
Change in Diet/Eating Habits	15	x	___ =	_____
Vacation	13	x	___ =	_____
Christmas	12	x	___ =	_____
Minor Violations of the Law/Fines	11	x	___ =	_____
			Total	____

If your total score is under 150, you are less likely to be suffering the effects of cumulative or chronic stress. You have less than a 37% probability of becoming ill due to a stress-related illness within two years.

A score of 150 to 300 means you may be suffering from chronic stress, depending on how you perceived and coped with the particular life events you experienced, and you have a 51% chance of incurring some type of stress-related illness within the next two years.

If your score is over 300, it is likely you are already experiencing some detrimental effects of chronic stress and have an 80% chance of developing a stress-related illness within the next two years. These scores were averaged over many people. The degree to which any particular event is stressful to you, personally, will depend on how you perceive it.

Adapted from "The Social Readjustment Scale" by Holmes, T.H. and Rahe, R. H. Journal of Psychosomatic Research, 1972, pp. 111-15.

⊕ Appendix C
Behavioral Signs of Stress

Individuals have different actions or behaviors that indicate to them that they are angry, tense, anxious or feeling some other negative emotion. Developing the ability to recognize these behavioral cues when they occur gives you the power to make conscious choices about how to handle the stress that brings them on. Circle all the behaviors you have used when you are upset or stressed. Put an **asterisk** in front of the action that is usually the **first** to occur.

1. Compulsive Eating
2. Increased Smoking
3. Increased Mistakes (at work or home)
4. Foot or Finger Tapping
5. Reduced Work Efficiency
6. Hair Pulling, Twirling or Cutting
7. Nervous Laughter
8. Chronic Tardiness
9. Increased Drug or Alcohol Use
10. Grinding Teeth (when awake or sleeping)
11. Overreacting to Things; Increased Irritability
12. Increased Fighting and Arguing (at work or home)
13. Crying
14. Poor Concentration or Forgetfulness
15. Lack of Enthusiasm
16. Constant Scratching
17. Nail Biting
18. Pacing the Floor
19. Sleep Problems (too much or too little)
20. Change in Social Habits (withdrawal from or increase in contact with friends and activities)
21. Repetitive Body Movements or Tics
22. Inattention to Grooming
23. Staring into Space/Zoning Out
24. Sighing
25. Swearing
26. Reckless Driving
27. "Bad" Thoughts (against self or others)

28. Apathy or Hopelessness
29. Being Suspicious or Paranoid
30. Cycling Thoughts or Worrying
31. Any other behavior you are aware of:
   _____

*"People are about as happy
as they make up their minds to be."*

~Abraham Lincoln

☮ Appendix D
"My Favorite Room" Visualization

It is best to be able to "just listen" to any visualization, such as the one below. Therefore, you may wish to either find a friend who can read it to you or read it yourself into a small tape recorder, then play it back when you want to use it.

Get comfortable. Either lie down on a bed or the floor or sit in a comfortable upholstered chair. Put your feet on the floor, let your head fall back and close your eyes...Here we go...

Come along with me to a house in the country. It is safe and hidden from view among the trees and hills, but you are able to find it easily.

It has a big front porch. You walk across the wide boards and hear them creak slightly, but you know they are strong and sturdy. There is a porch swing. You sit on the swing and enjoy the movement of swinging (say slowly "Back and forth, back and forth..."). You swing for awhile on the porch. (Pause).

After a time, you decide to go inside. You have a key for the door. Notice its shape and size. You fit the key into the lock and the door swings open.

You walk inside. Notice the floor. Is it covered with Linoleum or tile? Hardwood or carpeting? A long hallway leads you down to a room. Notice how your feet feel as you walk. (Pause)

The door to your room is closed, but opens easily when you turn the knob. You walk inside.

It is just as you left it! All of your favorite things are inside! There might be a fire in the fireplace, lighted candles, a warm blanket or quilt for your shoulders, your favorite beverage to drink, your favorite foods or snacks. You might hear soft music playing or a television with your favorite shows. You may find a Bible or other favorite book, letters to read or write, puzzles to work or crafts to make. You may just prefer to sit quietly and relax. (Long Pause—several minutes).

You know you can always return to your favorite room in your imagination. It will always be safe and warm, and you can take it with you in your mind. A warm and peaceful feeling accompanies your favorite room. Think of a word or phrase that represents this room, and this feeling of calm. Whenever you hear this word, you will feel calm and peaceful.

When you are ready, get up and leave your room, closing the door behind you. Slowly walk back down the hallway. As you leave the house, lock the front door behind you and walk past the swing and across the porch. When you are ready, you may open your eyes, feeling refreshed and full of energy, but you can always enjoy that calm and relaxed feeling by remembering the word or phrase you identified with your room.

Do not hesitate to visit your room anytime in your mind, or to use the word you associated with those feelings. These can operate as a tool to help you calm down when you are feeling stressed or frustrated. Use them to your best advantage.

If you like, feel free to record a brief description of your room below, to remind you of this exercise and enable you to access it easily when you most need to:

My Room:

_____

_____

_____

Snacks or Activities in My Room: _____

_____

My Word or Phrase for My Room:_____

Situations or Times I Will Most Benefit By Recalling My Room:

_____

_____

_____

☮ Appendix E
Simple Stretching Exercises to Reduce Stress

1. **Simple Neck Stretch:** To relieve tension in your neck, slowly turn your head to the right as far as possible. Hold that position for a count of 10. Return your head to face forward and then repeat to the left. Repeat several times on each side.

2. **Rolling Neck Stretch:** Stretch your neck by gently rolling your head in a half-circle, starting on one side, then dropping your chin to your chest and rolling your head over to the other side. Repeat in the opposite direction. Stretch each side five times. This is especially effective because so many of us hold our stress in our neck and shoulders and tighten those muscles accordingly. Loosening them in this manner can greatly relieve your physical stress.

3. **Shoulder Roll:** While slowly breathing in and out, draw your shoulders up toward your ears and move them forward in a circle. Repeat 5 to 7 times. In the same manner, roll your shoulders in backward circles 5 to 7 times.

4. **Hand Stretch:** Curl both hands into fists and hold tight for 7 seconds. Release fists and spread fingers wide apart. Hold for 5 seconds. Repeat 3 times. Try to do this at least once an hour when you are working with your hands, such as typing on a keyboard.

5. **Giraffe Stretch:** While standing, slowly breathe in while raising your right arm straight above your head. Keeping your arm raised, slowly breathe out. As you breathe in slowly again, stretch your arm as if it were a giraffe's neck, trying to reach a leaf on a tall tree. Breathe out slowly and gradually lower your arm back down to your side. Repeat with your left arm, then with both arms together.

(Appendix E, cont'd)
(Simple Stretching Exercises to Reduce Stress)

6. **Progressive Deep Muscle Relaxation:** This is a more extensive relaxation exercise and is best saved for the end of your workday or just prior to bed. Starting at your head, tense one of the main muscle groups around your face (eyes, jaw, forehead) for 5 to 7 seconds, then immediately let go of the tension. Relax as completely as you can for about 30 seconds before moving on to a new muscle group. When you finish with your head, repeat the tightening/relaxing process for the other muscle groups of your body in the following order—neck, shoulders, arms, back, stomach, buttocks, legs, and feet. It will take approximately 20-30 minutes to relax your entire body, and when you're through, if you've done it properly, you should feel like a bowl of warm spaghetti.

As you can see, each of these stretching exercises is easy to do and all except the last could easily be done in a work environment, such as an office, car, restroom or work area. Further, a number of these exercises can be fun to do with children, while teaching them life skills that will enhance their own well-being. Enjoying relaxation exercises with a partner can enhance intimacy. What do you have to lose, except your stress?

⊕ Appendix F
Event, Thought, Feeling Process Diagram

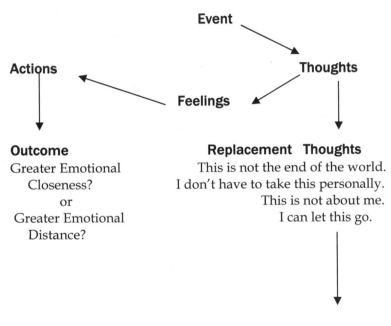

Event

Actions   **Thoughts**

                        Feelings

Outcome   **Replacement Thoughts**
Greater Emotional   This is not the end of the world.
Closeness?   I don't have to take this personally.
or   This is not about me.
Greater Emotional   I can let this go.
Distance?

More Positive Feelings
Calmer
More Accepting
More Neutral
More Relaxed

☮ Appendix G
STOP! Diagram

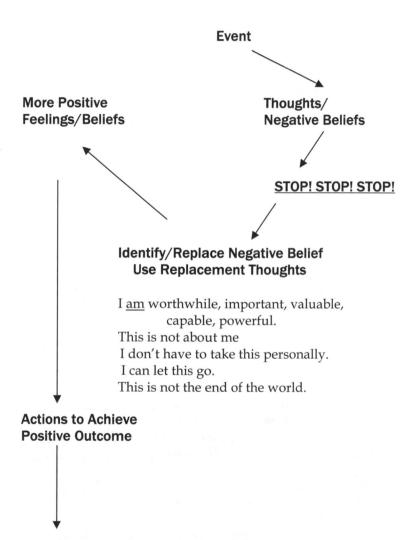

Event

**More Positive
Feelings/Beliefs**

**Thoughts/
Negative Beliefs**

STOP! STOP! STOP!

**Identify/Replace Negative Belief
Use Replacement Thoughts**

I <u>am</u> worthwhile, important, valuable,
    capable, powerful.
This is not about me
I don't have to take this personally.
I can let this go.
This is not the end of the world.

**Actions to Achieve
Positive Outcome**

Outcome: Greater Emotional Closeness!

⊕ Appendix H
Whose Decision Is It, Anyway?

An issue is open to negotiation between partners if it is not entirely one person's right to make the decision. If only one of the partners has the right to decide a particular issue, it may be open to discussion and input or feedback from the other partner, but not negotiation.

Read over the issues below. If you think the issue is one for joint decision making and open to negotiation between the two of you, check box 1. If you think the issue is for your partner, only, to decide, check box 2. If you think the issue is yours, alone, to decide, check line 3. Remember, an issue is still open for discussion and input between the two of you even if it is yours or your partner's to actually decide.

	1 Both Decide	2 Prtnr Decide	3 You Decide
1. Which friends can *s/he* be with?	____	____	____
2. Which friends can *you* be with?	____	____	____
3. Who cooks/ cleans during the week?	____	____	____
4. Who cooks/ cleans on weekends?	____	____	____
5. Will *s/he* drink, gamble, smoke or use drugs again?	____	____	____
6. Will *you* drink, gamble, smoke or use drugs again?	____	____	____
7. How much time will *s/he* spend on the computer or telephone?	____	____	____
8. How much time will *you* spend on the computer or telephone?	____	____	____
9. Will *s/he* drink on certain occasions?	____	____	____
10. Will *you* drink on certain occasions?	____	____	____
11. Who will find child care?	____	____	____
12. Will *s/he* buy a car with *her* money?	____	____	____
13. Will *you* buy a car with *your* money?	____	____	____
14. Will *s/he* get a job or change jobs?	____	____	____
15. Will *you* get a job or change jobs?	____	____	____
16. Will *s/he* go to school?	____	____	____

17. Will *you* go to school?   _____ _____ _____
18. Which guests or relatives may visit
    your home?   _____ _____ _____
19. How will children be disciplined?   _____ _____ _____
20. Will *s/he* go on a trip without you?   _____ _____ _____
21. Will *you* go on a trip without her?   _____ _____ _____
22. What is *her/his* paycheck spent on?   _____ _____ _____
23. What is *your* paycheck spent on?   _____ _____ _____

TOTALS:
    Number of responses for each: _____ _____ _____

    Does your partner agree with your responses?
Results: Only items 3, 4, 11, 18 and 19 are truly joint decisions.
However, all issues are open to feedback and discussion.
Please review Chapter Ten for further discussion of this quiz.

☮ Appendix I
How Jealous Are You?

Please use the following scale to circle your responses to the first 5 questions:

1	2	3	4	5
Not at all				Very Jealous

1. How jealous are you of your partner's **relationships** with members of the opposite sex?   1 2 3 4 5

2. How jealous are you when you see your partner **talking** with a member of the opposite sex?   1 2 3 4 5

3. How jealous are you when you see your partner **flirting** with a member of the opposite sex?   1 2 3 4 5

4. How jealous are you if you see your partner **dancing** with a member of the opposite sex?   1 2 3 4 5

5. In **general**, how jealous do you think you are?   1 2 3 4 5

Please use the following scale for the next 5 questions:

1	2	3	4	5
Never	Rarely	Sometimes	Occasionally	Often
1-2 times	1-2 X/Yr.	1X/Month	2X/Month	>2X/Month

6. How often do you get jealous of your partner's **relationships** with members of the opposite sex?   1 2 3 4 5

7. How often is your jealousy of your partner a **problem for you** even if you do not raise it with your partner?   1 2 3 4 5

8. How often have your and your partner **argued** as a result of your jealousy? 1 2 3 4 5

9. How often have you thought seriously about **ending** a relationship because of a partners' contact, behavior or attraction to a member of the opposite sex?   1 2 3 4 5

(Appendix I, Cont'd)

10. How often have you done things that have **surprised you,** or that you never thought you'd do because you were jealous at the time?   **1 2 3 4 5**

11. Are you more or less jealous in **this** (or your most recent) relationship than you have been in past relationships?
     _____ More   _____ Less
By how much?
1   **2**   **3**   **4**   **5**
Much Less   **Same**   **Much More**

12. Why do you think this is?
_____

13. Of all of the issues you and your (or your most recent) partner argue about, where does your jealousy rank in terms of **how often it comes up** or how important it is:

1   **2**   **3**   **4**   **5**
Never Mentioned   Middle of the List   At the Top

14. Has a previous partner ever had an affair or left you because of an attraction to another person?   ____Yes   ____ No

15. If yes, how many times has this happened to you?
Once   2-4 Times   Often/Every Partner

16. How much do you think that affects your ability to trust this partner?

Not at All   A Little   Some   Alot   Overwhelmingly

17. What are the thoughts in your mind when feeling jealous:
__She doesn't care about me. __I am not good enough for her.
__ She's just like _____. __Other: _____
__She wants to be with someone else.

⊕ Appendix J
Suggested Resources

Good Books On Anger and Relationships:

⊕ *Child Friendly Divorce*, by Diane M. Berry, MSW, LCSW, JD (Blue Waters Publications, 2004).

⊕ *The Dance of Anger*, by Harriet Goldhor Lerner, Ph.D (Harper & Row, 1985)

⊕ *Divorce Busting*, by Michele Weiner-Davis, MSW (Simon & Schuster, 1992)

⊕ *The Emotionally Abusive Relationship: How to Stop Being Abused and How to Stop Abusing*, by Beverly Engel (Wiley, 2003)

⊕ *The Four Agreements*, by Don Miguel Ruiz (Amber-Allen Publishers, 1997)

⊕ *Love Between Equals: How Peer Marriage Really Works*, by Pepper Schwartz, Ph.D (Touchstone, 1995)

⊕ *Passionate Marriage: Love, Sex and Intimacy in Emotionally Committed Relationships*, by David Schnarch (Owl Books, 1998)

⊕ *Romancing the Web*, by Diane M. Berry, MSW, LCSW, JD (Blue Waters Publications, 2005)

⊕ *The Verbally Abusive Relationship: How to Recognize It and How to Respond*, by Patricia Even (Adams Media Corp., 1996)

⊕ *When Anger Hurts: Quieting the Storm Within,*
by Matthew McKay, Ph.D, Peter D. Rogers, Ph.D &
Judith McKay, R.N. (New Harbinger Pubs, Inc.,1989)

⊕ *Why Does He Do That? Inside the Minds of Angry
and Controlling Men,* by Lundy Bancroft
(Berkley Publishing Group, 2003)

⊕ *You Just Don't Understand: Women and Men in
Conversation,* by Deborah Tannen, Ph.D. (Ballentine
Books, 1991)

Websites to Check Out

www.Alice-Miller.com
www.awareparenting.com
www.bluewatersfc.com (our clinic website)
www.bluewaterspublications.com (the publishing company)
www.endcorporalpunishment.org
www.naturalchild.org
www.nopunish.net
www.nospank.net
www.positiveparenting.com

How to Contact the Authors

Email: bluewaterspublications@lakefield.net
                (email is the best way to reach us!)
Telephone: (920) 683-3963
Fax: (920) 683-9624
Mailing Address: Blue Waters Publications
                P. O. Box 411
                Manitowoc, WI 54221-0411

Index

Book Order Form

Postal Orders: Mail completed form and check to:
Blue Waters Publications, LLC
P. O. Box 411
Manitowoc, WI 54221-0411

Email and   Please visit our website at
Credit Card   www.bluewaterspublications.com
*Orders:**

Questions: Telephone: (920)683-3963
Fax: (920)683-9624

Please send me the following books and articles:

*I understand I may return any of these materials for a full refund—
for any reason–with no questions asked.*

___ A Peace of My Mind $15.95
___ Child-Friendly Divorce $17.95
___ Romancing the Web $13.95
___ Positively Managing Your Stress (article) $5.95
___ Soothing the Self (article) $3.95

Please send me free information on:
___ Other Books   ___ Seminars   ___ Consulting

Name: _____
Address: _____
City: _____ State: _____ Zip:_____
Telephone: _____
Email Address: _____
Sales Tax: Please add 5 % for products shipped to Wisconsin addresses.

Shipping: Please add $3.00 for the first book and $2.00 for each
additional book or article shipped.

* If you wish to pay by credit card, please visit our website
(www.bluewaterspublications.com) at which that option is
available. Thank you.